Messages Men Hear

Messages Men Hear:
Constructing Masculinities

Ian M. Harris

Taylor & Francis
Publishers since 1798

UK   Taylor & Francis Ltd, 4 John St., London WC1N 2ET

USA   Taylor & Francis Inc., 1900 Frost Road, Suite 101, Bristol, PA 19007

First published 1995

A Catalogue Record for this book is available from the British Library

ISBN 0 7484 0229 2
ISBN 0 7484 0230 6 pbk

Library of Congress Cataloging-in-Publication Data are available on request

Typeset in 10.5/12pt Times
by Solidus (Bristol) Limited

Printed in Great Britain by Burgess Science Press, Basingstoke on paper which has a specified pH value on final paper manufacture of not less than 7.5 and is therefore 'acid free'.

Dedication

This book is dedicated to my father, Murray George Harris, without whose love this study would neither have been conceived nor completed.

Contents

Part III Differences Between Men

Contents

Acknowledgments

Research for this book has been ongoing throughout the 50 years I have been developing my own gender identity. There are literally thousands of people who have inspired the findings presented in the following pages. Perhaps most important are the close male buddies I have had throughout my life, friends who have inspired me about the value of both men's attempts to improve this world and the importance of male friendships.

Early in the 1970s I attended my first men's group, which was formed as a way of allowing males who were relating to women experiencing the challenges of the women's movement, to explore their own gender conditioning. I have subsequently been in four other men's groups and have for three years been in a group that grew out of a New Warrior weekend here in Milwaukee, Wisconsin. I am very indebted to all the participants in these groups who have challenged me about my own male behavior and taken risks to explore different aspects of their own gender conditioning. Without the insights gained from close introspection about the demands of masculinity within these groups, a study as intimate about the way men think about themselves would not have been possible.

Messages Men Hear is both my product and a product of a variety of social movements, begun in the 1960s and 1970s, that started to challenge traditional gender conditioning. These movements have been largely led by feminist academics and activists. I am very grateful to women scholars who have broken ground in terms of understanding how the extremely important category of gender affects human behavior. Their insights into the subtle nuances of gender conditioning have helped create some general theories upon which this study is based. I am also indebted to men within various branches within the modern men's movement who have encouraged me to complete this study.

The actual research project that formed the basis for this book began in 1982 when Claire Halverson, a multicultural trainer, came to my class, 'Changing Male Roles', and asked students (male and female) to list two messages they had received about their own gender conditioning. Their responses were so fascinating that the author decided to launch a detailed study into the influence of cultural messages upon male behavior.

This research would never have been completed without the assistance of the School of Education Research Office at the University of Wisconsin-Milwaukee. Under the leadership of Phil Smith, who provided guidance for the statistical aspects of this study, data from nearly 1000 questionnaires were analyzed and tabulated. This office made possible funds to hire Doris Peterson to help transcribe some of the 96 interviews conducted with participants in this study. I am particularly indebted to Mary Loveland, a neighbor, who without pay transcribed many of the interviews upon which this study is based. Cathy Nelson, from the School of Education word processing pool has revised numerous drafts of this manuscript; while Lois Lee, the program assistant from the Department of Educational Policy and Community Studies, has offered support in many ways. She has typed the bibliography, helped with tabulating data, and suggested alias names for respondents.

I would also like to thank my wife, Sara Spence, and my family who have been very supportive of this research throughout the 13 years it has taken to get this project from initial glimmerings to a completed book length manuscript. Sara, who works in a community health clinic where she sees on a daily basis the results of dysfunctional male behavior, has always considered it important to gain accurate understanding into why men behave the way they do. Her patience and belief in this study have helped me overcome many of the inevitable obstacles in a project as massive as this.

Introduction

Messages Men Hear describes the results of a study that attempts to answer the question: Why do men behave the way they do? (See the Appendix, for a discussion of methodology.) Male behavior is strongly influenced by gender role messages men receive from their social environments. This study interprets the responses of 560 men in the United States to 24 dominant male gender norms or male messages. Individuals participating in this study were asked to indicate how influential each message was at age 18 and how that influence has changed.

Male messages express gender role norms that tell men how to behave. The identities of boys, when they are born, are like unshaped balls of clay. Boys are born into a particular class status, cultural group, or race that helps determine their identities. Interaction with norms for male behavior helps them figure out how to behave as men. Males participating in this study have described male messages as a force propelling them in certain directions, like a spring in a watch, influencing their choices.

Men have penises, grow facial hair, and possess sex-linked characteristics acquired from their genes, but becoming a man is much more complex than growing a beard, having a lower voice, becoming bald, or learning the pleasures associated with a penis. As each man matures, he constructs a gender identity, which determines how he feels about himself and his masculine responses to the world. Gender is a social construction. A person's sex is determined by biology. A man's gender is to some extent determined by his biology. Because of his masculine features, he is exposed to a world where facts of gender are taken at face value. His raw sexual features are imbued with symbolic content and social meaning that, among other things, attempts to differentiate men from women.

The process by which an individual learns to become a member of society, called socialization, involves the imposition of social patterns upon behavior. The socialized part of the self is the identity. As a man matures, he forms a gender identity which should be distinguished from his sexual identity. The former refers to how he understands, relates to, and internalizes masculine behavior, while the latter refers to how he sees himself and behaves as a sexual being. Men have sexual aspects to their personalities, and their sexual behaviors can vary enormously, as can their complex gender identities. *Messages Men Hear* describes how men construct their gender, not their sexual identities. In this book only Chapter 6, 'Lovers', will refer to male sexual behavior.

Every culture has a gender system that contains shared expectations for appropriate male behavior, social norms, or roles, that vary from culture to culture. A central thesis of *Messages Men Hear* is that these roles for masculinity are complex, dynamic, and contradictory. Although the construction of masculinity tends to be regarded as natural and inevitable, individual men and the societies they inhabit are constantly reproducing their understandings of masculinity.

Organization of the Book

Messages Men Hear is divided into three parts and ten chapters. The first part, 'Learning to Be a Man', contains three chapters explaining how men form their gender identities. The second part, 'Acting Like a Man', has five chapters that describe men's experiences with these messages. The third part, 'Differences Between Men', consists of two chapters discussing the wide variety of responses men have to dominant cultural norms.

The first chapter 'Cultural Messages' provides an overview for the 24 modern male messages used in this study, placing them within patriarchal cultures and shifting economies.

The second chapter, 'Message Sources', answers questions about who sends these messages, providing information about the role of culture, peers, and family members. This chapter includes a discussion of how boys who have absent fathers construct their male identities.

The third chapter, 'Becoming a Man', describes the process by which a man develops a gender identity and adjusts that identity to changing circumstances throughout his life. Statistical data about developmental changes in a man's gender identity came from a scale that asked men to indicate how the influence of each message changed during the course of his life. These responses will be referred to in the text as 'over time'. 'Becoming a Man' provides a general framework for male gender socialization, places various responses to male messages within that framework, and summarizes the development of a man's gender identity in a table that presents chronological stages for identity formation.

The second part of this book, 'Acting Like a Man', contains interviews with specific men that help explain how they relate to the male messages presented in this study. A statistical technique known as factor analysis helped organize these male messages into five distinct factors. Table I contains the 24 messages used in this study, organizing them into different chapter titles derived from this analysis, and rank orders those factors according to how influential they have been in the lives of the 560 men who participated in this study.

Chapter 4 describes that aspect of masculinity, standard bearing behavior, considered most influential, while Chapter 8 describes that aspect of masculinity, rugged individualistic behavior, rated to be least influential. Within each chapter the presentations on separate messages are rank ordered according to the means listed to the right in Table 1.

Chapter 4, 'Standard Bearers', tells how men carry on traditions by passing their respect for standards on to others, revering traditions of excellence, and caring for the well being of others.

Table 1   Rank Order of Masculine Factors

Message	Average at age 18	Average over time	Sum of Means[1]
Standard Bearers			
Scholar	2.70	2.66	5.36
Nature Lover	2.46	2.80	5.26
Be the Best You Can	2.74	2.39	5.13
Good Samaritan	2.55	2.36	4.91
average			5.17
Workers			
Technician	2.23	2.05	4.28
Work Ethic	2.99	2.14	5.13
Money	2.27	1.79	4.06
Law	2.17	1.57	3.74
average			4.30
Lovers			
Breadwinner	2.42	1.76	4.18
Nurturer	1.96	3.02	3.98
Faithful Husband	2.04	1.88	3.92
Playboy	2.25	1.42	3.67
average			3.94
Bosses			
Control	2.45	1.88	4.33
President	2.35	1.85	4.20
Hurdles	2.26	1.92	4.18
Adventurer	2.38	1.70	4.08
Sportsman	2.34	1.74	4.08
Be Like Your Father	1.71	1.46	3.17
Warrior	1.58	1.26	2.84
average			3.84
Rugged Individuals			
Self-reliant	2.37	1.75	4.12
Stoic	2.30	1.59	3.89
Rebel	1.69	1.95	3.64
Tough Guy	2.11	1.24	3.35
Superman	1.71	1.30	3.01
average			3.60

Because men tend to define themselves by what they do, work is an important component of men's lives. Chapter 5, 'Workers', describes various expectations men have for themselves as providers, what they have to do to earn money, and the discipline demanded of them to perform at work.

Chapter 6, 'Lovers', discusses how men relate to others – their friendships with other men, fathering, and romantic relationships.

Chapter 7 'Bosses', describes those messages that prompt men to succeed, take risks, seek power, and accomplish heroic tasks. This chapter explains why men strive to climb to the top of various social structures.

Chapter 8 in this section, 'Rugged Individuals', reflects an image of a man standing alone, bearing the tribulations and difficulties of life with a stiff upper lip and not admitting to weakness. Messages within this factor, often glamorized by the media, create many problems for men.

The final part of this book, 'Differences Between Men', discusses diverse aspects of masculinity. The experience of being male is not uniform. Although any culture contains common norms for masculinity, individual men interpret dominant cultural expectations, adopting unique gender identities. This section discusses some of the variations in male gender identity that come from the different ways men are raised. It summarizes the five different themes for male behavior presented in this book.

Chapter 9, 'Different Lenses', explains how men from different generations and residential areas respond to male cultural expectations. Individual men interpret male messages differently, according to values within their subcultures. This chapter describes how generational differences and class background influence how men respond to gender-role expectations. Although some of the special conditions of minority men from racial and ethnic groups and the experiences of gay men are presented in this chapter, a discussion of how men from those groupings interpret masculinity is not relegated only to this chapter but sprinkled throughout the book. Racial designations are provided for all of the 96 men (four for each message) interviewed so that the reader can appreciate how men from diverse backgrounds view the dominant cultural norms examined in this study.

Chapter 10, 'Message Therapy', draws some conclusions about the importance of these messages. Understanding the role of these messages in men's lives helps unlock secrets about why men behave the way they do and allows men to achieve a sense of authenticity.

Throughout this book tables are presented describing how this sample of 560 men responded to dominant cultural norms. When comparisons are made between groups, only those results that are statistically significant (p is less than 0.05) are presented.

Messages Men Hear is based upon the self perceptions of males about dominant cultural norms in the United States. These perceptions have been measured by a questionnaire and interviews. The respondents in this study may or may not live according to the reports they have provided. Empirical verification of the way these men live their lives is beyond the scope of this research project.

Background of Author

The author himself is, of course, a participant in this study. His values and experiences are reflected throughout *Messages Men Hear*. This author was born in New York City and spent his first four years in Manhattan on Park Avenue. His father was English, a retired foreign service officer, and his mother was a fashion model who grew up in Indianapolis, Indiana. When he was four, his family bought a small truck farm in New Jersey and moved to Bergen County, an area which in the 1950s was fast becoming a suburb. He attended public school for grades K-8 and a prep school, Englewood School for Boys, for high school. He earned his undergraduate degree at St John's College in Annapolis, Maryland in 1967 and his doctorate in 1975 in Foundations of Education at Temple University in Philadelphia. He avoided serving in Vietnam by becoming a teacher. From the years 1968 to 1974 he taught math and science at a public high school in a tough, racially mixed neighborhood in West Philadelphia. From 1975 to the present time he has been a professor of Educational Policy and Community Studies at the University of Wisconsin-Milwaukee. Ian Harris lives in an integrated, inner city community in Milwaukee, Wisconsin. The father of a grown daughter and stepson, he married his current wife in 1981. He is author of *Peace Education* (Harris, 1988) and co-author with Paul Denise of *Experiential Education for Community Development* (Harris and Denise, 1989).

Ian Harris has had close male friends throughout his life. In 1975 he joined his first men's group. In 1977 he became involved in the National Organization for Changing Men (now known as National Organization of Men against Sexism). Since 1978 he has taught a course entitled 'Male Identity: Education and Development'. In 1979 he helped host the sixth national conference on Men and Masculinity at the University of Wisconsin-Milwaukee. He is a review editor of *Changing Men* (one-fourth of the proceeds from *Messages Men Hear* will go to support *Changing Men*). He has written numerous articles and reviews on masculinity. He has been a counselor in a Batterers Anonymous program and a trainer in the New Warrior experience, a growth weekend for men developed in Milwaukee, Wisconsin. His mission is to enable people to create and enjoy peace.

As a man growing up in the United States, this author has been influenced by all the messages described in this study, the most important of which has been 'president', a message that has propelled him to spend thousands of hours investigating the phenomenon of male gender conditioning. In addition to teaching classes on male identity and participating in men's groups, the author decided to write a book that would explain male behavior. In his attempt to present findings that reflect the experiences of a broad sample of men in the United States, the author has spent seven years in the field as a scientist talking to other men about how they have formed their gender identities. Because of the strong influence of the 'scholar' message, he will present the results of this study as accurately as possible.

Masculinity lives within a discourse that is extremely complex, containing reverse and counter discourses. Based upon the responses of 560 males in the United States to a questionnaire asking them about their responses to male cultural norms, *Messages Men Hear* presents an interpretation of masculinity in the western world. This sample contains men who come mostly from the middle class and the Midwest portion of the United States. These well educated, bourgeois men are in power positions where they help influence global standards for male behavior. This sample does contain representative individuals from minority groups, but most of those individuals are employed. This author does not attempt to speak for all men. In researching this book, Ian Harris has combined the latest theories about gender identity with his practical experiences as a teacher and facilitator of men's groups. He has gone out of his way to include many voices, so that this book does not just represent his opinions about masculinity, but there are still many voices to hear from, many counter tales to be told.

Note

1 The scores provided under the heading 'Sum of Means' are derived by adding together the means for the two scales which measure how influential these messages have been to men. The first scale allowed a man to indicate how influential a particular message was when he was 18 (on a five-point Likert scale going from no influence to dominant influence); and the second scale allowed the same man to indicate how the influence of that message had changed in their lives (on a five-point Likert scale going from much less influence to much more influence).

Part I

Learning to be a Man

Chapter 1

Cultural Messages

'The more I learn about the world, the more I feel we are fed a bunch of crud about who we are supposed to be.'

28-year-old unskilled laborer (Hispanic)

All boys are born innocent, capable of becoming Charles Manson or Dr Martin Luther King Jr. With constant love and nourishment boys have the capacity to grow into cuddly teddy bears. With hatred, abuse, and abandonment they can become fierce grizzlies. Young boys become men by responding to situational demands and social pressures. Surrounded with expectations about how they, as men, ought to behave, boys have to sift through various demands placed upon them by their culture, their associates, their teachers, their friends, and their family to construct their own gender identities.

Gender identity has been defined as 'an individual's own feelings of whether he or she is a woman or man, a girl or a boy. In essence gender identity is self attribution of gender' (Kessler and McKenna, 1978, p. 8). At an individual level a boy constructs his gender identity based upon his biology which influences messages he receives from his environment about how he ought to behave. Through language people develop classifying schemes which differentiate objects by gender (Lindsey, 1990). Each man constructs his own identity in relation to specific gender notions deeply embedded in his culture. These notions are coded into messages with specific configurations that spell out specialized patterns of conduct. To learn a role it is not enough to acquiesce to routines immediately necessary for its outward performance. A young boy must be initiated into the various cognitive and affective layers of the norms appropriate to that role. Each role carries with it a socially defined appendage of knowledge and a repertoire of acceptable and unacceptable behaviors.

Humans develop mechanisms of social control that include sanctions and retribution (Berger and Luckmann, 1966, p. 61). Roles represent and protect institutional order. Because of the overwhelming need of society to prepare the next generation for the social order, males and females are groomed to fit different adult roles. By conforming to roles, boys participate in their social worlds. Their conduct is subject to enforcement through a highly developed series of gender codes that spell out how males and females behave.

Not only does the social definition set up a pattern of behavior that is culturally consistent with whatever sex the child is told he or she is; it also instils in the child the never-to-be-forgotten feeling that being male or female is something to work at. to accomplish, and to be sure not to lose, rather than something one is biologically. (Bem, 1993, p. 148)

Young boys are rewarded by their parents and teachers for conforming to gender-role standards. Playmates congratulate peers for performing like men. Mentors pat them on the back for their 'masculine' achievements.

Concepts of masculinity, which provide beliefs about how men ought to behave, are constructed at many different levels both in society and in the minds of individuals. A masculine ideology generated by news media, artists, teachers, historians, parents, priests, and public figures dominates how men think about themselves. Because men in any country tend to share cultural histories, they may receive similar notions about how to behave. These common understandings of masculinity constitute dominant cultural norms.

Children who internalize social norms become cultural natives as members of particular social clans with traditions that define right and wrong. Boys from different subcultures – classes, kinship networks, ethnic groups, regional enclaves, religious communities – view the dominant ideology for masculinity with different lenses. From these perspectives they construct complex gender identities full of idiosyncratic interpretations of masculinity that contain common threads derived from dominant cultural norms and subcultural influences. These identities contain complicated notions about male behavior. Male gender identity, the subjective sense men develop about their own and others' masculinities, can be conceived as a man's interpretation and acting out of how his social group interprets masculinity. A man's gender identity has four distinct components that can be represented with the following equation:

gender identity = biology + dominant cultural norms + subcultural influences + unique circumstances

'Biology' refers to the physical characteristics of a boy or girl by which he or she is sex typed. These biological aspects are interpreted within a complex maze of social beliefs:

From the moment a child is born, he or she is exposed to a world in which the facts of gender are taken at face value. A boy's genitals are the first sign of his membership in the category male. Such categorization is not simply a label – it affects the way in which he defines his differences from the category female. (Brittan, 1989, p. 14)

Gender is such a powerful category that it sometimes overrules biology, as in the case of transsexuals (Stoller, 1985). Thus, a person with female genitalia and body characteristics might identify as a male, responding to masculine norms. Roles added to biology create a complex gender system.

'Dominant cultural norms' refers to patterns of masculinity promoted within national boundaries. Concepts of appropriate masculinity differ between countries like Chile, the United States, Nigeria, Saudi Arabia, and Japan. Although each country supports specific notions for how men ought to behave, different countries have similar notions for male behavior. Gilmore (1990) has argued that almost all cultures create ideals and norms about appropriate male behavior that serve ultimately to insure the survival of the culture. Elected officials, sports stars, literary figures, and popular actors help establish national norms for male behavior. Such depictions of men, together with values promoted by government, churches, and educational institutions, provide commonly understood notions of masculinity. In spite of these common images masculinity is not a uniform concept. Every country contains many dynamic and diverse concepts of masculinity.

'Subcultural influences' refers to an individual's membership within an ethnic or cultural group, e.g. Italian, Norwegian, inner city, suburban, Southern, working class, etc. Each of these different groups has a unique set of expectations for appropriate male behavior. These expectations, influenced by dominant culture, represent a variation with different emphases upon certain roles.

'Unique circumstances' refers to the environment in which a boy is raised. How do his father and mother behave towards him? Is his father domineering? What is the son's role in the family? Do his parents promote conformity to a particular church's teachings? What behaviors do other men within his environment exhibit? The tremendous variety of these different circumstances provides a rich diversity of masculinities, so that men raised in the same country within similar subcultures will have divergent views of appropriate male behavior.

Popular and unpopular notions of masculinity are subject to the winds of social change. All the same, masculinity does contain certain core concepts within cultural traditions as broad as advanced technological societies which include the United States, Canada, Japan, and European nations. Men in these cultures have formed identities in relation to the demands of surviving in an industrial world that is shifting to an information based economy. Challenges men face within technological societies differ from those men experienced before the discovery of electricity and from those men who live in primitive circumstances face on many parts of this planet. This is not to imply that one set of understandings about how men ought to behave is better than another, rather that different cultures contain differing norms for masculinity.

Cultural myths contain male messages that set forth prescriptions for how men ought to behave. These cultural myths have deep historical roots within a Western tradition that goes back to the ancient Greeks. Masculine myths containing male messages are invented stories about the deeds of men, passed down from father to sons. They praise the accomplishments of male heroes in movies, in songs, and in men's writings. Male myths contain noble standards for male behavior beyond the reach of most men, as well as standards that manifest degradations of all sorts. Like other myths, the origins of male messages lack rational explanation. We are neither sure where these myths which portray superhuman aspects of masculinity began, nor are we clear about why our society values them. They are celebrated because we want men to exhibit certain qualities portrayed by the myths.

In a modern technological world these cultural myths are extremely diverse and contribute to many different types of male behavior. In the United States myths from African and Spanish speaking countries provide role models for young boys forming their gender identities. In Great Britain immigrants from the former commonwealth countries provide diverse interpretations of masculinity. In France settlers from Africa provide their own cultural traditions about how males ought to behave. In Germany Turkish workers bring their masculine myths into Teutonic culture. Male messages that define masculinity contain complex and contradictory norms reflecting a wide variety of cultural myths, each with its own specific history and values.

Dominant Cultural Norms

The following 24 gender-role messages set standards for appropriate male behavior in the latter half of the twentieth century. Although this list has been generated in the United States, it has universal application. Because of the power of the US media, these messages are hegemonic, heard around the world, contributing to masculine ideology as men strive to conform to messages of modernity broadcast by popular media. This list is not exhaustive. Men receive many more messages than those listed below. This list is, however, representative of dominant male gender norms in modern technological societies.

The messages listed below, which have been generated from a diverse sample of men, also apply to women. These cultural norms are not exclusively male. The categories 'male' and 'female' do not exist isolated from each other. Although many women hear the same messages, this book will not discuss the influence of these messages upon females. Rather, it will present gender norms that a sample of 560 men in the United States rated as being influential in their lives. In this list those male messages that are considered traditionally masculine are labelled with a 'C' because they reflect what Clyde Franklin has called 'the classical man' (1984).

Male Messages

C *Adventurer:* Men take risks and have adventures. They are brave and courageous.

   Be Like Your Father: Dad is your role model. Males express feelings in ways similar to their fathers.

C *Be the Best You Can:* Do your best. Do not accept being second. 'I can't' is unacceptable.

C *Breadwinner:* Men provide for and protect family members. Fathering means bringing home the bacon, not necessarily nurturing.

C *Control:* Men are in control of their relationships, emotions, and job.

Faithful Husband: Men give up their freedom when they get married.

Good Samaritan: Do good deeds and acts. Put others' needs first. Set a good example.

C *Hurdles:* To be a man is to pass a series of tests. Accomplishment is central to the male style.

C *Money:* A man is judged by how much money he makes and the status of his job.

Nature Lover: Love of outdoors. Respectful treatment of plants and animals. Harmony with nature.

Nurturer: Among other things men are gentle, supportive, warm, sensitive, and concerned about others' feelings.

C *Playboy:* Men should be sexually aggressive, attractive and muscular.

C *President:* Men pursue power and status. They strive for success.

Rebel: Defy authority and be a nonconformist. Question and rebel against system.

Scholar: Be knowledgeable. Go to college. Value book learning. Read and study.

C *Self-Reliant:* Asking for help is a sign of weakness. Go it alone. Be self sufficient and do not depend on others.

C *Sportsman:* Men enjoy playing sports, where they learn the thrill of victory and how to compete.

C *Stoic:* Ignore pain in your body. Achieve even though it hurts. Do not admit weakness.

C *Superman:* Men are supposed to be perfect. They do not admit mistakes.

Technician: Men relate to, understand, and maintain machines. They fix and repair things around the house.

The Law: Do right and obey. Do not question authority.

C *Tough Guy:* Men do not touch, show emotions, or cry. They do not let others push them around.

C *Warrior:* Men take death defying risks to prove themselves and identify with war heroes.

C *Work Ethic:* Men are supposed to work for a living and not take handouts.

The fifteen classical messages – 'adventurer', 'be the best you can', 'breadwinner', 'control', 'hurdles', 'money', 'playboy', 'president', 'self reliant', 'sportsman', 'stoic', 'superman', 'tough guy', 'warrior', and 'work ethic', 63 per cent of the male messages used in this study – describe traditional standards of male behavior. These classical messages point to a man often portrayed in Hollywood movies. Like Clint Eastwood or John Wayne, he is tough, adventurous, and neither backs down from conflicts nor shows his feelings.

The other nine messages ('be like your father', 'faithful husband', 'good samaritan', 'law', 'nature lover', 'nurturer', 'rebel', 'scholar', and 'technician') have not received much discussion in gender-role literature. They indicate that modern expectations upon men transcend classical standards for male behavior. Although some of these ('be like your father', 'faithful husband', 'law', 'rebel', and 'technician') appear throughout western culture they are non-traditional, not having been seen as dominant messages. Four ('good samaritan', 'nature lover', 'nurturer', and 'scholar') have not appeared in descriptions of male conditioning (David and Brannon, 1976; Doyle, 1983; Farrell, 1986; Pleck and Sawyer, 1974). Males who stated that these messages have influenced their constructions of masculinity indicate that masculinity is not uniform in its expectations, containing only classical notions of appropriate male behavior. These four messages plus 'be like your father' 'faithful husband' and 'rebel' point to a type of man not often celebrated in popular culture. He wants to be like his father if he receives nurturing from him. A faithful husband pursues a committed, mutual relationship and not casual relationships for his own convenience. A good samaritan cares for others. A nature lover, concerned about the fate of planet Earth, nurtures plants and animals. A rebel questions social conventions. A scholar investigates different views of reality in his search for truth.

The above list of messages indicates that masculine gender role expectations are not limited to unemotional, aggressive responses to the world. As Robert Brannon has stated, 'It would be a mistake to assume that the male gender-role is a totally negative influence on the millions of individuals who grew up under its influence' (1985, p. 312). A man's gender identity includes both male and female characteristics (Freimuth and Hornstein, 1982). Male messages have both positive and negative aspects. In order to produce more nurturing individuals who will live in harmony with the life forces on this planet, the positive tendencies that already exist within the male psyche will have to be reinforced.

The Influence of Male Messages

Gender-role messages men receive from their surroundings are like scripts an actor follows in a play, except here the drama is a man's life. They are prescriptions for masculinity that influence the way an individual develops. Many men described these messages as a driving need. Earl, a 44-year-old therapist (Caucasian), described the 'playboy' message as a guiding light. Ralph, a writer-visionary (Caucasian), said that his whole life was affected by the 'adventurer' message. John, a 26-year-old short order cook (Caucasian), said that the 'self-reliant' message had influenced him for a long time. It was hard to break that pattern. He said, 'Following this message is like taking orders from people who love you. Except when you get older, the orders come from yourself.'

An 18-year-old high school student, Bruce (Caucasian), who came from a chaotic home with little stability, described gender-role messages as rules about how to live. Bruce felt he never got instructions when he was younger. 'I'm basically trying to write my own rule book,' he said, 'because I'm in a world that doesn't have one.'

Male messages set standards. Achieving these standards is virtuous for men who try to reach the challenges they set for themselves to become presidents, scholars, supermen, playboys, rebels, warriors, and sportsmen. By age 9 or 10, young boys develop identities that include goals they hope to accomplish. These identities provide direction for their lives. They travel through life as if driving a bumper car in an amusement park. An 'I' at the center of their being gets crashed into by a variety of unforeseen events – other people, crises, and circumstances that alter an individual's direction. As this car travels throughout the span of an individual's life, the 'I' at the control puts his foot on the accelerator, applies brakes, and steers toward particular goals. As Keith, a 32-year-old merchant-marine officer (Caucasian), stated:

> Life is a journey trying to find what is comfortable and satisfying. Life is like a car that you wind up, and it hits a wall, and bounces back and just keeps moving. The wall is being bored or not being happy with where I am.

When men reach such 'walls' they redefine their identities, devaluing certain messages received when younger and emphasizing others to choose new destinations for their journeys.

Sam, a 29-year-old Vietnam veteran (Caucasian), explained how male messages influenced him:

> We were raised with a certain script, and if we follow the script, we are told, life will work. What do you do when it's obvious to you that the script is not working? You keep working the script, because that's all you've got till the script just gets torn out of your hands, and you have no choice but to try something else, try a new script. We have plenty of scripts floating around in our heads. You either write a new script, or you realize you don't need a script. The process for me was to write a new script and find out that didn't work, and write a new script until I found a way of acting that brought me some satisfaction.

He followed his most important message, 'tough guy', into the special forces as a member of the Seal Team in the Navy in Vietnam, where he experienced the horrors of combat. Upon returning to civilian life he felt alienated from his wife and family and became increasingly isolated from friends. Finally, when he realized the 'tough guy' message was causing problems, Sam reoriented his life to become a counselor of Vietnam veterans. In his contemporary life, being tough involves taking risks, making himself vulnerable and confronting people with the reality of their behavior, but it no longer means hurting others.

Ricardo, a 31-year-old ex-con and Vietnam veteran (Hispanic), said his most important message was 'adventurer'. He remembered getting the message when he was two or three years old, when his mother and aunts would say he was just like his uncle, who was in jail, had been married two or three times, and had kids 'here and there'. Ricardo's uncle came home seldom but never to stay. Ricardo stated:

> Later on in life I started identifying with a lot of characters like Tarzan,

and Johnny Weissmuller and Steve Reeves who used to play Hercules, and I started identifying with figures like that on the TV and in the movies.

Ricardo remembers in his early teens that being an adventurer meant getting chased by cops, stealing bikes and cars, and conquering women. In high school he had to be the first one to have a gun, the first to drop out, and the first in his neighborhood to go to Vietnam, where the 'adventurer' message compelled him to take risks, volunteering for special assignments in the Marine Corps. Ricardo came home a hero. He settled down, got a job in the Post Office, and married, but dropped everything to join the Indian struggle for self determination at Wounded Knee in South Dakota. When he returned, he became a drug dealer, another adventure. His uncle taught him the ropes. Drug dealing led to prison, which he describes as 'a great big adventure':

> I remember when I went to prison. I was twenty-five at the time. It seemed like as soon as I hit prison it was like a great relief, like I had fulfilled something. Like I had become just like my uncle. I was a nail biter through most of my life. As soon as I arrived, the first day in county jail I just stopped biting them. It was like a spell breaker to me. I had finally fulfilled that destiny, or message that was given to me.

Five years in prison taught Ricardo about the bad side of the adventurer message. Upon return to civilian life, he became involved in a minority drug counseling program, where he used his leadership skills to help other men overcome their addictions. He reported that the influence of 'adventurer' message has not disappeared, but rather has a new emphasis in his current life.

This study demonstrates the conflicting nature of modern standards for male behavior. Messages such as 'playboy' and 'faithful husband', 'law' and 'rebel', 'nurturer' and 'stoic', place contradictory expectations on men and lead to what some researchers have described as gender-role stress, which comes from difficulties men have trying to live up to standards implied within these messages (Komarovsky, 1976; Pleck, 1976; Sargent, 1985). Not all men in the United States are faithful husbands. (A 1986 poll cited in *Esquire* stated 51 per cent of middle class and upper middle class men have had at least one extramarital affair.) The 'faithful husband' message indicates that men who commit adultery might feel guilty cheating on their wives. Men who lead criminal lives may feel remorse because they have received ethical messages to respect the law.

These messages create tensions within the minds of men who feel they ought to live up to the behavioral standards implied within them. Just because men receive certain messages does not mean that they will act in accordance with the behavior described by that message. Gender-role messages are scripts that set normative standards men carry around in their heads and try to realize. Such scripts help men organize information, determine plans, and set priorities, but the actual course of their lives may deviate considerably from scripts adopted in younger years. Once men assume adult tasks, they may not behave in accordance with various messages they learned as children, but the messages still tug within their psyches.

An example of how these messages may not be exhibited within an individual's life was provided by Mac, a 55-year-old African–American who had spent most of his years in jail. Even though Mac had never attended college, his most influential message was 'scholar'. His mother had instilled in him the value of a good education. Mac in his fifties tried to get into college to respond to the deep influence of this message.

Men feel frustrated when they can't realize deeply cherished messages. Joseph Pleck (1981) has pointed out how the dominant paradigm for masculinity in the United States induces strain. Male gender roles are contradictory and inconsistent. Violating roles leads to social condemnation and negative psychological consequences. Males who do not feel they live up to the impossible demands of masculinity suffer from low self esteem. Men like Mac often attempt late in life to realize goals they had as young boys. Historic changes in concepts of masculinity also cause gender-role strain.

Shifting Masculinities within a Patriarchal Social Order

A man's gender identity is formed in relation to his culture that contains patterned ways of thinking, feeling, and reacting that form the basis for his world views. A social culture evolves over time as a manifestation of evolutionary mechanism (Sahlins, 1976). Males grow up within cultures that have both implicit and explicit male messages that constitute masculine ideology. Classical male messages socialize boys to be aggressive:

> Take the example of male aggressiveness. The socialization case is that aggression is learned. Men learn that is both rewarding and expected to behave in an assertive way. Boys grow up in environments which encourage certain kinds of conduct, rather than others. They learn to be 'men'. Aggression, from this point of view, is a response to specific kinds of experience. Men will only behave aggressively if they have learned it is appropriate to do so. The implication is that a society's proper functioning depends upon the inculcation of aggressive patterns of behavior in young boys. (Brittan, 1989, p. 7)

As the twentieth century draws to a close, males are faced with a bewildering array of male models. This study indicates that norms about appropriate male behavior vary from classical messages that men ought to be aggressive, tough, unemotional, success oriented, and macho to notions of men being nature lovers, nurturers, and scholars. Classical messages support patriarchal order in modern societies.

> Patriarchy is the power of fathers: a familial-social, ideological, political system in which men – by force, direct pressure, or through ritual, tradition, law and language, customs, etiquette, education, and the division of labor – determine what part women shall or shall not play, and in which the female is everywhere subsumed by the male. It does not necessarily imply that no woman has power, or that all women in a given culture may not have certain powers. (Rich, 1976, p. 48)

Men have created patriarchal societies that grant privileges to those males who follow the dictates of classical masculinity. A patriarchy is a social order established by males to benefit themselves. The word 'patriarch' comes from the Greek word for father. Thus, a patriarchy is a world in which fathers rule, where women have subordinate roles. Patriarchy in Western nations benefits some, but not all white males, while women and people of color occupy secondary social status.

Historic ideals supporting rugged notions of patriarchy may not fit contemporary social conditions. Male aggressiveness towards nature and towards fellow human beings is proving dysfunctional. Male aggression may have had value in pioneer settlements where men hunted and protected loved ones but in modern societies male aggression causes considerable misery as in inner city areas in the United States, in Northern Ireland and in the former Yugoslavia (just to name several of many tragic situations). Twentieth century men have to adapt to highly sophisticated technological societies. Forty years ago in a patriarchial social order men could count on their wives staying home to take care of children. In contemporary families mothers also work, so many fathers must assume parenting responsibilities. In an industrial era brute male strength produced material comforts. Today, in large corporations, managers negotiate settlements within agreed upon limitations established for business contracts, drawing upon their intellects and emotions to resolve disputes:

> I'd say that most males in my age group grew up under the old frontier spirit – strong, low display of emotions, first at everything, hunter and provider way of thinking. This attitude towards masculinity proved essential in frontier American society. The earlier years of America were harsh and crude; sometimes brutal. The varying climate, natives, and wildlife, coupled with miles of isolation made social graces and emotional display very low on a list of survival priorities. This is, however, the twentieth century. We are said to be a very technological and civilized group of people. Men like myself have re-examined our attitudes towards American life and the male in society. Each of us can strive, with less criticism and scrutiny, to change or develop our genuine feelings and personalities.
>
> 34-year-old service worker (African–American)

As the twentieth century draws to a close the ideology that supports patriarchal notions of masculinity faces challenges, a condition noticed by the researcher Joseph Pleck (1976) who distinguished between the traditional male role (characterized by physical strength, impulsive behavior, display of angry emotions, and strong male bonding) and the modern male role (characterized by intellectual and interpersonal skills, emotional intimacy with women, prohibition of anger, rational control of behavior, and weak male bonding). These changes reflect a revolution in gender-role norms that calls into question traditional patriarchal values inherited from previous centuries.

Males in postmodern societies are adapting to the demands of life in advanced technologies by rejecting, reformulating, and replacing some of the classical messages listed above (Keen, 1991). In response to the realities of a changing world, males are creating new gender roles. The evolution of nontraditional male messages can to some extent be attributed to various challenges to classical concepts of masculinity mounted during the 1960s and 1970s, challenges that came from feminists who felt excluded within a patriarchal world order, challenges from men from ethnic/racial groups who rejected the dominance of white males, and challenges from gay men who questioned heterosexual hegemony. Such challenges threaten the privileged status of white males who benefit from a patriarchal status quo.

The problems associated with the patriarchal societies have been well documented. Feminists have pointed out how patriarchy retards women's development. The demands that patriarchy places upon males are also damaging (Goldberg, 1976). In the United States men have a life expectancy 10 years less than women. They suffer from cancer, heart attacks, and major diseases more than women. Males have higher rates of alcoholism, drug abuse, and assault. More men stutter. More men are homeless. More men end up incarcerated, and three times as many men commit suicide as women. Living up to the demands of patriarchy takes its toll both upon men and women.

In the 1970s, middle class men in western societies began to question classical demands of masculinity that sustain patriarchal societies and have started to redefine dominant male messages. At the beginning of the 1990s, a small, diffuse, tentative, and passionate men's movement exists – one that can be divided into left, right and central camps, according to how supportive its various branches are of feminism.[1] Men involved in this fledgling movement are discovering their wounds, questioning their socialization, challenging some of the tenets of patriarchy, and mounting a political agenda to focus on male concerns. Although few men identify with this movement, its existence portends deeper social rumblings. Many men who have had no contact with the various branches of this movement are staying home to look after their children, doing more housework, attending college to train for more meaningful jobs, pursuing political causes, changing careers, and in many other ways trying out new roles.

Riane Eisler stated in *The Chalice and the Blade* (1988) that the inchoate men's movement trying to redefine masculinity from its patriarchal basis is a sign that classical paradigms supporting western civilization are collapsing. Current challenges to classical notions of masculinity that undergird patriarchy indicate forces pushing for change. This struggle to create new gender norms for masculinity is extremely important. Because social organizations are so structured that men are in leadership positions, societies tend to follow the desires of men. If we are to move from our current patriarchal social order, which represents a garrison state (where individuals retreat from the social order into well-armed enclaves), towards a social order that represents a beloved state (where individuals demonstrate compassion for those less fortunate), men are going to have to come to grips with social norms that support patriarchy and confront the various agents that socialize them into destructive patterns of behavior. Without understanding both the social norms that influence male behavior and the process by which men form their gender identities, modern societies are in danger of perpetrating a social order that is hurtling towards an impending doom of desperate poverty, escalating crime, environmental destruction, and ethnic warfare. Who is giving men messages about how to behave?

Note

1   For an in-depth discussion of the trends within the modern men's movement, see Kenneth Clatterbaugh (1990), *Contemporary Perspectives on Masculinity: Men, Women and Politics in Modern Society.*

Chapter 2

Message Sources

> I feel that I and other men have learned well the messages we have been
> given. For this we should not be blamed. Rather we need a massive
> effort (bootstraps) to learn about ourselves, about women, and the skills
> required to both adapt and be critical about our changing roles and social
> norms.
>
> 45-year-old professional (Caucasian)

From millions of environmental cues each man develops standards for his
behavior. Jonathan, a 41-year-old community organizer (Caucasian), acquired
the male message 'be the best you can' from his parents:

> I think the example was that my parents were both very demanding of
> each other. So it was a two-sided message. It was coming, one, from
> their example; two, from everything they said. If there's any one
> consistent message we always got it was that you're good and capable
> and intelligent and should be everything you possibly can.

He explained the influence of this message in the following terms:

> So I willfully reinforce it in my own life, as compared with some
> messages that one buys, has bought, and continue to influence you, but
> you wish hadn't been so strongly influential, or you've worked to get
> them out of your life. Or you're constantly influenced by them but
> unaware of them. Or you're influenced by it and you think some of it's
> okay but you'd rather change it and struggle with pieces of it.

Men learn male messages in many different ways. In constructing their
gender identities, boys adopt messages that appeal to them and conform to
cultural norms they think they should emulate, even though they may not be
appealing. Some messages are directly taught. Others are learned by example.
Many men are not explicitly taught these messages, but rather pick them up by
observing male behavior. Harry, a 29-year-old computer consultant from
Cincinnati (Caucasian), said that everything was implied in his family, that there
was no communication:

But as far as thinking back to the early years, I just have to say at least in my family there wasn't real communication, where you sat down at the dinner table and things were discussed; it wasn't like that. Things were more relayed in an implicit way, where you were supposed to know your place. You were supposed to pick up on these things and know your place in the family and society.

Some participants in this study lived in environments where the behavior implied by the messages was omnipresent. This was especially true for men who grew up in rural areas where there was little deviation from standard norms. Sam, who grew up in Montana, observed the men around him being tough guys. Ed, a farmer in Iowa, stated that the 'breadwinner' message was the most important message in his life. All men in his community strove to support their families. These men do not so much remember anybody telling them to be tough guys or breadwinners, but rather they learned these messages by a kind of osmosis from their surroundings.

Gil, a 50-year-old Navy veteran raised in Hawaii (Caucasian), described learning the 'technician' message from his grandfather, a carpenter:

I learned many things from him when I used to visit him and my grandmother in the summer time. I would go with him and he would show me. I watched what he did. I had an uncle who was an electrician and he showed how to do a lot of things, at 9, 10, 11 years old.

Observing these men taught Gil how to become a competent technician fixing things in the Navy and in his current life repairing things around his own house.

The Role of Fathers

For most boys their most powerful teacher about masculinity is their father, who plays an enormously important role in their development, modeling how men behave. Psychologists have established that children will model their most nurturing parent, or parents who are nurturing (Bandura, 1969).

Many commentators about male behavior assume that men get their standards about how they ought to behave from the media (Farrell, 1986). To be sure, the media provide many models for male behavior, but media influence is far overshadowed by the influence of the family as demonstrated by Kirk, a 48-year-old Lutheran pastor (Caucasian), when he described how he learned the 'superman' message:

My father was really demanding; not in a harsh way, but his expectations were really high. I would imagine that the two sources for this message were my father and my older brother, also the school system I attended, my pastor, and finally from the society in depictions such as the comic book hero Superman (in that order).

Many men stated that their home environments dominated their under-standing of appropriate male behavior. Keith saw his father as his hero and strived to be like him, internalizing his father's values, preferences, and behavior:

> He was my hero and role model. But it does surprise me, because I don't think I realized until just recently how much, because I thought they were the things I thought I should do: Go to Alaska, go to sea – those were the things young men did, because that's what my father had done.

The behavior valued by fathers gets passed on to sons. This study included three pairs of fathers and their grown sons. One of these pairs included three generations – a grandfather, father, and a 19-year-old son. In this particular case the father, an executive with a computer company, mentioned that his father was a grocer with his own store who spent considerable time away from home. The executive continued this pattern with his own children. All of the sons exhibited behaviors which their fathers valued.

The way these messages get transmitted from one generation to the next was illustrated by Mark, an 18-year-old high school student (Caucasian), who learned the 'nature lover' message from his father. His mother and father divorced when he was in first grade. After the divorce his father used to take him on hikes. Mark explained:

> And he'd always spend time, like look at a flower for five minutes. It was his patience, his emphasis, his appreciation of nature that rubbed off on me. He just liked to be out there with me. When we would go out for walks we would talk. He'd ask, 'How's school going?' It's kind of like the association with having a good talk with my dad, being out in nature, so I put two good things together. Now that my dad has died, I have started to think about the things he taught me. He didn't really tell me 'This is bad. This is good.' But taught me through example. I really plan when I have children to give the same message my dad taught me.

Boys who admire their fathers internalize their standards.

Why do young boys emulate their dads? Keith described his fear of doing something wrong and of being criticized. Young boys want their parents' acceptance because they want their love. They strive to get their parents' affection by doing those things which they think will earn parental approval. Parents contribute to the process of gender-role conditioning by rewarding children.

Boys earn their fathers' approval for gender appropriate behavior. Dick, a 48-year-old retired Navy commander (Caucasian), described himself as a little boy trying to avoid his father's criticism. 'I'm aware of that, and I'm happy with that,' he said. 'This little boy wants to do good, wants to feel he's considered a good kid, you know, an okay person.' Al – a 55-year-old chemist (Caucasian), father of ten – described how he learned the 'work ethic' message:

> I have this driving need to achieve because I was seeking approval from
> my parents, and I wasn't getting it. I got good grades, working real hard
> because that's what they wanted me to do.

Sons learn masculine behavior from their dads because father's constant
presence provides a dominant image for masculinity. Parents present to their
children the way the world is and pass on to their offspring codes of conduct.
Another reason why young boys emulate their fathers was provided by Johnny,
a 41-year-old lawyer (Caucasian). He stated that young boys wanted to be like
their fathers because their fathers were loved by their mothers. In other words,
young boys are envious of their fathers who have their mother's love. They not
only want their mother's love, but want the love of women, so they conclude the
way to get their mother's love and the love of other women is to be like their
fathers.

Young boys inherit their parents' dreams. Earl mentioned that his father had
been sexually frustrated in his marriage. As a consequence Earl's most important
message was 'playboy', where Earl feared getting tied down into a marriage
situation he could not escape. Some parents set extremely rigorous standards for
their sons and insist their son meet those standards. A 58-year-old investor
(Caucasian) commented,

> The 'shoulds' were rammed down my throat in my youth; learning to
> stuff and deny my true inner feelings in order to placate parents' anger.
> Absence of strong males in my youth contributed a great deal to a long
> period of confusion and denial.

In many cases, boys are severely punished for not behaving in ways that
meet father's approval. Sam talked about living in fear as a young lad, trying to
live up to the 'tough guy' message, to be something others wanted him to be. He
feared if men in his community would find out that he was not tough, they would
pick on him.

Boys often rebel against their father's stern injunctions to behave in a
particular way. An example of such a rebellion was provided by a 46-year-old
service worker (Caucasian):

> At age 18 my image was formed as a rejection of my father, his values,
> and everything for which he stood. Now, I see myself adopting many of
> those traits and assimilating them into my personality and behavior.

A man's relationship with his father is extremely complex. As men mature,
they re-evaluate their dads. An opinion given by a man at age 20 might vary
drastically about the same father at a different age, as indicated by Jesse, a
57-year-old baptist preacher (African–American) who grew up in rural Texas.
His father, a baptist minister, never finished school and was fundamentalist in his

beliefs. He would not let his son date, go to dances, and party with his friends. Upon reflecting about his father's values and standards, Jesse said:

> At the time I was growing up I thought he was from another world. I thought he had sort of dropped out of space. I didn't know the word alien then, but if I had known it, I would've declared he was one. I used to think, 'How did he get like this? When I'm grown I'm never going to be like that guy'. But as I grow older, I realize that he was very sound. I find the advice my father gave me becomes more and more important.

Jesse, as he matured, developed a whole new appreciation of his father's behavior.

Men's relationships with their fathers are diverse and cannot easily be characterized. Messages passed down from father to son are not always positive. Two men interviewed for the 'be like your father' message indicated that they had a counter-dependent relationship upon their father's values. They were told when they were young that they should act like their fathers, but they did not respect their fathers; therefore they were trying in their adult lives to be entirely different types of men. One man who said he hated his father stated that he did not want to make the same mistakes his father did. A counter-dependent relationship implies that an individual is rebelling against injunctions to behave in a particular way.

Sons want to bond with other men. Many men have a deep longing for paternal love. Sons unable to become friends with their fathers feel great pain. Many sons deny this pain by romanticizing and idealizing their relationships with their fathers. Some boys do not know much about the inner lives of their fathers and feel that in order to win their father's approval, they have to be successful. Most sons show their love symbolically to their fathers by trying to achieve in the world, and not expressively through words and emotions.

As important as fathers are in a son's development, sons have the ultimate responsibility for their own development. Becoming a father can help a man understand his own father's limitations. As a man struggles with the stresses and difficulties of being a father, he can better empathize with his own father's behavior and learn to accept his father's limitations.

Samual Osheron (1986, p. 7) in his book, *Finding Our Fathers*, describes a study by Jack Sternbach in which Sternbach characterized how fathers relate to their sons. Below is a summary of that study:

- 23 per cent of fathers were physically absent from their son's upbringing;
- 29 per cent of fathers were psychologically absent;
- 18 per cent were austere, unrealistic, and uninvolved with their sons;
- 15 per cent were dangerous, frightening, and out of control; and
- 15 per cent were appropriately involved.

With these kinds of statistics and through his own research, Osheron concludes that in the United States the dominant experience of fathers and sons is one of distance, estrangement, and pain. From the lack of closeness that characterizes most father–son relationships, men have deep wounds, accompanied by an underlying sense of sadness that comes from leaving father behind as men mature. Men spend their lives trying to heal the pain of these wounds.

A man's attempt to reconcile himself to his father was captured in John Barth's first novel, *The Floating Opera* (1967), in which the hero started writing letters to his father in order to communicate about his life. After his father died, he continued the correspondence. Many men's attempts to get close to their fathers similarly fail. They have difficulty accepting that loss. From that primal experience they learn not to trust other men and spend their lives unable to achieve emotionally close relationships with males.

This sense of alienation of sons from fathers was commented upon by Arcana (1983, p. 6), who concluded about the father–son relationship:

> Sons are unrealistic to hope for spiritual presence and emotional nurturance from their fathers. Men are not trained to care for children – or for adults, really – and they are not part of daily family life, so that even those men who are, as one mother said, 'misfit' are hard pressed to spend enough time with their families to give and get loving.

Men who are not trained to be nurturing may not achieve nurturing relationships with their sons.

When Fathers Aren't Around

With a rapid increase in the divorce rate today over one third of first marriages end in divorce. As a result, sons are likely to spend less time with their fathers. Some experts have estimated that as many as 12 million children in the United States do not live with their fathers (Streiker, 1989). The following indicates what percentage of children continue to see their fathers after a divorce, indicating the extent of father deprivation in the United States (Osheron, 1986, p. 224):

- 50 per cent of children have no contact with father
- 30 per cent had only sporadic contact
- 20 per cent saw their children once a week or more

Eighty-eight per cent of children who are part of divorced families end up living with their mothers. Father's absence can have a profound effect upon a son who feels rejected because his father does not choose to spend time with him. Boys need a sense that it is okay to be a man. When they do not get that from their fathers, they tend to be confused about their masculine identity, as evidenced by the following statements:

> Very influenced regarding male conditioning by lack of father figure during formative years – prior to age 18. Parents divorced when I was

1 year old. Father did not (or very rarely) utilize visitation privileges and chose to move out of state. Raised by my mother in home with three sisters and no brothers. This caused great male identity concerns during years prior to age 18.

Lost father at an early age (14); used peers as role models.

I never knew my father. My mother tried to teach me to hate my father, and I have a very poor self image as a result.

Fathers can play an important part in a young man's development because they provide standards for masculinity by which boys can judge the world. But fathers are not the only role models available for young boys trying to figure out what it means to be a man. Older boys, siblings, and images depicted on the media provide important images of masculinity. Young boys, whether or not they have a present father, study the behavior of men in order to learn about masculinity:

My father left my mother when I was 6 years old. My mother remarried when I was seven, had a stressful marriage, and divorced when I was 17. My stepfather was largely uninvolved with me. I therefore see myself as being 'self taught' as a man, largely – that has pluses and minuses.

My father was gone a lot when I was growing up, and my brother is five years older, so most of my 'conditioning' came from peers and the media and school. The media are, generally, a strong and unrealistic source of conditioning.

All men form a gender identity, whether or not their fathers play an active role in their lives. Boys can learn about appropriate male behavior from families other than their own. Hank, a 24-year-old college student (Caucasian), told about how he learned the 'faithful husband' message:

Probably on my own. Just my own thinking. You see it everywhere. I've never really been open with anyone, so everything I've been taught, everything I do basically, I've done on my own or even learned on my own. I might have observed it somewhere, but it seems like I've never had any input or really known the influence of anyone else. My father divorced my mother when I was young. (He certainly wasn't an example of a faithful husband!) I hung around with other friends and their families a lot. Since my mother was working, I was constantly down the block in a friend's house that had four boys. I basically ate lunch there. I was there every day in the summer, and after school in the fall and the winter. The mother stayed home to look after her children. This family had a real big influence on my values.

The gender-role conditioning process by which men learn male messages is much more complex than the story of Keith, whose father was his hero. Fathers in real life often do not live up to the glamorized standards depicted in such television shows as 'Ozzie and Harriet', 'All in the Family', and 'The Cosby Show'. Most men do not actively participate in the raising of children. Many absent fathers working outside the house leave parenting responsibilities to their wives. Other fathers who abandon their children are not around to become a role model for their sons. Many fathers feel they are outsiders in the home, that they are failures as parents, and hence retreat from the family as workaholics or alcoholics, because they feel they do not belong in a caretaking environment.

Given the inappropriate behavior of most fathers towards their children, mother's influence can be dominant. Even for those boys who lived with both parents, their fathers were most often distant figures not involved in raising their children. Some of the fathers of the men who participated in this study were punitive, with the result that their sons did not respect them very much. Research shows that fathers who behave inappropriately towards their children can create severe behavioral problems for their children (both boys and girls). Many children would be better off without such hostile fathers (Green, 1976).

The Role of Females

Women influence the formation of a man's gender identity. Mothers teach their sons about masculinity by telling their sons how to behave, modeling certain behaviors, and rewarding sons for their actions. Women reinforce messages through the approval, love, and friendship they share with men. Boys are likely to take their cues about how they ought to behave from mother who is often the only nurturing parent. Since most elementary teachers are female, women play extremely important roles in helping young boys adopt appropriate standards for their behavior.

A good example of how women become agents in the gender-role conditioning process, is provided by Steve, a 41-year-old Baptist preacher (African–American), talking about how he learned the 'control' message. He did not respect his father whom his mother used to push around:

> My mother not only dominated my father but she dominated other women as well. I liked that she was a strong woman, very energetic. She wasn't afraid to tackle anybody. I learned those qualities from her. That's where I got the control message, I guess, because I'm exactly the way she was.

Psychologists state that the early years are the most important years in an individual's development. Since most boys in the United States are raised by their mothers, women strongly influence male identities. The power of mother's influence upon a young boy is described graphically by Frank, a 44-year-old senior industrial engineer, telling how he learned 'law' message. He described his mother as the life giver, as the original nurturer:

When you're one year old, your mother is God; she is the law. I guess right now I think my mother had a much more profound effect upon me than my father. And in terms of this the way I would describe it is with this image I have: She is this huge gray rock, kind of buried under the ground, and my father's like a puppet dancing around in a colorful costume. But he's like real small, where she is huge. You don't even notice she is there, because my father is there all colorful and noisy.

The irony of Frank's story is that Frank's mother worked full time from the time he was in the first grade. His father, a factory worker, hurt his back, and spent much more time with his children, because he was disabled, than do most fathers. In spite of his father's active involvement in his life, Frank's mother was this huge solid rock, with subterranean influences upon his psyche. He described as a young boy trying to psyche her out and do what he thought was correct so he could get her approval. Her standards established the law in his household.

Most mothers take care of the day-to-day details in young boys' lives. As Warren, a 37-year-old carpenter (Caucasian), put it, 'As far as learning that certain things were right and certain things were wrong, I learned most of that from my mother.' Daily contact with these powerful caretakers dominates a young boy's superego, his sense of how he ought to behave. Some mothers help boys figure out how to behave by praising their sons. This was evidenced by Bob, a 44-year-old manager of a housing cooperative, whose most important message was 'technician'. He remembers getting praised by his mother for building elaborate structures with erector sets and Lincoln logs. Since mothers play such an important role in young men's lives, their praise is especially meaningful. Women continue to play a role as a reinforcer of particular behaviors throughout a man's life, as friends, as lovers, and as wives. Some respondents lived out their mother's dreams. Larry, a TV weatherman, mentioned that his mother was extremely devoted to him. She wanted him to be successful, and he felt that his ambition had been in part a desire to fulfill his mother's wishes. An example of the impact a mother can have upon a young man's life when the father has not been around at all was provided by Slim,[1] an 18-year-old high school student (Afro–American). When asked where he received the message 'nurturer', he responded:

From my mother, because my father left her and married someone else, and her father was real old-fashioned and never spent a lot of time with them. So she came up with the idea that a man should be loving and close to his children. She wanted to instill the message in me that I should both be loving to my wife and a loving father.

Slim's mother taught this message to her son both explicitly and implicitly by providing an example of how to be nurturing:

She always tries to be close to me. She knows that life at this time is real hard, and she always tries to be close and open and understanding to whatever I have to say. So I'd say, yeah, she really tries to the best of her ability to set an example for me to be nurturing.

Further evidence for the crucial role mothers play in the development of a man's gender identity comes from the following comments:[2]

Was raised by mother, grandmother, and other women. Few male influences other than peers, and many of them had no fathers.

Many young men have their fathers as role models, but my father was rarely ever home. My main role models were probably my mom, my friends' fathers, and the books I read. I know a lot of guys that grow up under their mothers turn out to be kind of prissy, but my mom encouraged me to take up anything I wanted. She wouldn't back off an argument, or take shit from anybody. She didn't teach me to be macho, but to do what I really want to do and stand up for what I believe in.

My mother was a strong influence in my life. She wanted me to be a journalist like herself. I got a journalism degree but found I really didn't like journalism work. My father owned his own business. I could have taken it over when he retired. However my father was so cold and nonsupportive that I had no desire to follow in his footsteps. I now drive a truck for a living and love it.

Women, more than men, were the ones who conveyed my most dominant messages to me. Men reinforced them.

My main message as a child came from my dominant mother about my passive father. It was 'don't be like your father'. This double bind still expresses itself in the complications I have in relating to men and women today.

Growing up male is not easy. As the last quote indicates, boys raised by overpowering mothers can be confused about their masculine identities. A divorced or deserted mother who sees her sons as a reflection of their father can respond negatively towards them. Satir (1972, p. 172) has pointed out that a boy treated this way will find it hard to believe 'that maleness is good' or that he is good. She warns:

Boys in a one-parent family probably face the greatest trap – being over-mothered, and/or getting the picture that the female has the dominant power in society, ending up with feeling that the male is nothing.

An overly demanding mother can create identity problems for boys, as indicated by the two quotes below:

My messages were double: 1) From my father, the model (and message) was one of self-sufficiency, giving to others, not showing feelings. 2) Mother wanted to keep me weak and dependent on her. That was especially difficult – and I was closer to my mother in growing up.

I've gotten into trouble in the past by trying to be the kind of man that women think they would like me to be.

Young boys are totally helpless when they are born. Somebody has to take care of them, a task called 'mothering', that is for the vast majority of boys in the United States carried out by women. A mother's role has been defined as follows: 'A mother is a person who takes responsibility for children's lives and for whom providing child care is a significant part of life' (Ruddick, 1989, p. 10). Mothers provide the primary source of praise, encouragement, and selfless service in a boy's life. They have primary responsibility for the well-being of their sons, whose whole world is initially interpreted by their mothers. As Forcey (1987) has pointed out, mothers often become goddesses in a young boy's eyes. Many men, after they leave the warmth of their mother's 'cocoon', seek nurturing women to take care of them.

A domineering mother provides an important developmental challenge for men who must cease being boys and grow into men. In order to feel secure about their masculine identities, boys must learn to assert their own identities as men, to develop their own standards for appropriate male behavior, getting approval from men, and not to depend solely upon women for a sense that they are okay. When mothers are overly critical of their fathers, young boys have difficulty identifying with their fathers and feel ambivalent about being men, as evidenced by the following quotes:

> I got quite a few mixed messages while growing up. From my peers I sensed what the male was 'supposed' to be, but at home it was totally different. My mother was very domineering and did her best to emasculate my father. This made it very difficult for me to understand or to learn what was expected of me.

> Most of my conditioning as a young boy and throughout my adolescence was subtle; I had very little contact with my father on an emotional level, and I received mixed messages from my mother because she attempted to invoke in me an attitude quite different than the basic make-up of my father. I really grew up with few strong ideas about what my manhood was about.

Contradictory pulls between the feminine and masculine are at the core of every man's gender identity. The influence of mothers creates what Carl Jung (1928) called 'the anima' or feminine side of the psyche. The masculine culture pulls boys away from their mothers, because they have to prove themselves in the world of men. Because many mothers want their sons to be expressive and aware of their feelings, many men have deep inside gender-role notions that contradict classical masculine expectations. Mothers who do not want their sons to be independent, obsessed by work, aggressive, selfish, or rigidly defensive hope their sons will be more committed to relationships – nurturers and faithful husbands, as opposed to playboys and supermen.

Sources for Male Messages

Table 2.1 indicates where men receive male messages:[3]

In Table 2.1, (P) indicates a person who was a primary caretaker for the person being interviewed. Sixty-three per cent of the men interviewed for this study indicated that they had received their most important male message from such a caretaker. All the other categories are secondary in the sense that their origins are outside the family.

An example of what the category 'all men in the family' means was provided by Wayne, a 49-year-old quality control inspector at a factory (Caucasian), when discussing how he learned the technician message. Wayne came from a big family, which he described as follows:

> Everyone was delegated a certain job. We were all shown how to do certain things when we were younger. And it was just normal – what was the norm in our household. I mean parents, both my grandparents lived next door. And my uncles and aunts rented from them, so there was a whole tribe of people, working around the house helping with the garden, taking the grease out, collecting eggs in the morning. You'd

Table 2.1   Sources for male messages

Origin	Number	Percentage
	96	100
All Men in Family (P)	6	6
Aunt (P)	1	1
Brother (P)	2	2
Church	1	1
Community	1	1
Culture	5	5
Father (P)	20	21
Grandfather (P)	4	4
High School	1	1
Just born with it	2	2
Media	5	5
Mother (P)	12	13
On own	16	17
Parents (both Mom and Dad) (P)	13	14
Peers	6	6
Uncle (P)	1	1

have to do your iron collections, paper, whatever. I always thought it was normal for kids to help out with the house.

The category 'community' implies the broader community in which an individual was raised. An example came from Randy, a Coast Guard electrician from New Hampshire (Caucasian), who described the small town where he was raised in New Hampshire. Not only did all the men in his family exhibit stoic behavior, but all his male friends had a hard time discussing their feelings and would not share weaknesses.

The category 'culture' describes tribal traditions within which a boy is raised. A good example of this category was provided by a 60-year-old professor, Phillipo (Hispanic), who was raised in a Chicano community in Kansas. Phillipo described how he learned the 'warrior' message:

Being Hispanic and being Mexican, Mexico's had a tradition of independence and the revolution and arms, so we have always admired, most of us, including the women, soldiers. Soldiering has always been considered a noble profession amongst us; and so my earliest recollections were admiring people like Pancho Villa, so that I grew up feeling it was very important to be a warrior.

With this category, the message permeates all parts of his environment.

The category 'just born with it' comes from two men who believed that they had always had the characteristics described by the message. Ralph provided an example of this when he described how he learned the 'adventurer' message:

Well, I think I got it from my genes. I'm reported to have been from the very beginning very intense and exploratory, and there are stories about how I walked around the living room without ever touching the floor, really walking or crawling to the edge of the sofa and jumping to the next chair. The second part comes from culture generally. Boyhood heroes like Davy Crockett. I was interested in the explorers. My general feeling about life was never really security oriented.

The other example of this source for a message comes from Bob, who believed he was born with certain aptitudes – math, reasoning, and spatial abilities – that formed the basis for his 'technician' message.

The category 'media' refers to men who learned that message from television, radio, movies, songs, and other media for popular culture.

As far as the culture and my life, I'd have to say that the media had a big impact on my perception of masculinity. Also, peer groups have been a factor along the way. I am sure that many men would have to say the same thing, since those two factors play an important role in just about every male's life.

As one man indicated, 'At present day TV has a great influence upon male character.' The types of messages so learned were traditional – warrior, tough guy, and superman:

> The role models or heroes when I grew up were tough guys – Clint Eastwood, Chuck Norris, James Coburn – each was quietly anti-social and expressed his feelings with violence.

> My father was gone a lot when I was growing up and my brother is 5 years older, so most of my 'conditioning' came from peers and the media and school. The media are, generally, a strong and unrealistic source of conditioning.

Only five per cent of the men interviewed indicated that the media was the source of their male messages.

A good example of how the category 'on own' operates was provided by Carl, a 43-year-old lawyer from Boston (Caucasian), who reported that his most important message was 'nurturer'. He had no recollection of anybody teaching him nurturing skills. After his divorce, when he had custody of his daughters, he learned to value nurturing. Another example comes from Alex, a 40-year-old machinist (Caucasian), whose most important message was 'nature lover'. He felt at home wandering around his parents' farm in Indiana. Nobody told him it was important to spend time in natural settings. He learned to love exploring that wilderness and carries his interest in nature forward to his adult life, where he gardens as an avocation.

The category 'parents' applies to situations when the respondent could not discern whether his mother or father had a greater influence. In these cases both parents valued the standards implied by that message. An example of such a response was provided by Doug, a 41-year-old campus minister (Caucasian) who learned the 'good samaritan' message from both his parents, although each taught a different aspect of it. His father was a pastor who had worked for the World Council of Churches and 'was very highly respected for the work he had done with the refugees. So I admired that value and motivation in working', he continued.

> From my Mom I got the message of personal care for other people. She was a very nurturing person, the type of mother who was a low profile kind of person, but who was really making the household go, and was present for the kids, for all six of us on many occasions when my dad was away. So they each conveyed this message in their own way; Dad in a more professional way and Mom in a personal way ... Yeah; I would say the message was not explicitly verbalized. But it was pretty clearly conveyed, implicitly. The climate of our household, the clear values of our family were to care for other people, have respect for others. Those sorts of values were reinforced.

This category 'parents' has many more cases than the 13 mentioned in Table 2.1. Including the responses from the categories 'father' and 'mother', indicates the true influence of parents upon their sons. Adding together these three categories, 47 per cent of the men indicated their parents had been their most important source for learning gender-role messages. The following quote indicates how a man can learn appropriate male behavior from his grandfather:

> While I came from an intact, two-parent family, my strongest male identification came from my paternal grandfather whom I visited (in the same city) every other weekend. He, not my father, was my model.

The category 'peers' refers to the influence of friends and acquaintances. An example of how men learn male messages from peers came from a man who grew up in suburban Philadelphia talking about the rebel message. His parents divorced when he was eight years old, an age at which he became a juvenile delinquent – hanging out with other boys, getting in trouble, selling pot, and becoming a respected leader in a group of teenagers. At the same time his father was refusing to support him, and he had little or no contact with his dad. He earned the respect of his peers by taking risks, many of which broke the law.

Boys learn about masculinity from many different sources, including the media. Popular culture conveys popular male models. However, the influence of popular culture is not as important as the influence of family members. Research shows that an individual inherits his view of the social order from his parents who present to their children the only conceivable world a young child knows (Berger and Luckmann, 1966). Parents and relatives are the primary senders of male messages to young boys, who construct their gender identities under the influence of adults who interpret social reality to children. Boys adopt the attitudes of the particular world presented by their caretakers. The media, the church, high school, the surrounding culture provide many messages for men about how to behave, but their influence is less important than the influence of family members. This does not deny the importance of the surrounding culture in setting standards for appropriate male behavior, but rather underscores the importance of the home environment. Findings from this study indicate that the influence of violent and destructive images from the media are offset by the influence of family members and intimate friends, who play a crucial role in the construction of a man's gender identity.

Notes

1   Slim was a research assistant of mine, helping me complete this project during his senior year. As I got to know him, I noticed how stereotypical some of his notions about men were. When asked how fathers behave, he would often refer to a television show, like the Cosby show, to provide examples to back up his notions. Boys who do not have fathers in their lives can acquire exaggerated notions of male behavior from the media.

2   These comments come from an open ended stem at the end of the questionnaire used

in this study. 'Use the space below to state anything you would like to say about your own male conditioning or messages in this culture that have influenced your identity as a man.'

3   In determining the source for these male messages, such a response would be categorized with the first source a respondent mentioned. It is possible that men learn these messages from many different sources. This section of the research project tried to pin down what the most important source was and did not try to exhaust all the sources of a particular message in a man's life.

Chapter 3

Becoming a Man

> I've finally realized that to me a 'man' is just about what you think you
> want to be, depending on your background and developed social
> attitudes. Seeing the many role models available helps to reaffirm the
> ideals held about male identity and can yield better self-feelings about
> the choices made.
>
> 28-year-old professional (African–American)

A key part of any person's identity concerns his or her understanding of gender,
comprehending social notions of gender, and applying these concepts accurately
to the self. A man's gender identity enables him to identify himself as a man
within a specific culture. While forming their gender identities, young boys
desire 'to imitate the masculine model, which leads to a deeper attachment to the
model' (Kohlberg, 1966, p. 165). This formation of gender identity includes sex
typing and continues throughout life. Through sex typing an individual comes to
acquire, to value, and to adopt gender appropriate behavior patterns. Sex typing
is similar to programming a computer. The process of sex typing places a disk
within the superego. This disk contains cultural messages that reflect the shared
rules of society. Male messages are the various files within the disk that translate
social norms into schemata, which establish guidelines for thinking and acting.
All of these files, stored in the superego, program a person to behave according
to culturally defined gender patterns that prescribe methods of associating with
others.

Each person's identity contains an idealized self, called the superego by
Sigmund Freud (1962). The superego provides internal standards for right and
wrong derived from the society by way of identification with parents, friends,
authorities, and literary figures. As the psychologist, Eric Berne, stated, people
carry around in their superegos scripts telling them what to do and what not to
do (1976, p. 156). These scripts contain rules of conduct internalized from the
culture.

Identities have aspects of both continuity and change. An identity establishes
an individual as a particular type of person. An 'I', an individual at the core of an
ever-changing world of inner experience, constantly strives to produce a picture of
the self that belongs to the identity and guides behavior. The ego organizes
experiences into various conceptual grids and categories (Mead, 1934). At the
same time that a person seeks order and predictability dealing with the external

world, that person finds growth a dynamic process engaging attention.

Each person's identity contains schemata, mental representations of experiences that tell how to behave, what to value, and what to avoid.

> Gender schema theory contains two fundamental presuppositions about the process of individual gender formation: first, that there are gender lenses embedded in cultural discourse and social practice that are internalized by the developing child, and, second, that once these gender lenses have been internalized, they predispose the child, and later the adult, to construct an identity that is consistent with social concepts of gender. (Bem, 1993, p. 138–9)

These schemata, internal representations of events, become abstract mental organization systems or memory structures that provide a basis for organizing information, making judgments, and predicting the behavior of individuals. They help people comprehend and react to events. As children mature, their schemata become more diverse, integrated, and sophisticated, resulting in a series of complex rules that help individuals connect events, organize information, solve problems, and make judgments (Perry and Bussey, 1984). These schemata constitute an identity that directs behavior.

Joseph Pleck describes the process of becoming a man as learning a set of rules (1976). As one participant in this study put it, 'The condition of being male is to strive to become a man.' A boy learns how to become a man by studying male behavior in his surroundings. He wants to become like other men and embodies what he perceives to be standards for male behavior. These standards come from gender roles nested in specific cultures. Gender-roles include rights and obligations in a given society (Lindsey, 1990). Male messages define those roles and set limits on male behavior.

Men learn about male messages both by being directly taught and by observing other males. Throughout their lives they receive feedback from peers, parents, and others about how well they are performing as men. Becoming a man involves much more than learning the skills associated with masculinity, e.g. how to play football. It requires the development of identity and personality attributes that direct boys towards appropriate male behavior (Martin and Halverson, 1981). Once a boy realizes he is male, he wants to behave like other boys and constructs a perceptual grid that will evaluate the world according to his developing notions of masculinity.

Messages to conform to what society feels is appropriate for males surround men from birth. Men receive reinforcement both verbally and nonverbally for performing according to gender-role norms. In some cases they are pressured or coerced to conform to certain standards, as in the Marines. Hogie Wykoff (1974, p. 198) refers to that part of the superego that drives men to conform to rigid gender-role stereotypes as a 'pig parent':

> The main job of the male Pig Parent is to police men into always having their adults turned on to do as their pigs say they should do, to be 'real

men'; that is, to be out of touch with their nurturing, intuitive, or fun-loving feelings.

Boys and men are enjoined to participate in masculine rituals to learn appropriate male behavior. Men develop a fear of not doing right as defined by commonly understood notions of how men ought to behave (Stoltenberg, 1989). They reinforce their male identities by having pleasant experiences in the male arena.

Jerome Kagen (1964, p. 144) has suggested that the acquisition of gender-role behavior is the single most potent and long lasting aspect of the socialization process:

> The degree of match or mismatch between the gender-role standards of the culture and the individual's assessment of his own overt and covert attributes provides him with a partial answer to the question, 'How masculine am I?'

Younger men, faced with standards promulgated in the media, are insecure about their gender identities. Boys are not accepted members of society as males until they learn the socially prescribed roles appropriate for their gender. They live with the innate dread of being inadequate, comparing themselves with males who do better in school, who are handsome, muscular, rich, successful, and attractive. Leonard Kreigel (1979, p. 34) put it this way: 'To be a man is to carry a tape measure by which you measure yourself in relation to the world'.

Influence of Male Messages Throughout Life

Dynamic individuals interacting with changing cultures alter their gender identities:

> Change in sex-typed traits occurs, in fact, through the life cycle. As individuals encounter the many life experiences that have sex role meaning – parenthood, same and cross-sex intimacy, experiences in work, adult psychological changes, and aging. These later life experiences enrich and loosen one's conception of oneself as a man or woman, or they can be occasions of still more distress, discomfort, and feelings of inadequacy. (Pleck, 1975, p. 173)

Individuals trying to maintain a coherent view of themselves play an active role in their own gender development. Sorting out cues from their surroundings they establish identities that exist both in a biological timetable and in an ever-changing social environment. Individuals adjust their identities to circumstances.

As they mature, men gain understandings about their identities. When men become conscious of their behavior, they question original prescriptions they received from adults and start to determine what kind of people they want to be.

They gain appreciation for their own personalities, learn to accept specific cultural norms, and reject guidelines for their behavior. The influence of male messages within a man's gender identity takes many different directions, as seen in Table 3.1. Twenty-nine per cent of the men interviewed stated that the influence of their most important male message increased. For these men that particular message had been a chief motivator. As Dave said, 'I keep getting new understandings about this message as I age.' They appreciated its effect upon their lives. As they matured, its impact became stronger.

A similar percentage said that the influence of a particular message decreased. An example of how a man abandons a particular message was provided by Leo, a 52-year-old professor (Caucasian). His parents had exerted strong emotional control over his behavior, a habit which he carried into adulthood by controlling relationships. Leo became aware of the negative aspects of this message when he experienced a series of crises where he lost control and became suicidal. When asked how functional the 'control' message had been in his life, he responded:

> Oh, it's been terrible. Absolutely horrid. The primary ramification is that people run like hell away from it. They just don't want to be around you. You wind up every time you turn around arguing with people in meetings and arguing with lovers because you're constantly trying to control. When you try to control the person you love, that's not particularly rational, reasonable, or adult love. But the thing that's more important about this, is they become resentful, start acting mean and ultimately take off.

Leo lost his wife of long standing. Now he describes himself as much more relaxed socially. He does not need to control every situation.

Twenty-one per cent of the respondents indicated that the influence of their most important male message had remained the same. Typically respondents who indicated this said that the influence of a particular male message had risen to a point in their lives, usually by the end of their twenties, and had reached a plateau. It exerted a constant pressure.

An example of how a message stays important but switches emphasis was provided by Tony, a 31-year-therapist (American Indian) discussing the

Table 3.1   Influence of male messages over life span

	Number of subjects[1]	Percentage
	70	100
Increase	20	29
Decrease	20	29
Stay the same	15	21
Stay important but switch emphasis	7	10
Fluctuate	3	4
Counterdependent	5	7

influence of the 'rebel' message in his life. He transformed the influence of this message from ten years earlier when he was a punk, a smart ass. At that time he had serious drug problems and used to love to party:

> Now, instead of my rebellion being defensive anger I turn my anger into love, into passion. Instead of using that angry energy to say 'fuck you' to everybody and everything, I am using it to get things done, to make things happen in the world.

Tony said that the energy he gets from this message feels the same but that he has learned to redirect it.

An example of how a message fluctuates was provided by Harvey, a 40-year-old unemployed American Indian who had participated in the struggle at Wounded Knee. He was discussing the 'warrior' message, which had appeared periodically in his life. As a young kid living on the streets, he used it to defend himself. When he was in jail this message was also an important part of his life, but now that he has grown older it is not a part of his daily repertoire, although if he puts himself in certain situations it surges forth within him.

The category 'counterdependent' refers to men who receive a particular message but decide they do not like that message so they act out in rebellion against its influence. In such cases the importance of the message has not left them. It still tugs at their psyches but rather than acting in accordance with it, they try to abandon it or define the message in their own terms. They are dependent upon the message insofar as they are actively struggling against it. The following quote from a 65-year-old retired man provides an example of counterdependent:

> In reviewing the list of messages, I seem to have received and listened to almost all. I did not adopt my father as a role model but rather rebelled against his role. (I thought – but not merely to the extent I thought.)

The parenthetical comment at the end of this quote indicates the power of the counterdependent category. Even though this man thought he was rebelling against his father, he could not free himself from his father's influence.

Table 3.1 indicates that constructing a masculine identity is an interactive process where the ego expands its understanding of an individual's capacities throughout life. As men age, they acquire different views of masculinity and adjust their schemata to reflect both body changes and a dynamic culture. Insights gained throughout the lifelong process of maturation influence how men see themselves.

Growing Up Male

This lifelong process of sex typing has 6 stages -- early childhood (ages 0–6), youth (ages 6–18), early adulthood (ages 18–30), adulthood (ages 30–40), maturity (40–50), and seniority (51–). A man faces developmental challenges as he passes through these stages.

Early Childhood

Gender-role socialization begins at birth. Because of gender preconceptions about what boys and girls should be, parents talk to and handle girl and boy babies differently. As soon as a baby is born, it enters a gender tracking system. A boy's biology will influence his gender identity because others label him as male. From infancy boys and girls receive different cues from adults in their environment. They are dressed in separate styles of clothing and given different toys. Parental approval for behavior that conforms to gender norms and disapproval for inappropriate behavior sculpts schemata within a child's gender identity. Children are acknowledged by peers for their gender-role behavior. Boys are told they are supposed to be 'rough, tough, and full of bluff'. Teachers and other significant adults relate to them based on notions of gender. A child's emerging sense of self is determined by others' responses:

> Because these responses tend to be sexually differential, male and female children's initial images of self are likely to differ. Although the child does not, at first, associate his or her emerging sense of self with sex-category membership, sex differences in early self-image may provide the foundation for gender identity. (Cahill, 1983, pp. 4–5)

Rudimentary understandings of gender identity start to emerge at about age two. By the time a boy is three years old he understands that he is a boy. He starts labeling others as boys or girls and correctly applies gender labels to himself. After a boy realizes he is male, he has to determine what type of man he wants to be. Developing a male gender identity takes an individual through certain stages. His next challenge is to understand social concepts of gender.

Boys face a developmental challenge when they reach the age of six, a time by which they have achieved gender constancy, a developed sense of how to apply accurately the concept 'male' both to themselves and the world. They make clear distinctions between the concepts of male and female and begin to no longer model their mother, who in most cases has been their most nurturing parent (Chodorow, 1978). At that point they have to figure out how to act like men and start modeling the behavior of men they admire.

Many men interviewed for this study indicated that they were first aware of male messages at age five or six, an age at which boys can correctly identify male attributes (Kohlberg, 1966). Some boys have little choice about what male messages to adopt. Kirk said, 'As I was growing up, when I was a little boy and through my high school, my parents sort of defined who I was. They had this ideal for me that they kind of built up.' Some men mentioned that they were aware of the influence of certain messages around ages five or six but were not conscious of this influence until they became adults.

Youth

At this stage of development boys learn how to behave like men. The types of gender identities they acquire will depend upon the male behaviors they observe. Boys try to conform to what they think are the standards for male behavior.

Research on sex-typing demonstrates that being a young boy can be stressful. Boys experience more physical punishment than girls. Boys are more closely restricted in their behavior and are punished for not adhering to traditional male behavior patterns (Weitzman, 1979). Gender-role socialization of boys is often characterized by negative prescriptions: Don't be a sissy; don't engage in feminine behavior. Boys push themselves to be masculine and bury their sensitivities (Jourard, 1968). Since it is harder to learn from negative structures than from positive models, boys are more anxious. They are asked to do something not clearly defined.

By the time a boy reaches puberty he has a fairly well found gender identity. Modifications may be made to this identity, but these changes will relate to the original schemata, complex notions of gender established by this time, that form a blueprint he carries throughout life. This plan is like a road map with clear directions that determine behavior.

At puberty a young man goes through another birth process. When he first came into the world his umbilical cord was cut, severing his physical tie to his mother, who was his lifeline. During the teenage years young men have to cut the apron strings that tie them to their parents. Many primitive cultures have complicated initiation rites of passage for males at puberty to signify this transition to the adult world (Van Gennep, 1960). At these rites boys are taken from their mothers, told about sacred traditions, leave the comfort of home, and enter the world of adult men. They abandon the security that comes from being cared for by mother and learn how to take care of themselves, which means figuring out not only how to provide for themselves, but also how to receive nurturing independent of parents. Many flirtations with puppy love are so cathectic with emotions during adolescence because the stakes are high. Young lovers anxiously try to find in each other parent substitutes who help young men withdrawing from parents feel good about themselves. Their ultimate developmental task is to learn how to love themselves.

During adolescence a young man tries out his gender identity in much the same way as he might try out a suit. He has a good sense of his likes and dislikes, his strengths and weaknesses – which he has had since the time he was 13. Some schemata within this identity are comfortable to him. He rejects others that do not fit. Every new endeavor helps solidify his identity. He tests his skills. Friendships reinforce his values. He may find in school certain subjects he likes which might provide the bases for career choices. Teenagers have fledgling identities they are casting about in the world to reinforce. They choose heroes who reflect valued characteristics. Edward, a 33-year-old (Caucasian) community organizer, thought all boys have superheroes. At age 13 he looked for male role models to reinforce his budding notions of masculinity. Skip, an unemployed African–American, described looking up to certain 'stars' in his neighborhood, when he was learning to value the 'rebel' message as a teenager. As men grow older, they outgrow their boyhood heroes.

During the teenage years peers reinforce gender-role schemata. Jack, a 33-year-old mortgage banker (Caucasian), described picking friends in high school to reflect the 'money' message. He described his school as being divided into different cliques – jocks, eggheads, junkies, and preppies like himself who chose careers in business. This particular group of friends still serves as an important reference point in Jack's life, reinforcing his interest in making money.

Early Adulthood

Until age 18, children are legally under the care of their parents. Because in the US culture a young man lives with his parents during his first 18 years, becoming an adult provides a key challenge. Living independently forces him to make his own decisions. Although he may not during this stage of his life move away from his parents physically, he sets his own goals, chooses how to achieve happiness, and controls his own destiny. In his early twenties Harry, a 29-year-old self-employed computer consultant, decided to define success for himself, separate from his parents' notion of success. His most important message was the 'president' message. He still wanted to be successful but dropped out of Wharton school at the University of Pennsylvania and enlisted in the Navy, which directly contradicted his father's script for success. Alex mentioned that once he got away from his parent's control it was:

> Okay, what do I want to do here? And it turned out to be different than what my parents wanted, but even that I didn't particularly perceive as rebellion, as much as it was making choices on my own.

In the stages of early adulthood men define themselves in the social order. During their twenties some get married or fall in love, trying to substitute for parental love. They may at this time leave the armed forces, graduate from college, go to prison, and start a career. If they are dissatisfied at work, they switch jobs, searching for a location to accomplish what they value. During this very tumultuous period young men seek a niche, or place to settle down, where they will spend most of their adult energy – a job where they can exercise skills and a home where they will be loved. Ultimately, each man seeks acceptance for the gender identity that forms the core of his being. Many previous attachments are abandoned because they do not complement his male schemata, his own sense of what is appropriate. Religious beliefs formed during childhood are sometimes neglected. Many men rebel against their parents' values.

The twenties are a time when men set direction for their lives, as indicated by a 32-year-old commercial artist:

> Peer pressure was the prime motivation when I was younger. In my late twenties I began not to care about what others thought and became more independent and to do my own thing.

One respondent, a 35-year-old fireman, said, 'I think most people don't become adult mentally until they are about 30.'

Adulthood

Adult development implies an episodic heightening of self-consciousness. People do not suddenly become aware of who they are but rather receive glimpses about themselves throughout their lives. These momentary understandings of the self contribute to clarity about identity. Becoming an adult requires being clear about values. Larry, a 33-year-old TV weatherman, described how men achieve psychological adulthood. He stated that his life had clear divisions:

> Up to the point that I went to college, it was defined for me by my parents. After that it was defined for me by my peers, and that corresponded to the time I was really trying to break away from my parents. It was a futile attempt at individuation at that point – just trying to break away and not knowing how to do it, sort of the rebellious stage – and that was when I got to go to college, and that's when my parents stopped defining hurdles and my fellow students and peers did.

> When I became 31 things started to become a little more internally guided instead of externally guided, but I think all the way through my first nine or ten years in the quote-unquote work world, everything was externally motivated, and it's not until a year and a half ago that I started to turn inward more for that guidance in defining for me what's a goal or what's going to be a hurdle.

> I think I gained a lot of respect and a lot more love for myself and was able to get more self-nurturing as opposed to relying on nurturing from the outside. Instead of relying on people saying 'Good job!' 'You're a good person – good job and here's a bone,' that kind of thing; like here's a reward – like when you train a dog or something – it became a lot more internal. I think a lot of it has to do with self-love, self-nurturing and realizing what I was not only as a person but also as a man and what that meant for me. So everything became more internal in terms of how I saw myself, and I relied less on other people defining things for me as upon me defining things.

An adult man defines his own values. Life experiences test the male messages that provide the core of his identity. If he experiences rejection, he adjusts his behavior to receive approval and transforms his identity. At this stage in their lives men winnow through the messages that constitute the schemata in their identities. They cannot abandon old messages, because they are so deeply buried within the psyche. Rather, adult men adjust them to fit life circumstances. This self definition comes about when the old inherited definitions no longer work.

Adults who achieve competence with their identities do not need others to tell them how to be. They can call the shots in life, choosing how to live. Reinforcement comes from within. During his thirties a man seeks competence in whatever arena he has chosen during young adulthood (Levinson *et al.*, 1978). He seeks affirmation in a chosen career, a family, and in community affairs – challenges that test the identity adopted earlier. Does it fit? Does he gain a sense of accomplishment from his chosen tasks? Is he respected by peers, accepted by fellow workers, and loved by friends? During this stage men adopt a standard of living commensurate with their peers. For some this means joining a club with other men from the office. For others it might include becoming active in civic affairs and/or living in a particular locale. For others it might involve being active in a union. Each subculture defines a set of appropriate behaviors that men imitate in their attempt to achieve acceptance for their competence.

If a man experiences failure in his attempt to achieve a sense of competence, he may abandon dysfunctional parts of his identity. If he loses a job, he may seek to change his behavior on a new job. If he is divorced or loses a lover, he may adjust his work hours so he can devote more time to personal life. These crises will be the most serious challenges to his fundamental sense of who he is.

Larry suggested a stage of development where humans no longer look outside themselves for a sense of how they are doing in the world. Carl, a 43-year-old lawyer from Boston (Caucasian), described how he set his own agenda after his divorce. He stated it this way:

> I've come to understand, much to my surprise, that one matures. (It's the same with a female as it is with a male.) You mature in sort of levels. There are conscious changes and changes that happen without even trying. And it seems to me they happen about every decade. You are not the same person at 40 that you were at 30. Even though all external things have remained the same, you just change, your values change, your objectives change; sense of self-esteem changes without working at it. It just happens. That's part of an evolutionary characteristic of what we call personality. It just changes.

Carl had learned to value certain male messages during his youth. As a mature man, he started to formulate his own gender identity based upon messages he valued. Rather than conforming to other people's standards about how he ought to behave, Carl in his forties has developed his own values that direct his behavior.

Adult men may become what Abraham Maslow (1968) referred to as self-actualized, where they no longer have to please others but are self-motivated to pursue those things they value. The following quotes reflect this adult process of self-definition:

> I think maturity plays a big part in how male messages formed my life. A lot of things have not changed that much. I just take a different approach to them now.

My parents were both raised Catholic on farms. Both are conducive to the male figurehead role modeling. Their ideas of behavior greatly influenced my early years. However, many lifetime experiences caused me to modify my attitude and approach to everyday life.

Cultural messages about what constitutes 'maleness' probably do not have a great deal of influence on my behavior, although they do cause me to second-guess myself on an after-the-fact basis at times. Disillusioned as I am with the way this culture presents any attitude, I've gotten to the point where it doesn't much matter any more how I 'measure-up'. I flat out don't give a shit any more.

People at this stage write their own instruction books, but their development does not stop. This time of self-definition helps a person get clear about identity, but an individual who has achieved such clarity may still question how to spend the rest of life. Some men, after they have achieved competence with their gender identities, go through a mid-life crisis where they tear up their male schemata and pursue a more deeply held set of values.

Maturity

Research studies indicate that not all men go through a crisis when they reach their mid years.

Contrary to our expectations, we do not find evidence for a universal mid-life crisis in men. Although men seem to accumulate the burdens of middle age at roughly the same place, they show variation in how they respond to these stresses. Some men do appear to reach a state of crisis, but others seem to thrive. More typical than either of these responses is the tendency for men to bury their heads and deny and avoid all the pressures closing in on them. (Farrell and Rosenberg, 1981, p. vii)

Mid-life cannot be clearly demarked at a particular age but rather represents a period when life problems and physiological changes cause a man to question his identity. Men at middle age reconcile the dreams of youth with the realities of the present, coping with declining vigor and agility. Responses of men to reaching middle age can vary from pride to cynicism.

Farrell and Rosenberg's classic study of men at mid-life indicates that only 12 per cent of men in the United States experience an identity crisis in their mature years. Fifty-six per cent deny that they are having problems and keep up a façade to hide their depression. Another 32 per cent achieve a generative stance to life where they have a positive sense of themselves. The majority of men experiencing crisis are from the lower classes, while men from the middle and upper classes are more likely to report that 'in general, life has measured up to expectations' (ibid., p. 82). The majority of middle-aged men deal with the stresses of mid-life by repressing their feelings and becoming hostile to the world around them. These men do not exhibit signs of overt crises because they deny troubling perceptions.

At the mid-life stage men question the value of particular male messages within their schema. Some individuals change their behavior to reflect new appreciations acquired from experiences. Skip, at age 42, discussed the influence of the 'rebel' message on his life:

> The rebel is still alive but that sense of urgency is gone and not as strong as it was. When I was much younger, the need to rebel was more urgent. Perhaps time has mellowed me and I've learned to set my own agenda.

As mature individuals, they stop blaming parents for their problems and take responsibility for their lives. At this stage in life men learn to live with their warts. They accept their circumstances.

Mature men adjust their lives to accomplish what they value during their remaining years. Some are relentless in pursuing their goals. Deep in their psyches they realize their mortality, that limitations exist in their universe. They have important tasks they want to accomplish before their biological clocks run out. For some men this sense of purpose has deeply spiritual roots. Most men at this time feel they want to leave a contribution to the world.

Men who participated in this study responded to interviews about the influence of male messages in varying ways according to their age. Men younger than 40 were fascinated by the whole notion of male messages. They had not understood their development in those terms, even though they were comfortable talking about the influence of their most important male message. They described with a sense of gratitude the interviews as enlightening because of what they learned about themselves.

Men in their forties were not awed by the interview because they were familiar with these messages. Some were tentative in their discussions, obviously enjoying thinking about aspects of their masculine development which they had not explored in much depth. They were more reflective than younger men. The thoughtful way men in their forties explored these messages evidenced deep understandings.

The 16 men who were 50 or older were confident and somewhat blasé about their messages. They did not speak hesitantly, and were clear as if they had thought about their messages. Al, a 55-year-old chemist, had struggled with the 'work ethic' message. He had rejected some extreme aspects of this message and no longer felt compelled to work 60 hour weeks. The message still provides a dynamic tension in his life. He is self-employed and works hard, but he has learned to reject those aspects of this message that made his life miserable. Older men reflected a conscious understanding of their various schemata that constitute their male gender identities.

Men older than 50 were no longer confused about the type of people they want to be. They understood their limitations and capacities. They had achieved a level of comfort with their identities. Two men in their seventies were sure with their answers. For these older men the interview process was going over 'plowed' ground. They had spent considerable time analyzing how they had gotten to where they were and understood well different aspects of their masculine identities.

Seniority

The later years are times of reconciliation, where men search their pasts to reconcile concerns. Before they die, individuals want to feel a sense of ego integrity, that their time on this planet has been worthwhile. Since they do not want to be remembered as villains or ogres, they attempt to right wrongs. Earlier in their lives many men were so devoted to their careers that they neglected family matters. This neglect can be reconciled by spending time with grand-children. Men who have acquired fortunes often become philanthropists.

Not all men achieve what Erik Erikson (1968) described as 'generativity' in their mature years. Generativity refers to a sense of contributing to the future. Ideally men would like to feel they have made the world better, that somehow their lives have counted. The opposite of generativity is stagnation, where men feel they have not made a contribution. Only one third of a broad sample of men at mid-life achieve a 'transcendent-generative solution' to the midlife passage (Farrell and Rosenberg, 1981). Many men are locked into mindless routines. Depressed, they despair about the future. Because of financial obligations they cannot realize their wishes. As they grow older, some men become angry and bitter for not being able to realize their dreams (Brown, 1987, p. 296).

The acceptance of the role of cultural messages in a man's life leads to integrity, a state of comfort with himself. Achieving ego integrity implies a high degree of symmetry between objective (social) and subjective reality (identity). This does not imply that men are satisfied with what they have accomplished. Rather it implies that they have grown to accept life as it is. They have mellowed and no longer want to crash through new barriers. Senior men maintain a precious psychological balance and accept their conditions out of habit. Living with acceptance is easier than taking risks.

Influence of Male Messages Over Time

Reflecting upon these responses to sex typing by men of different ages, gives rise to Table 3.2 which provides a chronology of how men form their gender identities.

Men do not go through these stages precisely at these ages but each man confronts the questions listed at the key levels. To some extent these stages overlap in different men's lives. The lines of demarcation between them are not always clear. Table 3.2 explains the stages of a man's life in terms of a search for meaning, not so much trying to answer the question, 'What is the meaning of life?' but rather answering the question 'What kind of man am I?' The answer to this question comes from understanding oneself as a man with certain values,

Table 3.2   A chronology of masculine gender identity formation[2]

Level	Stage (age)	Identity formation	Challenging question
Level I Learning how to identify by sex	Early Childhood Infancy (0–2) Preschool (2–6)	Unclear Achieving gender constancy Recognition of biological difference	Am I male?
Level II Formation of male gender identity	Primary School (6–12) Adolescence* (12–18)	Key period of formation Reinforce through peers	What is a man?
Level III Trying out identity	Early adulthood* (18–30)	Testing in world	Am I a man among men?
Level IV Affirming identity	Adulthood (30–40)	Form own self-concept	What is most important to me?
Level V Evaluating identity	Maturity (40–50)	The final test	Is this the way I want to be for the rest of my life?
Level VI Accepting identity	Seniority (51–)	Authenticity	Do I like myself?

* These time periods which encompass the years 13–30 will for many men comprise some form of rebellion against father's standards. The vehemence of that rebellion depends upon the quality of the relationship between fathers and sons. The more harsh, judgmental, controlling, and punitive a father is, the more angry and rebellious the son will be.

desires, and limitations. Men reach authenticity by accepting who they are.

Validation of these levels was provided by Michael, a 44-year-old real estate salesman (African–American), who described his life as having different phases. 'I think it's nice to have different phases in one's life', he said. The first phase was what he called 'growing up', which would be consistent with levels I and II in Table 3.2. The second phase corresponds with level III when men test their identities in the real world. Michael described this phase as being young without heavy responsibilities. 'I would say the second phase was probably college, which I extended for many years, through the sixties.' He explained, 'That was a time of values clarification, if you will.' The third phase of his life was a time of responsibilities. He became a father and worked real hard. This corresponds to level IV, where men achieve competence with the values they have adopted, a time of affirmation for a person's identity. Michael's children are practically grown (he has one son who still attends high school). He is looking forward to his last child leaving home so he can enter the next phase of his life, which he anticipates as a time of freedom, when he gets to do what he wants and won't be so burdened by the responsibilities of the previous phase. This corresponds to level V, where a mature man decides how he wants to spend his life, and level VI where he operates out of a clear sense of what is important. Michael does not anticipate that there will be great changes in his life in this next phase, but rather that without the financial and emotional responsibilities of raising children he will have more freedom to pursue his own interests.

Forming a male identity is similar to selecting a wardrobe. Mothers choose clothing for little boys. As these boys mature and gain a sense of what other boys are wearing, they begin to decide what to wear. When young men first enter the work force they select clothes to gain respect from fellow workers. Their clothes reflect their self images. What kind of man do I want to be? Wanting to fit in with the crowd, they choose styles similar to what other males whom they respect wear. Standards for male apparel are pretty well established in the United States. Teachers wear tweeds, Businessmen wear three-piece suits. Laborers wear jeans. Therapists wear casual clothes to make their clients feel at ease. The choices a man makes about what clothes to wear are dictated by styles promoted on Madison Avenue. Men in the United States, for example, are not free to wear the baggy pants worn by all men in Afghanistan, or the flowing robes of a Bedouin warrior. As men grow older they choose a style of clothing that fits them. Many reject fashion standards and select clothes that indicate their own preferences.

In a similar manner male gender identities are molded by cultures which hold beliefs about appropriate male behavior. Younger men not in control of their own destinies take direction for their behavior from adults. They decide the kind of men they want to be as they grow older and try out new behaviors. Their goals are dictated by past experiences and family history. What have significant others valued? What role models have influenced them? (How do other men dress?) Men experience their choices of how to live to be free, but those choices are limited by past experiences. The question of how to live a life is similar to opening a closet on a given day and figuring out what clothes to wear. However, adopting a gender identity is much more traumatic, anxiety driven, and painful. The kinds of human beings that children and adults become depend upon their daily experiences and social experiences that are preprogrammed by institution-alized practices. The process of social enculturation transfers a complex culture to the psyche of individual men through a process by which masculinity is constantly being constructed and reconstructed.

Notes

1   This table comes from interviews with men about their most important male message. Subjects older than 18 were asked how the influence of that message had changed over time. Table 3.1 has only 70 subjects because 26 of the men interviewed who were younger than 19 were not asked how the influence of their most important male message had changed over time.

2   The author hypothesizes that these levels and stages might also apply to women. Throughout this book inferences about human behavior can be drawn from observations of men. However, this author did not study women and is uncomfort-able making statements about human behavior which might apply to women. It is hoped that a female researcher would duplicate this study with a female sample to discover how the findings of this study apply to women. It is assumed that there are many subtle differences in social conditioning of men and women; therefore, conclusions will only be applied to men.

Part II

Acting Like a Man

Chapter 4

Standard Bearers

> I've always thought of males making the world we live in. It was their contributions – thought, actions and feelings – that have made all else possible, e.g. art, music, poetry, written word, laws, justice, etc.
>
> 45-year-old manager (Caucasian)

Men give more to the societies they inhabit than the children they sire. Whereas women reproduce life by giving birth to and nurturing children, men produce the world by promoting certain social standards that reflect the way they want the world to be. They reproduce a social order by cherishing certain values, a behavior classified as standard bearing. Men want to make their worlds better. Without this activity a social system decays, crumbles, or dies.

Observers of adult development, like Susan Krause Whitbourne (1986), have noted that human beings set goals for themselves. Living up to the standards inherent in these goals generates feelings of competence key to establishing an identity. Erik Erikson (1980, p. 262) observed that generativity is the key to an individual achieving ego integrity, which he defined as follows:

> The sense of identity, then, is the accrued confidence that the inner sameness and continuity prepared in the past are matched by the sameness and continuity of one's meaning for others.

Ego integrity comes from promoting standards valued both by the individual and the society. This sense of being meaningful implies a productive individual caring for future generations (Erikson and Erikson, 1981). Generativity is the opposite of self-preoccupation. Generativity can mean providing health for family members, being a breadwinner, or creating an environment that fosters growth. George Vaillant saw that the upholding of standards and passing them on to future generations is crucial to males' psychological adaption in middle adulthood (1977; Vaillant and Milofsky, 1980). Individuals unable to realize these standards stagnate.

Male standard bearers strive to realize ethical standards, produce lasting creations, improve the world, and devote themselves to excellence. Standard bearers reflect concern for higher order needs, not just survival. They derive a sense of worth by fulfilling meaningful social roles and have an unselfish concern for others' well-being. Standard bearers take pride in living up to their moral precepts, so that when they finish their lives they can feel they have been of use. They guide the next generation. As one participant put it, 'This is what I get up for every morning.'

Because each family has standards it cherishes, every father and grandfather has values he hopes to pass on to the next generation. Parents expect their sons to uphold cherished moral principles, reward sons for living up to those values, and are frustrated when sons don't conform to their expectations. Children internalize values from their parents which provide a basis for their morals. Male emphasis upon standards grows out of the superego, which directs how men ought to live their lives. Social standards learned from other males become the basis for a moral personality. The superego represents the ideal and strives for perfection.

During the 1980s this aspect of male behavior in the United States was captured by Tom Peters and Robert Waterman, Jr in their book, *In Search of Excellence* (1982). This best seller described the role of standard bearing in the corporate world, where excellence is defined as having high goals, thinking big, and respecting employees. The *Oxford English Dictionary* defines excellence as the 'possession of . . . good qualities in an eminent or unusual degree'. The drive for excellence abhors the average or mediocre, just as nature abhors a vacuum. Standard bearers have an enthusiasm that inspires others.

The category of standard bearer contains four male messages – 'scholar', 'nature lover', 'be the best you can', and 'good samaritan'. Popular media, which depict men as being rugged individuals, as bosses, as workers, or as lovers have almost totally ignored these aspects of the male personality. In a sense the standard bearing aspects of male identity are invisible, buried deep within the male psyche.

Scholar

Be knowledgeable. Go to college. Value book learning. Read and study.

Modern western civilization dating back to Descartes, the eighteenth century French philosopher, has always valued reason. Male rational abilities have generated scientific discoveries that have prompted the great technological advances that characterize modern life. Men's rational activities from the time of the Enlightenment in the sixteenth and seventeenth centuries have created the modern world (Seidler, 1989). In a high tech society the 'scholar' message stimulates men to do well in school and strive for academic credentials – certificates, diplomas, bachelor's degree, and advanced professional degrees.

Sixty-three per cent of the respondents to the questionnaire used in this study rated this message as having a strong to dominant influence in their lives at age 18. Only 6 per cent said it had no influence at that age. Scholars can be conformists, as indicated by the negative correlation with the 'rebel' message which increased over time. The 'scholar' message correlates with the 'be the best you can' message.

The 'scholar' message typifies standard bearing behavior when boys learn in schools to judge themselves by external standards, the grades they earn. Through grades young boys learn very thoroughly that success comes from performing up to certain standards. Adult men use this same behavior to judge other men who do not live up to their standards as inferior.

In a stereotypical sense, doing well in school is often chastised as feminine behavior. This tension in modern life between being a 'a man' and being a scholar is illustrated by the following quote from a 28-year-old entomologist (Caucasian):

> It became obvious to me *at a very early age* that if one's manhood was determined by his bravery, courage, and handling of his own death, then I would *never* be a true male. So I cursed my luck and grew to admire, then eventually lust for, other guys who I imagined were *'real males'* because they supposedly conformed to such rigid rules. Such oppressive thought patterns plagued me until I was 21. I was *never* attractive, *never* muscular, *never* athletic and so I *never* fit in with the 'true males'. I could *never* be myself and be masculine at the same time. I compensated for my lack of sexual identity and self respect by valuing book learning over physical ability. In fact, as a child I thought there were two types of people: smart wimps and dumb jocks. At least I was smart. I could still be something worthwhile.

A scholar values being smart over being tough. Scholars who lose themselves in books do not often feel the need to prove themselves in athletic contests.

The four men interviewed for the 'scholar' message were raised in an era where men were supposed to be aggressive. Richard Hofstadter (1963) pointed out in his book, *Anti-Intellectualism in American Life*, that true men worked with their hands, tamed the wilderness, and made fun of intellectuals. Cultural norms opposed to men becoming scholars were challenged after the Second World War with the growth of the large bureaucratic corporations, where men no longer made a living from the strength of their muscles and had to become organization men. High school diplomas and college degrees became certificates that ultimately became necessary criteria for success, as evidenced by the following comment written by a 19-year-old machinist (Caucasian), 'I have been influenced to go through college, get a job and support a family in the best way that I possibly can.' In a technological society education is the key to acquiring a secure job that allows an individual to fulfill the other requirements of the male role.

The urgency of the 'scholar' message for contemporary life was emphasized by Dean, a 18-year-old high school senior (Caucasian), whose most important message was money:

> My value of money is one reason I'm going to college. I know you need a good education to get a good job. If you get a good job it will pay good money, and to obtain those professional jobs which pay higher money, you need a college education. Coming out of college with a degree in

some field, you're going to almost always be entering a career that pays $30,000 and up and that's good money.

Jesse, a 57-year-old Baptist minister (African–American), demonstrated how the 'scholar' message had been deeply drilled in him as a necessity for survival. He had attended college on an athletic scholarship. He saw life as a series of hurdles to be surmounted. Education was one of them. 'You get an education and everything will take care of itself', he said. His parents taught him to do well in school in order to be prepared for anything that came his way.

The influence of this message upon men ranged on a continuum, where, on one side, men like those quoted above value the 'scholar' message as a practical necessity to get ahead, while on the other side, men read and pursue scholarship for enjoyment. Phil, a 74-year-old retired corporate lawyer (Caucasian) for a fortune 500 firm who lived in Western Massachusetts, typified the recreational scholar. His father was an artist. He attended an exclusive Eastern prep school and graduated with undergraduate and law degrees from Yale. In describing how he learned the 'scholar' message, he said: 'I don't know where I got it from. I know I've always been motivated to try and do very well academically in schools.' Phil received satisfaction from doing things well. His high performance standards carried into his work, where he wanted to do a 'proper, correct job, not second rate'. He stated that the influence of the 'scholar' message was just as strong in his retirement as it had been in his early years. He spends most of his time reading *The New York Times* and other newspapers and magazines so he can keep up with the world.

Mac, a 55-year-old ex-con (African–American), valued this message because his mother read to him and encouraged him to read. As a young boy he used to spend hours in the local library where he joined a book club. Reading became an adventure. He would escape into wondrous lands and places, enraptured with fictional plots and heroes. As a young man in a black inner city neighborhood, his peers thought he was strange:

> They perceived me as aloof, or whatever. Even thinking I'm special because I read a book or something. Vocabulary gets in the way. It doesn't even have to be big words. Saying 'thank you' instead of 'thanks' sounds too stilted to some people.

Mac was aware from a very young age of the importance of the 'scholar' message. In describing how this message influenced him when he was growing up, he said:

> You've got to study. Otherwise you'll be called dumb. And a dumb Negro gets called a nigger. And then you're wide open to anything. That's not even a person. You can get killed that way, if you're deemed that, so I'm trying to at least never be a dumb one.

As a young lad, Mac loved to read, but his curiosity and desire to learn did not lead him to college. His peers were angry at their segregated society and rebelled. Mac had gone to jail six times which kept him from fulfilling his goal of going to college. In prison he taught himself two different languages and spent his spare time reading. Scholarship was not a profession for Mac, but a way of life:

> To me scholarship is only an answer to curiosity. I'm interested in everything there is, so I read at the highest level I can find. That's been my sole purpose for scholarship.

The lives of scholars are a series of questions. Those male scholars like Arthur, who have scientific minds, solve problems through experimentation – formulating hypotheses, testing them out, and then reformulating them. Arthur – the only professional scholar interviewed for this message, a 44-year-old biology professor who grew up in rural North Carolina (Caucasian) – learned this message on his own 'because there was no push at all to make good grades or go to college'. No one in his family went to college. His stepfather was a mechanic. Arthur remembered no positive role models in terms of inspiring teachers prior to going to a two year college. In describing how he learned to value the 'scholar' message, Arthur said:

> I knew that there was no way I wanted to stay in that little dusty hot town that I grew up in; there was just nothing for me there. Once I got to college the world opened up and I starting seeing that there was more to life than what I had thought there was. I had a very boring existence prior to that. Some of my college classes were very interesting. I'd never thought of things like that ... Once I started doing research there was nothing else I wanted to do.

Arthur enjoys being a scholar. He pursues his own interests and is free to be inquisitive. He is his own boss, answerable to himself and does not have someone standing over his shoulder telling him what to do. He remarked about the relationship between the 'scholar' message and standard bearing behavior:

> I get paid for doing what I want to do, sitting around thinking. I feel like I am a professional as opposed to a worker, and by being a professional I have to live up to certain professional standards which imply living a certain way, keeping an open mind, and always trying to see the other person's point of view; always trying to be objective, having an analytic mind.

The essence of being a scholar is the search for truth. Arthur did not like the word 'truth'. He said it was too value-laden. He preferred to characterize what he did as describing the world the way it is.

Many men – philosophers, poets, mathematicians, scientists – have dedicated their lives to the pursuit of truth, which implies a particular way of looking at the world. Religious converts discover the truth, often becoming zealous about promoting it. A real scholar understands, though, that each new insight into reality, is only a resting point on the path of curiosity upon which his mind will travel throughout his life. Each new truth provides new standards. For many men being a scholar implies constantly seeking new insights and ways of understanding the worlds they inhabit.

Many men do not live up to the demands of gender-role messages they receive when they are little boys. Just because the 'scholar' message is rated by men as being the most important in their lives does not mean they become scholars. This research does not state that just because a man receives a message, he becomes what that message implies. It does, however, state that these messages provide direction. Seventeen per cent of the men who participated in this study said the 'scholar' was the most important message in their lives. The influence of this message is so high because parents tell their sons to achieve in school, a message that is reinforced in educational institutions. The high rating of this message provides evidence for the powerful effect of schools upon men. No other message is so uniformly reinforced. Being a scholar or doing well in school is the hallmark of middle class status.

Nature Lover

Love of outdoors. Respectful treatment of plants and animals. Harmony with nature.

We are all descended from people who worshipped the Earth. Wilderness has always played an important role in the male experience. History is full of earthy male figures, protectors of forests, gods of the woods, streams, and fields. Between the city and the wilderness lies a middle ground that has always nourished the human race – what might be called a garden, a farm, or a meadow – where men derive sustenance from natural processes. Evidence of the importance of the 'nature lover' message in the United States comes from all the men who like to garden, from the popularity of house plants, and from interest in the land expressed by men who live in rural and suburban environments. All of us have male ancestors who have lived directly from the Earth.

A nature lover is a husbandman. Webster's dictionary defines the husbandman as 'one who plows and cultivates land' and husbandry as 'the care of the household, the cultivation of plants and animals and the management of a farm, especially domestic animals'. In *The Annotated Walden* Thoreau says, 'ancient poetry and mythology suggest that husbandry was once a sacred art' (1970, p. 294). This research demonstrates that the archetype of husbandman as someone who cares for the natural order is still important, even though most men today do not make their living off the land.

Mark, an 18-year-old student (Caucasian) at an urban public high school, hinted at why this message is so important for men. He associated the 'nature lover' message with fond memories of his father. He used to take walks in the woods with his father and learned that in nature he could forget his problems. Many parents reinforce this message in young boys by urging them to be kind to animals. Mark referred to this, 'When I was a little kid, this message meant I shouldn't kick animals; I shouldn't kill ants under a magnifying glass.' Parents who give their young boys pets hope to teach them respectful treatment of animals. Many parents take their boys to zoos to appreciate the wonders of the animal kingdom. Some boys learn to value the 'nature lover' message through scout activities. A 32-year-old craftsman (Caucasian) mentioned, 'The greatest influence was boy scouting. My scoutmaster taught me how to treat and appreciate the out of doors and be concerned about environmental protection.'

The 'nature lover' message involves the private lives of men, their secret thoughts about being human in a bountiful universe. Men interviewed for this message described feeling good about themselves in nature, where they unwind by observing natural processes. Tim, a businessman from Iowa (Caucasian), felt that men like to get away from the pressures of life and be by themselves in the woods, where men have good feelings about themselves and are rewarded by many pleasant moments exploring nature's wonder.

For all the men interviewed for this section being in nature has a spiritual dimension of awe – wonder at how insignificant the human world seems to be in comparison to the natural world. Pete, a 32-year-old unemployed auto body repairman from Iowa, expressed this by stating that the natural world was beyond his power. It was something he could not create. Some wonderful force (God) had created our universe. Mark mentioned that being out of doors had taught him that all life is sacred:

Nature is all-encompassing for me. Nature connects with everything that happens in our world, in the way we act, what we eat and drink; what we wear; and how we feel about different stuff; how we relate towards other people; what we do when we grow up. It affects every part of our lives. People should be more respectful of it. It's made me more compassionate than any other message. Nature is an example for me about how our life needs to be lived.

Dave, a 45-year-old university professor (Caucasian) who had grown up on a farm in New Jersey, stated that he always felt insignificant in nature:

That's where I learn what ephemeral creatures human beings are. We don't live very long and all our civilizations die out, but these wonderful trees live forever. They are born; they die; they rot; and they contribute to the soil which nourishes other forms of life. It's a beautiful process of continuity. Within such a time span our problems do not seem very great.

Mark also mentioned that being in the natural world gave him a fresh perspective on life:

> When I go out in the woods, I'm getting back to the basics of human nature, and what the world is all about; or where it started. So it helps me clear my mind, because when I am relating to other people in the human world, a lot of things get in my mind that aren't really that important. When I go out in the woods I realize how minimal those things are so I can take a new stand and start over.

He went on to say that there was a certain morality that came from relating to nature. Being in nature had made him more compassionate.

Bill, a 30-year-old unemployed laborer (Caucasian), thought that the human world was different than the natural world. He felt comfortable in nature and ill at ease in social situations. Bill, like all the other men interviewed for this message, loved to escape to natural settings. He described himself as a loner, suffering from agoraphobia, who felt good in a natural environment. Bill was raised in Northern Michigan and had an alcoholic father. When he was young, he used to love to sit at the side of Lake Superior and reflect about life . He said that such experiences made him much more understanding of other people. Now, living in a large city, he still seeks to console himself by the shores of Lake Michigan:

> When I get depressed I will go for a walk. I will try to find a secluded area. It's very comforting. It makes me feel at ease, and I can just look at the lake, the sky, rocks, sand, anything, and it just makes me feel better.

Being a nature lover helps Bill deal with the stresses he experiences in the city.

For Alex, a 40-year-old machinist (Caucasian), being in the woods had an intellectual component, where he learned about different plants and natural systems. Each woods has a character to be discovered. No two woods, or two moments in the same woods are alike. Alex referred to the woods near his house where he grew up as his space, a playground where he spent many pleasant hours during his youth climbing over trees and playing in water. He could do as he wished in comfort away from his demanding parents. He finds being in nature relaxing because he can set his own agenda. He talked about getting away in the woods to escape people's attempts to control him. In nature he was on his own, free to do what he wanted.

Joshua, the only professional gardener interviewed for this message, used to be a Wall Street broker. A graduate of Williams college, he left the glamorous life in New York City when he was 33 to live on an Indian reservation in Arizona:

> When I left Wall Street I went straight to the reservation where I visited the Pueblo people. There I met a grandfather and a young child both of whom socked me with some things that were so fundamental and so simple that I've been on that trail ever since.

As a young boy Joshua used to play in the woods. He grew up outside New York City, and although he did not know many Indian people, used to have fantasies about Indians living in those woods. Becoming a gardener in his adult life has enabled him to live close to nature. He says that as he has grown older, he has become clearer about what is important:

> As I have matured I've just been able to define much more specifically for myself what is important to me and what is relevant to not only me but my people, to my species and to other species, recognizing all the while the interconnection and the interdependence of all these things.

He confirmed a close relationship between the 'nurturer' message and 'nature lover':

> I nurture the soil as I grow things. Doing it in such a way that I know that my legacy will not be Rockefeller Center or the Pyramids, but it will be better soil for future generations. Knowing that that which I discard will hopefully be disposed of properly as possible, trying to be fully conscious of these endeavors full time.

For Joshua, the key component of 'nature lover' message is respect for all forms of life.

Not all boys feel comfortable with the 'nature lover' message. The 29-year-old doctor quoted in the previous section had this to say about his early experiences with this message:

> My father instilled in me a great love of nature, and I have pride and no regret. However, I learned from my peers that nature-loving and masculinity were mutually exclusive. You were supposed to conquer nature, not love it. They taunted me and called me 'Mother Nature' all through elementary and junior high school.

Eight per cent of the sample surveyed here said this message had no influence on them when they were 18. Many men have destroyed nature by extracting profit from natural systems. The 'nature lover' message correlates negatively with the 'tough guy' message and the 'money' message, which suggests that aggressive men oriented towards making money may not value the 'nature lover' message. Over time there was a stronger negative relationship between 'tough guy' and 'nature lover' and a negative relationship between 'nature lover' and 'superman', which implies that tough macho men may not be nature lovers. Just because 5 per cent of the men in this study said 'nature lover' is their most important message does not mean that all men, or even the majority of men in the United States respect animal rights or worship natural processes. Of all the messages, this message had the second highest increase over time, meaning that, as men grow older, they become more appreciative of nature. It also had the second lowest variance score, indicating that men's feelings about nature do not shift wildly over time, but rather stayed fairly constant, at a level where they love being out of doors and have a high regard for plants and animals.

The importance of this message indicates that men in contemporary times yearn to be connected with what is natural in environments where they can experience both the wilderness outside and their own wildness. Contact with nature awakens men's senses. By coming in contact with the unplannable, the uncontrollable, and the incomprehensible, they can renew themselves. In the wilderness of nature men encounter their own wild natures. A refreshing experience with the incomprehensible stirs deep emotions and makes men humble.

Be the Best You Can

Do your best. Don't accept being second. 'I can't' is unacceptable.

This extremely important gender message for men demonstrates how the superego works. Parents tell their children to strive to be the best they can, to be honest, to tell the truth, not to give up, and to obey standard moral scriptures – all that goes with being a good person. This message implies not only doing a good job, completing tasks well, but also moral and ethical standards of goodness, as in 'being the best person you can'.

Parents reward their children both consciously and unconsciously for conforming to this message. All four men interviewed for this section said they had learned this message from their mothers. Jonathan, a 41-year-old community organizer from the Boston area (Caucasian) said, 'My mother was a perfectionist at the things she did – homemaking and gardening. The nonverbal message was perfectionism.' His father made a deliberate effort to teach him to be the best he could in all things. Other fathers provided a silent example of this message by doing the best they could in their own lives. One participant in this study, Leroy, quoted his grandfather who exemplified the commitment to excellence implied by this message with the following expression, 'Once a task has begun, be it large or small, do it well or not at all.'

Men find and create outlets to demonstrate their masculinity by being the best they can in a variety of arenas. They hope their performance will impress others so that they can gain the respect of men. Roy, a 34-year-old brewery electrician (Caucasian), said he learned this message from sports, where he had for years competed to be the best he could in a variety of playing fields. The 'be the best you can be' message connotes men striving for perfection, doing everything to the best of their abilities.

This particular message provides a motor that drives men by providing standards of accomplishment in every aspect of their lives, from being a good worker to being a good husband. Sixty-two per cent of the respondents said that this message had a strong to dominant influence on them when they were 18, and only 3 per cent said it was of no influence at age 18. Correlations for the 'be the best you can' message indicate how widely this message spreads across the expectations for men. The relationship between this message and being successful is illustrated by the correlations with the 'president' message and the 'hurdles' message. As men mature, they become more interested in being the best they can. Many of the more serious male concerns associated with being productive citizens – like 'breadwinner', 'good samaritan', 'law', and 'work ethic' – do not score significantly with younger men but do correlate with 'be the best you can' significantly over time. The influence of this message increased over time.

Striving to be the best dooms many men to failure. Because the standards implied by this message are internal, they can seldom be accomplished. There are always higher levels of achievement. Jonathan said that this message was a little bit like pursuing outer space. There was always something beyond and you can never rest on your laurels. A 61-year-old businessman from Baltimore commented that men do not love themselves because they have such high standards that cannot be met. An 18-year-old high school student observed, 'I believe in trying to do my best in everything I do. If I don't give 100 per cent, then I usually get upset.' A curse of being the best you can is that there are always new horizons to conquer. Being the best you can drives some men to expect perfection of themselves. They stubbornly do not recognize that they and their bodies have limitations until suddenly they have heart attacks, back problems, nervous disorders, mental lapses, or some other crippling problem that might have been prevented if they had been more cautious about their own limitations.

Throughout his life, Jonathan's high principles have been demanding both upon himself and others. He explained. 'It's not very satisfying sometimes because I can always look at what I did and say "I could have done more." People need to consider their own imperfections without guilt.' As an activist who spent his full time working for social justice, he felt particularly frustrated because, 'When you're trying to save the world and the world ain't saved, it's hard to turn around and look back at what you did and say "Wow, I did a great job!"' More recently Jonathan had begun to question the orientation towards perfection which he received from his parents. He acknowledged his parents' weaknesses, which he said they tried their best to hide not only from their children but from themselves:

> You not only try to be the best you can, but you hide from yourself the things you're not doing very well. I think I've outgrown that to a great extent. I sometimes tend to be superficially self-critical, which is a way of protecting some of the deeper, ah, warts. If you confess to the wart on the surface, you can hide the fact that you've got a tumor. I think we all have tumors deep inside, because none of us is perfectly developed.

Jonathan felt that as he matured he has been able to find his 'tumors', those parts of his identity where he has not been able to achieve what he wanted, and admit them to himself. He sees that the process of achieving authenticity demands acknowledging such fallabilities.

Paul, a 58-year-old director of development for a large private university in the Northeast (Caucasian), described the influence of this message upon his life as driving him to take challenges, not so much in order to be successful materially, but rather in order internally to gain satisfaction from having met those challenges. He felt he learned this message from trying to get the approval of his father who, like the popular movie star Gary Cooper, was a silent figure who never rewarded his son for his accomplishments, so Paul always thought he was not doing enough and had to strive harder to win his father's approval. Paul felt that this message implied living up to the best of his abilities. He had attended Yale law school, not so much because he wanted to be a lawyer, but because it was a challenge. Whereas some men might be satisfied with what he had achieved and rest on their laurels, Paul would move to some new arena to take on new challenges. He described this aspect of his life as the wonder of new accomplishments, of being the best he could by pushing forward into new horizons with new standards and goals to achieve. He felt that being a nonachiever was being a nonperson. In Eriksonian terms introduced at the beginning of this chapter, being a nonachiever would imply that a man who did not have standards he was trying to achieve would not achieve ego integrity.

Marty, a 54-year-old executive at IBM (Caucasian), had also attended a private school which expected him to excel. He said that he could not excel in sports so he used extracurricular activities at school and youth programs at church as arenas in which to prove himself. Marty provides a good explanation about how the rewards for being the best you can are not external:

> I don't remember any kind of recognition. I got support from my folks. I just think it was an inner feeling of accomplishing things, many times succeeding despite what others seemed to feel. I never got any support from the guys in grade school. They could care less. I rarely found anybody who would come up and say, 'Hey, great job! Glad you did it.'

Marty's desire to be the best he can comes from deep within and forms an integral part of his personality.

Marty liked working at IBM because that organization expects the best of him. 'It was a perfect match for me,' he said, 'because IBM maintains a very solid spirit of competitiveness. There's constant pressure to perform.' He enjoys the challenge of a business that constantly expects him to achieve his best.

Tom, a 68-year-old engineer from Long Island (Caucasian), said that this message had dominated his life. He linked it to being a faithful husband and a good breadwinner, providing for his family. He had applied the 'be the best you can' message to work. 'I always try to do my tasks as well as I can, develop a program with no bugs in it. I not only did a job, but a very good job', he said. In his later years he regretted that he that spent so much time obsessively trying to produce results and wishes he had not ignored his personal life. He felt his relationships with other people, family and friends, had suffered because of this message and admitted that for most of his life his identity had been bound up with the attitude that 'any job worth doing is worth doing well.' The influence of the 'be the best you can' message is so powerful that he could not conceive of letting go of it, but he could conceive of redirecting it. Two years ago he became active in the men's movement and started to question how devoted he was to his work, saying, 'Maybe I shouldn't be so serious about this stuff.' He now would like to apply this message to personal relationships:

> I think I had it to an obsessive degree. I guess the message I got was 'be the best you can at doing things'. I think the message should have been 'be the best you can to be supportive, to be helpful and to nurture'.

Tom had fulfilled his father role by being the best breadwinner he could. He wishes that he had spent more time nurturing his four sons instead of being busy all the time.

Tom mentioned something about this message that other men collaborated, that having the 'be the best you can be' message does not necessarily mean a man is ambitious. Tom had tried being a supervisor, which he did not enjoy because it involved no technical work. He had good friends at work but was much more interested in technical fields.

Jonathan is the only man interviewed for this section who spends his full time trying to improve the world. As a community organizer he strives to realize his mission, which is to promote justice. Jonathan gets motivation for his work from his belief that human beings as a species are capable of improving themselves. He explained it this way:

> Being the best you can has something to do with the human condition. What are humans here for? I think we have the capacity to do great things in a horrible world, a world that has been made horrible by man's inhumanity towards other human beings and the environment. Human beings don't have to destroy themselves. They can use their creative energies to improve life on this planet. It's a faith statement, that human beings are fundamentally good, which I can't prove anymore than some can demonstrate that human beings are fundamentally bad. Human beings will always strive as a race to survive by dominating adversity.

Jonathan's belief in being the best he can is not just an individual statement but also a social statement about the capacity of the human species to be the best it can by promoting justice to create a better world. Just like individuals who grow from a state of dependency under the care of their parents to developing fully mature egos with internal standards, societies grow away from the control of tyrants by attempting to fulfill standards for democracy, freedom, equality, justice, universal well-being, prosperity, and literacy. Such social goals become norms in a society and affect the behavior of individuals, like Jonathan, who adopt those standards for themselves. Like good samaritans they try to create a better world for future generations.

Good Samaritan

Do good deeds and acts. Put others' needs first. Set a good example.

In the New Testament (Luke 10:33) a Samaritan rescued a man who had been robbed and beaten and was lying by the side of the road. This good Samaritan was praised by Jesus for his compassion, for showing mercy to a poor, wounded stranger, for being a good neighbor, and expressing concern for a fellow human being. In the 1980s Robert Bellah *et al.* wrote a book, *Habits of the Heart* (1985), which tried to capture the spirit of times in the United States. These authors discovered that Americans care deeply for others. Through intimate involvement with community and family life, US citizens gain meaning and coherence for their own lives. Cooperative action to create a just society evidences 'good samaritan' behavior. Men who are 'good samaritans' strive to improve their local communities. The very notion of a democratic society expressed by Thomas Jefferson and other 'founding fathers' of the United States depends upon notions of public virtue, that individuals within a democratic society will strive for the common good.

The 'good samaritan' message correlates positively with the 'law' message and 'nurturer' message, which means that men who are good samaritans uphold the social order and care for others. The influence of this message increases over time with significant correlations with 'be the best you can', 'breadwinner', 'control', 'hurdles', 'law', and 'work ethic'. At age 18 the 'good samaritan' message has a negative correlation with the 'rebel' message. Over half the men who responded to the survey instrument used in this study indicated that the 'good samaritan' message was a strong to dominant influence in their lives at age 18. Only 4 per cent said it was no influence. Does this mean that half the men in the United States are good samaritans? This would be a surprise. Men are not often depicted doing good deeds. How do they manifest this concern for others? What kind of activities do good samaritans carry out in order to act neighborly towards their fellow human beings?

Males demonstrate their concern for others in a variety of ways that range from being kind to being involved in political causes. They give to charities, volunteer at their children's schools, serve on boards, become deacons at church, and participate in politics. A recent Gallup organization poll reported that 75 per cent of American households contribute to charitable causes, and 98 million Americans volunteered 20.5 billion hours to these causes in 1989.[1] Many men, although they may desire social justice, lead lives so full of other concerns that they do not devote themselves to social causes.

Gary – a 37-year-old construction worker from Mississippi (African–American), one of 13 children – said that the 'good samaritan' message was the most important message in his life, but he neither actively worked for social causes nor volunteered time for charitable interests. For Gary this message was a credo. He learned the 'good samaritan' message from his relatives in the rural community where he grew up:

They was good people. You know they would try to do anything they could to help you if you showed them that you were worthy and weren't trying to use them. And I'm the same way, you know. It just gives me joy to be able to help somebody get where they are going in this world. What else is life all about?

Gary hates someone who lies. To Gary the opposite of a good samaritan is a man who does anything to get ahead, who ruthlessly climbs over other people to pursue his own goals. 'I don't want to be used,' he said. 'And I don't want to use anybody else. I wasn't raised abusing people.' He does not like to see young men making girls pregnant and abandoning their children. Gary sees a strong relationship between the 'good samaritan' message and the 'self reliant' message. He thinks people ought to be able to take care of themselves and not rely on other people for handouts. He would like to see the country changed so the average man can have a life for himself and his family. Gary used to be active in the Civil Rights movement, but his current job is so exhausting that he has little time for causes. He works so hard because he wants to make sure that his son 'gets a better shot at life'.

Emilio, a 24-year-old student (Asiatic), tried to be a good samaritan but became exhausted by the demands of helping other people. Emilio was brought up in a Catholic tradition in which 'you don't hurt anybody and you try to help out as much as possible'. He had been taught the value of sharing. He lived with his grandmother, a social worker in the Philippines, for four years when he was a little boy. Emilio is a good listener, and people like to tell their problems to him. He was a house counselor in high school and became a dorm counselor in college.

Emilio's career goal is to become a doctor so that he can help others:

I don't want to be a physician. I want to be a missionary doctor where I can help kids. I like taking care of people. If it boils down to the bottom line, I think I will take care of anybody.

When Emilio was a teenager he used to walk around the streets of Boston talking to bums. One of his heroes was John Kennedy whom he admired for founding the Peace Corps. When asked what he thought a good samaritan is, he replied:

Do unto others as you want them to do unto you. You don't lift a finger against anybody else unless you have to defend yourself. To defend your body and soul you have to be prepared to fight but everything else you try to ignore. You have to know exactly what's wrong and what's right to the point that you don't hurt the other person. Try to do the best you can so the other person will eventually find something that will steer him the right way.

Rick, a 48-year-old man who suffered from Parkinson's disease and was disabled[2] (Caucasian), learned to be a good samaritan from his mother who was very loving and made him feel secure. For him the 'good samaritan' message contained a series of moral precepts: Do not be self centered; put others' needs first; and set a good example. This message had such a profound effect upon his life that he quit engineering school when he was in college (he was number one in his class), and became a public health official. He decided against social work because he had a reputation for being a sensitive person:

> I was aware that I have a history of becoming very involved in other people's situations, including their problems. Consequently, I have wound up paying for it many times with some combination of financial, emotional, and physical loss. I thought to myself, 'Don't go into social work; don't go right smack into the field that you feel so susceptible to being manipulated.' Most people who've known me tell me that I'm the most sensitive person they've ever known in their lives.

In addition to his job in public health, Rick spends time volunteering for a variety of agencies. He is involved in the social concerns committee at his church and volunteers at both an alcoholic treatment center and a food bank. He hopes his efforts will improve the world.

Doug is a professional good samaritan. A 41-year-old campus minister (Caucasian), he had grown up in a household of good samaritans. His father, a Lutheran pastor, worked with refugees for the World Council of Churches. Doug explained that the 'good samaritan' message was 'implicit in that you do what you can for people who are in need of aid, who are not able to do for themselves'. This message of caring for others was conveyed through the climate of his household. In college he found he was more interested in working with people than in abstract concepts:

> I spent one summer working in a poor neighborhood in St Louis with people who had migrated there from the Appalachian region; and really found that a lot more satisfying, and it began to raise questions in my mind about how people came to live the way they do; what sorts of systems result in inequities, injustice, and so on. So I think that sort of reinforced the message; but I think the message had kind of been there waiting to be fed for quite a while.

From such experiences he became outraged by injustice and has devoted his life to trying to create a better world. The 'good samaritan' message permeates Doug's whole life, how he sees the world, and how he responds to events. It demands that he act for justice and not just believe in justice. Doug understands well that being a good samaritan has some drawbacks. He is suspicious of institutions and often feels challenged to question authorities in the public sphere as well as his church:

> There are times when it would be a lot more comfortable not to question authority; it might even be more profitable to go with the flow.

I could probably be making more money in another field.

Doug also feels that this message has put him at odds with his family. He feels he does not have much security and is living with less because of his devotion to the 'good samaritan' message. 'It's a pain in the ass,' he said. 'I sometimes would like to go with the flow.'

In spite of these difficulties and the lack of external rewards, many men spend time passionately caring for a cause trying to improve the world. Many men have within them deep feelings of wanting to be successful at being good people. A 44-year-old auto mechanic (African–American) said he enjoyed fixing cars because he liked helping people. A social worker from Texas (African–American) who works in the evenings and weekends as a real estate broker enjoys having the extra money so he can tithe and support various social causes financially. A 39-year-old county employee (Hispanic) feels the 'good samaritan' message gives his life direction. He wants to help other people know they can do good things in this society. A 32-year-old salesman (Caucasian) noted, 'Man has a responsibility to help others less fortunate.' Dave, the university professor mentioned earlier in this chapter, sees a relationship between the 'good samaritan' message and the 'president' message. The president has power to improve the world. He seeks fame and glory so that he can be influential and wants to be known for doing good deeds. Another man, a 27-year-old unemployed laborer (Caucasian), saw a relationship between the 'good samaritan' message and the 'superman' message. Superman worked hard to conquer the forces of evil.

Conclusion

Not all men are like Doug, able to achieve careers where they devote their energies to improving the world. Most men find themselves overwhelmed by responsibilities and find few opportunities to express their concerns for justice. However, some men, like an acquaintance this author met in an industrial bowling league, spend their spare evenings volunteering for their son's boy scout troop. A classmate of this author, who is the president of a large trucking firm in New Jersey, finds time to be chairman of the Board of Trustees of his high school and recently spearheaded a $7 million campaign to build a new library. Every day millions of men contribute their efforts to give something back to the communities they inhabit. Their stories are dramatic and heroic, even though they are not commonplace. This behavior is not very visible because, as one high school student said, 'I think there's too much stress on the "macho" image of men and success in the modern world.' This research indicates that the most important thing for many men in the United States is living up to the expectations of being a standard bearer, which is manifested in their family lives as well as their work.

Standard bearing behavior for men has four main aspects to it – generativity, love, excellence, and satisfaction. Men who are standard bearers recreate the social order. They uphold the traditions and embody the culture with their action, values, and decisions. Men are stewards both of the earth and the social orders they inhabit.

Every human being is born with a capacity for love. Standard bearers care for all forms of life on this planet. They are rescuers, helping others in need. Being a standard bearer implies acting out of feelings of love, which are reciprocated, so that a man who cares for others receives care from others and is able to love even more. Standard bearers are motivated by a desire to excel. Not satisfied with the status quo, they strive to improve the world. They care for quality and strive to be the best they can. If they fail the first time, their strong desire to see their internal standards realized motivates them to try again. Their dedication inspires others. Like a farmer in New England building a stone wall, standard bearers take great care to build something that will last, a monument to their time here on Earth, even though farmers do not leave their names by the stone walls they build. They take satisfaction from being able to make a positive contribution. Admiration from other people is a by-product of standard bearing behavior. Men who are standard bearers get their rewards from realizing those standards and not from pleasing others.

Standards held within the superego create a dynamic tension in men's lives. There are always new degrees of excellence to be achieved, new problems to be solved, and new challenges to be met. A true standard bearer never rests on his laurels. This behavior, so often ignored in the popular media, reflects the innermost dreams of men. It enriches their lives and contributes to future generations.

Notes

1   *The Milwaukee Journal*, November 25, 1990, p. G2.
2   Rick maintained that his disability had not affected the way he responded to these messages. In other words, he had the same standards for male behavior within his gender identity in spite of his crippling disease.

Chapter 5

Workers

> The messages I received from my environment were that men were only important as providers, that work came first, and work was where one's true identity as a man came out and was judged.
>
> 33-year-old craftsman (Caucasian)

Work defines men. When young boys are asked the question, 'What do you want to be when you grow up?', the answer is not a general statement like 'a loving person', but rather a job title like 'an engineer', 'a pilot', 'a policeman', or a 'businessman'. When asked, 'Who are you?' a man will respond, 'I am a carpenter,' or 'I am a machinist.' Men's work plays a key role in the construction of their identities and often includes more than a job. For many men their most important work lies outside their jobs – building their own home, raising money for a church, supporting a theatre group, or writing a novel – and gives their lives purpose. Men take great pride in their work and identify themselves with the goals they set in the world of work.

Through the exchange of labor men earn money that allows them to take care of their needs. A man's work provides both for basic needs – food, shelter, clothing – and higher order needs. How much money he makes places him in the social order – the type of neighborhood he lives in, the style of clothes he wears, the vacation he takes, and the car he drives or does not drive. Work is not only a way of earning money. Men who achieve success with the expectations of the messages in this factor are more likely to achieve ego integrity than men who are unable to retain jobs, or men with low status jobs, or men unable to achieve competence within their work. The aggregate high scores of the messages discussed in this chapter indicate that men value being good workers, and look to their careers to build a positive self image as well as a comfortable standard of living. Those men who are not able to earn money and acquire good jobs will feel bad about themselves precisely because of the importance of the work ethic. Men who have been laid off or fired commit suicide at higher rates than employed men (30 times the expected number), and have bouts of depression and major illnesses. Not having a job is devastating for a man's ego (Brenner, 1976).

The Protestant work ethic states that human beings are fallible and unworthy. Men who believe this try to dignify themselves through hard work and bury themselves in activities believing that work success will bring happiness (Seidler, 1989). According to this Protestant work ethic, men try to prove themselves to overcome their inherited sense that their basic nature is rotten and evil. They do not know how to stop because they think they can only achieve worth through hard work (Weber, 1958).

Work takes a heavy toll on men who often pride themselves on being male machines (Fasteau, 1974), able to tackle anything, taking great risks to prove themselves on the job. Many manufacturing and farm jobs are dangerous, where males are injured from handling equipment or straining themselves. Other jobs involve chemicals that introduce toxins into men's bodies. Office jobs are stressful which can lead to higher rates of heart attacks. Most men overlook these dangers because of their need to earn money, but such risks contribute to the higher rate of mortality found among males.

With roughly 80 per cent of the fully employed men in the United States working for someone else, most male workers feel alienated from their jobs (Brenton, 1966, p. 93). Such alienation comes from feeling powerless and without control, where males who take orders are at the mercy of management. Many men feel their work is meaningless because they produce goods which have little value other than making profit for those who own the means of production. Truly creative jobs are relatively few in number (Brenton, 1966, p. 194):

> Thus, for the tremendous ego investment a man makes in his job, the great emphasis he places on it in terms of his masculinity, the work he does will not, generally speaking, reward him commensurately.

Most companies are structured hierarchically, so that only a few men can occupy positions of power at the top, while the vast majority of men feel a sense of failure because they cannot occupy prestige positions (Harris, 1986). Some social scientists have indicated that as many as 80 per cent of male workers in the United States are unhappy with their jobs (Terkel, 1974).

The 'worker' category of messages being discussed here does not describe men striving for success, an aspect of male behavior that will be discussed in Chapter 7, 'Bosses'. The aspect of male behavior described in this chapter is that of an hourly wage earner who gets up every morning and does what his boss asks him. The difference between workers and bosses is the difference between a guard on a football team and the quarterback. The guard does all the slave labor that enables the quarterback to gain glory. Men who perform menial tasks in order to survive do not become stars.

The 'Workers' category of male messages consists of the following messages – 'technician', 'work ethic', 'money', and 'law' – that paint a picture of a man who is skilled, who works hard, who values work because it allows him to make money, and who obeys the rules.

Technician

Men relate to, understand, and maintain machines. They fix and repair things around the house.

The United States has a proud tradition of male technicians. Benjamin Franklin, Alexander Graham Bell, and Henry Ford are just some of the men lionized in popular culture because of their technical achievements. In ancient Greek mythology, Hephaestus represented this archetype. The god of the forge, he made beautiful things with his hands (Bolen, 1989).

Technicians are self-reliant. They build and repair automobiles. They do not rely on car mechanics and enjoy helping friends repair cars. Many men in office jobs play the technician role on the weekends, fixing things around the house or pursuing a hobby, like furniture stripping, that allows them to use the 'technician' message in recreational pursuits.

Technicians are craftsmen – men who build devices with great skill. A technician may be an inventor. He might be a furniture-maker, an engineer, an electrician, a car mechanic, or an electronic wizard. He will be a problem solver who uses his brain to master machines. A technician is also an artist who creates masterpieces for the enjoyment of others. The 'technician' message correlates with the 'breadwinner' message, the 'warrior' message, and the 'work ethic' message, meaning that male technicians use their skills to support their families, feel that their skills provide them with a mission in life, and value working as a way to display their craft. Over time the 'technician' message had a positive correlation with the 'hurdles' message, which implies that as men who value this message grew older they feel they had to pass a series of tests. The influence of this message showed a slight increase over time, which implies that men valued this message more as they grew older. Forty-four per cent of the respondents said this was a dominant to strong influence when they were 18, while 10 per cent said the 'technician' message had no influence in their lives.

Wayne, a 49-year-old inspector in a machine shop (Caucasian), typified how the 'technician' message has changed its influence during the latter half of the twentieth century. Wayne, who was raised on a farm in an area now that consists mostly of affluent suburbs, was the second oldest of seven children. 'Everybody had their own responsibility', Wayne explained. 'I always thought that was normal, but maybe that's because it was a bigger family.' Young Wayne was expected to contribute to the maintenance of the family farm. His father built the house they lived in and did all the electrical work. His grandfather was a carpenter, who taught the young boys how to fix things.

As a craftsman, Wayne developed a habit of visualizing jobs and working them through to the end. He enjoys the intellectual challenge of having a job to do, conceptualizing how to do it, and completing it well. His first job was with International Harvester, where he worked as a machinist. Wayne ultimately lost this job when International Harvester closed the plant and moved south. Afterwards he worked at a steel mill where they told him to just 'push the stuff through, good, bad, or indifferent.' He said, 'I told them goodbye. I won't do this. First of all, I might've killed myself, and second of all I don't need a job that bad that I'm just gonna put crap through. So I quit.' Wayne had had a variety of jobs. He had taken odd jobs painting houses. He even had his own food concession in a tavern and had worked as a chef in a fancy restaurant downtown.

At age 49, he is earning less money than he had ten years ago. The factory at which he works was recently bought out by a company that has a record of bankrupting four previous businesses. Wayne hates working for a poorly managed company:

> That's why I don't like this job at all. They've changed managers four times this year. Everyone in management has a title but none of them has more than a high school degree. A tooling engineer works in the tool room. But he's not even a journeyman tool and die maker. They just keep moving people around and they don't have a right title in the first place. I mean education.

Wayne feels bitter about the 'technician' message, which has caused him a series of frustrations. He thought that learning a skill would provide stability, but he now has carpal tunnel syndrome and can no longer work long hours on a machine. The insecurity of his current life bothers him. He has no pension. All his friends with blue collar jobs have also suffered:

> They lost their jobs. There's a lotta people my age that are not working, or they're working at minimum wage jobs. Because they didn't go for their education and they had all those good jobs for all those years. Their companies are gone, and they don't have any other skills. And they're guards for $5.00 an hour. They used to make $15.00 an hour.

He now takes most pride in his house, which he and his roommate have remodeled. His backyard displayed beautiful flowers around a patio he had built.

Wayne's roomate, Gil, a 50-year-old Navy veteran, raised in Hawaii, the oldest of eight children, said that the 'technician' message was important in his life. Wayne and Gil had been living together as a gay couple for 15 years. Gil's father spent a lot of time at sea, so Gil was the repairman around the house. Gil enjoyed doing favors for others and got personal satisfaction out of being a technician:

> At the end of the day, when I do a project, I can go to bed at night and say I did it; I accomplished something. Or I can look forward to the next day, picking up again and enjoying it. The routine, it's almost like a ritual. The routine of getting in there and doing it; that's the part I take satisfaction from.

Gil was too small to play basketball, and not strong enough to play football; so he gained a masculine identity as a boy scout, earning merit badges for doing technical things well. His high level of skill made him a leader among boys.

Bob has a more scientific approach to the 'technician' message. A 44-year-old manager of an inner city housing cooperative, Bob grew up on a farm in rural Wisconsin where he helped with electrical wiring, painting and laying of linoleum. As a boy, he built a tree house in the backyard and looked up to his older brother who became an engineer. Bob ran all the audio equipment for school productions and worked on the stage crew. While he was in high school he made money fixing things for people. He ultimately earned a degree in architecture with an emphasis on civil engineering.

Bob saw that he had gained two things out of the 'technician' message. On the one hand, he was able to earn a living from his technical skills. On the other, he learned a set of what he called 'secondary skills':

> I learned how things go together. Knowing how electricity goes together; knowing how the woodwork in a house goes together; knowing how plumbing goes together; knowing how to take a kit of separate parts and putting it together, all belongs to the technician. (I'm good at puzzles.) It's a process by which you know that any kind of design or set of decisions has a logical order. I've often said I'm an organizer of inanimate objects.

Bob now applies these skills to the political realm, trying to figure out who has the power over issues relating to the housing cooperative, so he can influence decision makers in ways that will benefit the co-op. He feels that a knowledge of computers is essential. Computers are a technician's dream because they perform technical tasks so quickly and easily.

Bob felt that a drawback to the 'technician' message was that in his environment everybody was so busy working that nobody took any time for social activities. He said his parents never went out to movies or parties. They basically worked and came home. When he was young, he never developed close friends, and in his adult life he has somewhat the same pattern. His family, wife and children, are important to him. He works hard at his office and when he is home he works on technical projects which do not allow much time for a social life.

Gerard, a 44-year-old automobile mechanic (African–American), earned his livelihood from being a technician. He enjoys helping people in his neighborhood. Gerard saw a strong relationship between valuing the 'technician' message and standard bearing behavior. Gil captured this aspect of the 'technician' message with the following statement:

> I want the world to remember me by something I physically made. Maybe somebody will pass it on to somebody else. I think of many great people who have made things with their hands which have been passed down. I think of my grandfather as a great man because I can go to a small town and look at some of the houses he built and say my grandpa built that house. I saw my mother do a lot of sewing. I have some of the things she made. I cherish them. I look at them and say 'This is a representation of what my mother was. These things are important to me'.

The 'technician' message allows men to be generative, creating things that leave an impression and taking pride in their accomplishments. Technicians mold parts that are used by others. They take pride in those parts working well. They build artifacts and structures that last for generations.

Work Ethic

Men are supposed to work for a living and not take handouts.

The 'work ethic' message is an extremely important male gender-role message. It had the lowest variance score for all the messages which implies agreement among the participants about the importance of this message. Seventy-four per cent of the respondents said this was a strong to dominant influence when they were 18, the highest rating at that age of all the messages. Only 3 per cent said it was of no influence at age 18. The 'work ethic' message is characterized by the Horatio Alger myth which states that if a man works hard he will be successful.

The 'work ethic' message has wide scope, covering many different aspects of men's lives. At age 18, men see a relationship between having to work hard and support a family ('breadwinner'). They also see a relationship between working hard and gaining control. Over time 18 per cent of the respondents see a relationship between these two variables. Some men who work hard do not show emotions ('tough guy' and 'stoic'). Over time the 'work ethic' message has a positive correlation with over half the messages in this study, indicating the importance of work in a man's life where its influence spreads to his leisure time ('sportsman'), social involvement ('good samaritan'), and family life ('breadwinner'). The correlation between the 'breadwinner' message and the 'work ethic' message over time is one of the strongest in this study.

The 'work ethic' message seems to be handed down from generation to generation. Al, a 55-year-old chemical engineer, commented that all his children were industrious; some had two jobs while others worked 60-hour weeks. Eric, a 53-year-old head of an advertising agency (African–American), described how he got the 'work ethic' message from his grandfather:

> I spent a lot of weekends and Sundays at my grandfather's house. Industry was real important for him. I saw him being industrious and was impressed because his life seemed to be working. All my grandparents were industrious. My Dad didn't make much money but never missed a day of work in 25 years.

Eric said that he had been rewarded for his own industriousness in the Air Force with a commission and had learned that you get something for working hard. He saw the 'work ethic' message as a matter of survival. 'People who don't work hard get screwed,' he explained.

In addition to hard work the 'work ethic' message implied for Eric a certain code of behavior. 'It's meant keeping agreements,' he said. 'It's agreeing to what you said you'd do, you do, even though it's not stated.' The 'work ethic' message also implies honesty, that you do not 'bullshit people'. 'If you say you're going to do something,' Eric explained, 'you do it. I've always tried to be like that.' Eric is also a perfectionist. 'Yeah,' he said, 'I try to do everything perfectly. I don't beat myself if I don't, but I really try to.' Eric concluded his interview saying, 'Don't leave home without the "work ethic" message,' meaning that he relied upon it and looked for it in others. Having this message was as important as wearing clothes. You would not want to be caught naked in the street, nor would you want to have to earn a living without having this kind of dedication to work.

Al worked hard to provide for his family. Al, the father of ten children, was the fourth in a large family that lived on a farm in southern Indiana. He felt overwhelmed by financial responsibilities and gets tense when he does not have enough money to pay bills.

> Mom and Dad were both hard workers. We had a family of ten children which put an enormous amount of pressure on my Dad who was always complaining about being constipated. I find that I get constipated when I'm under stress, which suggests to me that my Dad must have been under stress all his life, simply because of that pressure to earn enough money to support the family. My mother always insisted that we work very hard. I got very little time off around home because we were expected to take care of the house, the garden, and the livestock.

Al was a type-A personality. An overachiever, he could not sit still and felt he always had to be doing something. Al enjoys doing physical work and gardens every summer to experience the gratification of 'getting things done'.

Al saw a negative relationship between the 'work ethic' message and pleasure. When he was young he felt very frustrated sexually and would work long hard hours as a way of releasing his frustrations. (Having been brought up in the Catholic church, he thought it was a sin to masturbate.) As an adult he felt a similar frustration with the 'work ethic' message. 'I would like to be able to stop and have more fun than I do,' he said. 'I find there's lots of things I enjoy, but I don't find enough time for them and that aggravates me.' The 'work ethic' message has a negative correlation with the 'rebel' message implying that men who work hard are obedient. They do not break the rules. It also has a negative relationship over time with the 'nurturer' message which implies that men buried in their work have a hard time achieving intimacy.

Other men felt that the 'work ethic' message afforded them pleasures because they had money to buy things they wanted. Sid, an 18-year-old public high school student (Caucasian), worked as a head bus boy at Chuck E. Cheese and thought this message made him independent. He did not have to count on handouts from his parents and was able buy a stereo and a car:

> So now I have this car which costs a lot of money to run. I just can't

drive it anyplace and buy five tapes. I go to the record store and buy one tape but half the fun is driving there by myself, and being responsible for car insurance and any car repairs. I think it's pretty pleasurable. I only have one chance to be on this Earth; I'm only going to be 18 once. I'd rather be 18 and be able to do things I want to do than be 18 stuck at home and depend upon other people for driving. I don't like the idea of having my Mom give me money. Every once in a while she says, 'You've been good; here's a couple of dollars. Go out and buy yourself a new pair of pants' or something like that. Even when she does that and I know I've been good, I feel there's something missing to that money, since the full value of that money is not really there. When I work ten hours and get my paycheck, then I go out and buy something I want. I know that money has some value because I worked for that money.

Sid gets more from his work than money which enables him to buy things. He gets good feelings:

When I walk into Chuck E. Cheese and see all the things I've done. I see the walls I've painted, and I see the good bussers I've created, and the other good workers I've created. I've spent the last two years there and I've got a lot of time and money invested in Chuck E. Cheese.

A good standard bearer, Sid wants to leave something behind. 'I've worked very hard to train employees', he explained. 'I don't want to build something up and as soon as I walk away it's going to fall. I want it to last a while.'

Mario, a 31-year-old shift worker at an oil refinery in Texas (Hispanic), took great pride in his work and talked in glowing terms about how he benefited from it. He feels the 'work ethic' message provides a direction and purpose to his life. 'I have to get up in the morning and go to work', he said. 'I don't question it. It's helped me cope with my problems on a day to day basis. I roll with the punches.' Mario is a technician who feels good about 'being part of a select group in the nation who knows how to operate a refinery'.

Mario is single. He makes good money and, like other respondents to this survey, finds a strong correlation between 'work ethic' and 'money'. He enjoys having the freedom to pursue his own interests and being able to throw himself into his work, not having to answer to anybody, but he finds the erratic hours demanded on his job make it hard to maintain a long term relationship:

I come from a very male oriented industry. We pay a heavy price. We've some of the highest incident rates of drug abuse, alcoholism, and divorce. I think a lot of us don't really understand the type of changes the industry puts us through. We're willing to do the work, but the consequences come later. Me being a good example. I lost a woman that I deeply loved. There were other problems too, but this was one of the major problems. With anything a person does to make a living there's going to be some kind of debt to be paid.

Like many male workers, Mario realized that he had to put up with many difficulties and problems at his job. This was expressed also by Otto, 73-year-old retired brewery worker (Caucasian), who said that the 'work ethic' message had forced him to buckle down:

> I guess it's one of the things the work message does some times. You have to put up with all kinds of shit from your boss. Some times you get awful disgusted but you can't take out your frustration 'cause you got to bring home the pay check.

Otto worked two jobs until he was 55 to support his family. He came home from the night shift at the brewery and laid down for a couple of hours before he went to his day job. In spite of the difficulties he said, 'You feel pretty good about your life, that you had the work ethic. You take pride in your work and the ability to provide for your family and things like that.'

The future of the 'work ethic' message may be in some jeopardy. Many jobs that reward men for hard work are disappearing. Many young boys neither live with their fathers nor do they have male role models who value the 'work ethic' message. The following table which compares the mean scores for the 'work ethic' message for men of different ages clearly indicates a decline in the importance of the 'work ethic' message among men in the United States.

This decline could be due to many factors. It could be that younger men have not experienced the responsibility of maturity and do not understand the value of work. Similarly older men could appreciate how much they gained from work. In many poor families men have not been able to hold steady jobs, so young boys are not learning respect for the 'work ethic' message. This is especially a problem for minority men who face discrimination which keeps them from getting jobs. Fewer than half the African–American men under 24 have a job today (Kunjufu, 1985).

Wayne provided another explanation for this decline. As had many of the men interviewed for this chapter, Wayne learned his work habits on a farm, where there were clear rewards for work. On a farm men plant crops that feed them. They sweat in the hot sun and bring in the hay. They fix machines. They directly experience the benefits of working hard. In a technological society many men may not feel connected to their work, so the importance of the 'work ethic' message declines.

Table 5.1   Average response to work ethic message

Age	Mean	Cases
19 or under	2.4242	99
20–29	2.8868	106
30–39	3.1013	159
40–49	3.1593	113
50–59	3.3095	42
60–69	3.3750	24
70 or over	3.5385	13

With high levels of unemployment, underemployment, and part time employment, younger men may lack role models in their families that can teach them to value work. The pattern whereby large corporations are shifting manufacturing jobs abroad may be forcing many men in advanced technological societies to re-evaluate the importance of the Protestant work ethic.

Money

A man is judged by how much money he makes and the status of his job.

Men who live in competitive worlds are valued by how much money they have. Money bestows status. Those that have money are envied, while many who have little feel worthless. Wealthy men like Andrew Carnegie, Rupert Murdoch, Nelson Rockefeller, and Donald Trump are heroes. Popular television shows demonstrate the lifestyles of the rich and famous.

Ron, a 31-year-old unemployed man (Caucasian), was consumed by concerns about money. Ron lived at home with his parents. He had been working a variety of odd jobs since graduating from high school:

> Any goal you have, money is going to be the seed for it. It won't grow or be healthy unless you have enough money to support your goals. If you don't have money you can't go to school. Without money you can't go to the bars and have a social life.

Ron even needed money to work out at the YMCA. All the different events that gave his life direction required money. Without money it was hard to have a good time.

Ron was obsessed by money. He was constantly worried about his financial situation.

> You know that old saying, 'Money isn't everything', but you can't live without it. You have to survive with it. You have to work hard and I'm constantly worried about my money situation. I'm in a constant panic about money.

Ron understood clearly the relationship between the 'money' and the 'scholar' message:

> I didn't go to college, so I found that's a major factor with money and the scholar. These two messages go hand in hand. They're pretty vital. If you don't go to college, how are you going to manage your life? Where are you going to go?

Not having a college education has clearly hurt Ron's chances of finding secure employment.

Michael, a 44-year-old school social worker (African-American), worked hard for his money. He spent his spare time as a real estate agent, so his life would be more comfortable. Michael saw money as a convenience:

Not having money is terribly inconvenient. Not earning enough money that allows one to care for one's family is demoralizing. Poverty is destructive. I don't think amassing large amounts of money is important, but being without it is terrible. If a man could not support his family adequately, feed and clothe his children, it would be very difficult for that individual.

Many men in this study commented on the relationship between the 'breadwinner' message and the 'money' message. As Michael pointed out, having children made him take the 'money' message more seriously because of the 'awesome responsibilities involved in being a father'.

Michael grew up in a small town in Texas that was, in his words, highly stratified. He envied the rich people in his town who had their private planes, and said that the sordidness of Dallas was an important symbol in his life. Michael enjoys being able to go places and buy things. He takes pride in paying his own way. Michael sees a relationship between the 'money' message and the 'good samaritan' message. 'It makes me feel good to help other people', he said 'That's a very, very important part of my life.' Michael prefers to give money anonymously:

For me it's just a feeling that that's just what we are here for. I think we all have to help each other. And I think that is why we have a lot of poor, demoralized, emotionally sick people because people have not taken the time to care.

He participates in political campaigns and gives money to candidates of his choice:

In terms of charity I think it is important to give both time and money. I think that I as an individual have an obligation to support community groups and give both money and time to community issues. I do that as much as I can.

Men compete fiercely for positions that confer wealth. Jack, a 33-year-old real estate banker (Caucasian), said this competition began in high school, where the influence of this message went sky high as soon as his peers started to divide up into cliques. He associated with a group of boys who knew they wanted to be business majors, so they could earn good money. Jack's father, whom he described as an extreme workaholic, was a doctor. His male friends have similar positions working for business firms. Their values reinforce his desire for money.

Jack feels that men who show off their wealth are insecure:

I don't like it when someone pulls out his wallet in a restaurant and starts throwing around $100 bills. Those people have to have luxury surrounding them or they don't feel luxurious. In some ways I think they are insecure people. If you took their money away they wouldn't know what to do. If you took my money away, I would just start over. I don't *need* the money. It's nice. It's very nice as a security blanket.

Jack uses the 'money' message to judge the character of others:

I figure if you can't manage your money, you can't really manage much else in your life. Money, to me, is the easiest thing to manage. It's the easiest thing to mismanage, too. So I won't condemn anyone that can't manage his money, or be a responsible person, but for the most part, if you have a grip on your financial situation, be it poor or rich, you can still handle yourself. That tells me a lot about the person.

Jack thinks that men who cannot manage their money lack self-control. Those who work hard can stand on their own two feet and manage their affairs with dignity.

Although money plays an important role in Jack's life, he sees that the success that comes with money is a drag because people are drawn to the outward aspects of a man's personality. People are attracted to a rich man not because of his character but because of his wealth. In Jack's experience, the more money a man has, the harder it is to find a secure man. Jack grew up in an affluent community and has discovered that rich people are used for their money and do not have happy relationships. They are working so hard to get money that they have no time to enjoy it. Jack feels that happiness comes from inside and not from owning material possessions. Having a healthy mind and body is more important than having money.

Jack's ambivalence about the 'money' message is reflected in the population of men who participated in this study. Of the 560 men who filled out this questionnaire, only one said the money message was the most important male message in his life. As Jack suggested, money may be a cornerstone to a man's life, but it does not seem to be central to his identity. The 'money' message was rated as the thirteenth most important message at age 18 with 9 per cent of the men saying it had no influence at that age. Slightly less than half the respondents said it was a strong to dominant influence at age 18, and the influence of this message decreased over time. The 'money' message had the fourth highest variance score over time which implies that as men grew older they had a wide degree of different responses to the influence of this message.

The location of the 'money' message within this chapter implies that men work because they need money, which is necessary to fulfill many of the other requirements of the male role. At age 18, respondents indicated a negative relationship between this message and 'nurturer' and 'nature lover', implying that the desire for money blocks enjoyment of some of the more nourishing aspects of the male gender-role. Many men feel it is important to have money in order to fulfill their familial tasks as husbands ('breadwinner' and 'faithful husband'). They also feel men have to jump over hurdles and, as they get older, have to deny their feelings ('stoic') in order to earn money. Power and prestige ('president') comes from having money, and men appreciate this more as they grow older. Men feel that having money helps them control others, and they feel this more strongly as they mature.

Men value other aspects of their gender identity more than they do the 'money' message. Men realize they have to earn money, but this study indicates that making money is not the most important thing in men's lives. Working hard to earn money may not be that satisfying, while the hours men have to give to their jobs take them from other more enjoyable pursuits. Money, rather than being an end in itself, a goal for a man's life, seems rather to be a tool that allows men to achieve what they value. Men who do not have money have little value.

Law

Do right and obey. Don't question authority.

The 'law' message was not a very popular message with the respondents to this survey. It had the third lowest rating in response to the question: 'What is the most important message in your life?' This is to a large extent because this message became less influential to men as they grew older. In the process of becoming adults, men challenge the laws they acquire when they are younger and establish their own set of rules based upon their experiences, as explained by Dick, a 47-year-old retired Navy Commander (Caucasian):

> The influence of the law message went down as I matured and aged because as I got to know myself better I started to pick my own rules. I gradually gave up following other authorities and came to a point where I was happy with myself and where I was in life.

Over time the 'law' message had significant correlations with the following messages: 'be the best you can', 'breadwinner', 'control', 'faithful husband', 'good samaritan', 'hurdles', 'money', 'president', 'sportsman', 'stoic', 'tough guy', and 'work ethic'. These correlations paint a picture of a particular type of adult male – an authoritarian personality, who lives by the rules to meet his family obligations, who tries to control the behavior of others, who works hard and jumps over hurdles to get ahead, who gets paid for being obedient, and who denies his feelings. These authoritarian men enforce rules and represent a legal system upheld by men – policemen, judges, parole officers, and lawyers – critical of those who do not obey rules. Some social scientists have even suggested the rule following behavior is particularly masculine, that women are more permissive regarding rules that men feel ought to be obeyed (Flugel, 1970).

Dick had lived by the rules. In the Navy, where he built a successful career protecting the laws of his country, he was promoted for his adherence to laws.

Dick had a very strong father figure. Because his mother died when Dick was young, he was raised by his father whom he described as being very stern. In order to get his father's approval, he had to toe the line. Dick mentioned that the 'law' message would be just the opposite of the 'nurturer' message, a feeling that was collaborated with other men as there was a negative correlation between these two messages. A man who values the 'law' message lives up to his obligations. Dick felt there were no strokes for people who obeyed society's rules, just cold prickles for those who disobeyed; therefore most people obeyed the law because they feared punishment.

Frank was a similar man, a 44-year-old senior industrial engineer (Caucasian) who had spent the past fifteen years working for General Motors and the ten previous years in the Marine corps. For Frank the 'law' message meant, 'It's real important that you do everything just like it's supposed to be done.' Frank had been raised in the Catholic church where he acquired a fear of not doing things right. Frank thought there were two levels to this message. One was punitive, where an individual would be punished for doing something bad and the other was moral, where an individual would feel disgrace for being bad. He said, 'There's the act itself which is bad but the shame that's associated with the act is probably a bigger force.' For a man who feels he ought to be doing right, breaking the law creates moral pain. Such individuals can see themselves as unworthy because of their sins.

Frank explained how the 'law' message had played a key role in his career. He had been an extremely conscientious rule follower until his thirty-third year, when he had a nervous breakdown. Because he was such a loyal employee he had been promoted rapidly at General Motors. Frank had learned the hard way that he could not please all the people and described his life as a 'self discovery journey in terms of pleasing and not pleasing people.' Trying to do the right thing all the time had been a tremendous burden. Frank said that the 'law' message resulted in him having a certain inflexibility that he did not like. He felt his life was highly structured.

Warren had learned the 'law' message from his mother. A 37-year-old home repairman (Caucasian), Warren said that both his parents had set a good example by obeying rules. He explained, 'From caring and nurturing I learned the right thing to do.' Warren also had received the 'law' message from Catholic schools:

> I went to parochial school when I was eight or nine, and they put you through a very strict indoctrination, and I got the impression that behavior is black and white. It's either good or it's bad and you're wholly responsible for what you do. The good guys go to heaven and the bad guys go to hell.

Television had also played an important role in how Warren learned the 'law' message:

> Television stressed the importance of being tough and aggressive. I picked up on TV having certain heroes – Wyatt Earp, Perry Mason,

Westerns, Highway Patrol, movies and things like that – stereotypical portrayals of good and evil.

Many popular male figures in the media culture, men like Eddie Murphy in 'Beverly Hills Cop', Matt Dillon in 'Gunsmoke', Don Johnson in 'Miami Vice', Telly Savalas in 'Kojak', and Mr T in the 'A-Team' are heroes because they enforce laws.

Warren thought that without laws there would be social anarchy. His respect for the law led him to be patriotic. He said, 'I think we live in a pretty good country and a certain amount of compliance with the law is necessary in order to hold it together.' He respected the law without question up until the time he was a teenager, when he found out he was gay:

> I just somehow did not feel that the law was protecting me. It's like you always had to be careful, like you can't walk hand in hand like a man and woman could. You can't show affection openly in public like a man and woman could, and these constraints, plus the things I have read in the newspaper about the way police hassle gay people when they haven't broken any law, I guess to a great extent has made the law less important to me.

As a mature individual, Warren feels he is more able to draw his own conclusions about right and wrong. At his age he is critical of some aspects of the law because it excludes people.

Warren had left the Catholic church since he had become gay, an experience which he said 'had forced me to question everything'. He started to read Eastern philosophy and now considers himself a Buddhist, which has given him the perspective that the universe is constantly changing and there is no place for static laws. Warren now believes in Karma, a law of cause and effect. For every action taken in this world there is a reaction. If you do wrong to someone, it will come back to haunt you. He believes that human nature is governed by the laws of Karma, but that our true nature is eternal and beyond the law.

Heraldo, a 39-year-old service worker (Hispanic), had experienced a variety of reactions to the 'law' message. His parents were migrant farm workers. He was raised in a tough inner city neighborhood. He had learned respect for the law from his parents. His father conveyed his own sense of right and wrong by being disappointed when he or one of his ten siblings would do something wrong. When Heraldo was 18, he enlisted in the Army and went to Vietnam where he began to rebel against the social order and began to feel 'very, very disappointed with the laws that were written':

> It was during the time when there was a lot of negativity because of the war in Vietnam. There were some laws that weren't for everybody. There were certain people who were privileged who were excused from the law and could do things that to me were not correct. I felt if we were to believe in and die for these causes and these laws, then everybody

should be subject to them and not just a certain few. I began to see other things about how certain people manipulated the law; in many ways it was circumvented for whatever use people had for it. So I was disappointed for a long time.

After Vietnam Heraldo became an outlaw. He was very discouraged about his society. 'When I came back from Vietnam,' Heraldo said, 'I basically stayed at war. I began to experience hatred in a way that just overwhelmed me. I was willing to do harm.'

Heraldo got out of his lawless state by working with youth in his neighborhood as a little league baseball coach. He tells young boys that the street games they are playing are dangerous, and has regained respect for the law by making a positive contribution. Heraldo says he feels good when he can help others. He is very concerned about youth in the inner city. He feels kids today are confused and he wants to help them to understand they can have fulfilling lives living by the norms of society. Heraldo feels there are good reasons for obeying the law:

You have to obey the law; and there is a good reason for that. If we didn't, if there wasn't law, well obviously then we'd be in anarchy. We want to respect each other as neighbors; we respect each other's property, we respect each other's person.

Heraldo has learned that there are consequences for breaking the law and that there are no shortcuts.

Because humans themselves are imperfect, the social systems they create are often unjust. In trying to create a more just social order men appeal to higher order laws, which Heraldo refers to as the 'laws within'. Some see these laws as coming from God. For others they are part of the moral nature of human beings. In a democratic society laws should allow a wide variety of opinion. Men like Martin Luther King Jr, acutely aware of the lack of justice in some laws, feel they must practice civil disobedience in order to promote a more just world order.

The 'law' message contains ethical principles. All men are taught to adhere to certain moral precepts. Many children learn their morals from their fathers. The placement of this message within the factor, 'workers', implies that men who are good workers are also obedient. They do not question authority. As children, they 'do what their parents tell them'. As grown men, they are faithful husbands and law abiding citizens. Forty-four per cent of the men said this was a strong to dominant influence when they were 18, while 12 per cent said it had no influence at all at that age, which indicates that not all men respect the law, a statistic that may help explain why crime statistics are so high. If 12 per cent of the men do not respect the law when they are 18, this suggests that in a city of a million men, 120,000 might be prepared to take the law into their own hands in order to get what they want – a situation that contributes to drug dealing, shop-lifting, stealing cars, sexual assaults, defying parents, challenging authority, and breaking the law in order to prove their manliness. This disrespect for the law in the US culture is not just an inner city phenomenon. Cowboys, pioneers, and settlers in the West have a proud tradition of taking the law into their own hands, as has been demonstrated by historians (Dubbert, 1979; Filene, 1975) and in novels like *The Ox-Bow Incident* (Clark, 1940). Less than 1 per cent of the respondents to this questionnaire indicated that the 'law' message is the most important message in their lives.

Conclusion

The 'workers' category of male gender conditioning is undergoing changes. Table 5.1 indicates a changing pattern in the work ethic. Younger men do not seem to value working hard as much as older American males. Men like Ron and Wayne, without college degrees, have no security in advanced technological societies which have high levels of unemployment. One out of five men in the United States in the 1980s lacks the skills and knowledge to function effectively (Lloyd and Hetrick, 1987). In 1980 slightly more than half the men in the United States were employed full time (others were retired, below the age of employment, in the armed forces, or employed part time). Of those that are employed, 45 per cent are in blue collar occupations, 27 per cent in non-professional/technical occupations, and 13 per cent in service and farm occupations. Only 15 per cent of the men in the United States work in the professional white collar occupations so often flaunted on television (Harris, 1986). Studies that monitor television programming have indicated that pro-fessional and managerial occupations are overrepresented and blue collar jobs underrepresented compared to the actual labor force (Butsch and Glennon, 1983). Most television shows inaccurately depict American males as upwardly mobile successful workers, rewarded for their labor with luxurious living standards. The images men carry around in their heads about the rewards of work differ from the realities they face trying to hold a job in postindustrial societies.

Because men in modern societies are influenced by the various social messages that encourage them to be duteous workers, to obey the law, to become technically competent, and to work in order to earn a living, they have not yet learned how to achieve identities independent from their job titles. Work is crucial. With a good job a man will earn enough money to participate in the consumer society and buy goods that provide status. Meaningful work allows men to be generative and creates the possibility of a man achieving ego integrity. However, in a postindustrial economy many men who define themselves through accomplishments on the job and/or material success provided through employ-ment will be insecure because of layoffs, shifting unemployment, lack of job security, and poor pay. In this postmodern world the 'worker' aspect of masculinity creates many problems for men attempting to construct healthy gender identities.

Chapter 6

Lovers

Men are lonely.

Men are isolated.

Men validate their feelings through women, not through men.

Beware of discussing your feelings with other men.

If your wife wants to have an affair, she will find another man who won't refuse. Don't trust men with your woman.

Men lack courage of conviction and will individually succumb to pressure by other men.

Men look outside for a father, but forget to father themselves.

Every man fears that every other man has a bigger penis and knows how to use it better.

48-year-old professional

Each man has within a little boy wanting to be loved. In order to receive both the comfort and security provided by love, men have throughout their lives a variety of different relationships with other human beings – parents, children, colleagues, lovers, and friends. Many observers of social behavior have criticized men's inabilities to relate warmly to other human beings (Farrell, 1974; Fasteau, 1974). Men are seen as being instrumental in the world, achievement oriented, working hard to achieve goals and get rewards. Women, on the other hand, are described as being expressive, relating to the world emotionally through their hearts (Lindsey, 1990). Miller (1983) estimated that one out of every eight men in the United States has a close male friend or buddy. Since 40 per cent of the marriages in the United States end in divorce, it is easy to put these two statistics together and get a picture of American men without close friendships, unable to achieve intimacy.

Men do have friendships, yes, but their relationships with other men are usually built around competition, not emotional sharing. Male play, where men compete with peers, tests their skills, helps men relax, and provides enjoyable recreation. Men play a variety of games together, but relationships founded on sports fields provide an arena where men prove themselves rather than an arena for self-disclosure. Competition plays an important part in men's lives, urging males to perform at their highest level but does not lead to trust. Garfinkel (1985) stated that men have a hard time forming friendships because they are so busy competing with each other. As the quotation at the beginning of this chapter indicates, men who fear other men will steal their wives or outperform them, have a hard time making friends because they fear other men will stab them in the back.

Men are not taught how to be lovers, to be expressive, to share, to show affection, and to become companions. As do all human beings, men have the capacity to love, but this capacity is not developed. Gender role researchers have pointed out that all people have masculine and feminine traits (Schaffer, 1981). Because men are taught how to be workers and to be bosses, their gender identities do not respect their feminine sides. David and Brannon (1976, p. 12) have pointed out how the anti-feminine element is a key component of masculinity. They described this element as follows: 'No Sissy Stuff: The stigma of all stereotyped feminine characteristics and qualities, including openness and vulnerability'. Bem (1974) has established that those persons who are best adjusted to the world value both masculine and feminine aspects in their own personalities. Those men who deny their feminine nurturing sides are emotionally illiterate. They are not in touch with their feelings; they try to dominate and do not admit vulnerabilities, which allow closeness to others.

The way men express their capacity for love is reflected in four messages – 'breadwinner', 'nurturer', 'faithful husband', and 'playboy'.

Breadwinner

Men provide for and protect family members. Fathering means bringing home the bacon, not necessarily nurturing.

The tension in men's lives between the instrumental and expressive sides of their personalities is best expressed in the 'breadwinner' message, which characterizes one way men relate to their families. Rather than emotionally caring for family members, men provide for them. They work long hours, which keeps them away from spouses and children. When they return home from work, they are often too exhausted to relate to their family members. This dilemma was described by Farrell (1986) in his book, *Why Men Are the Way They Are*, where he posited a ninth grade class of boys and girls at some high school in the United States. Some of the boys would be attracted to some of the girls. However, those girls would not be attracted to their classmates. They would be more interested in older boys who drive cars, who star on the sports team, who participate in student government, or who have had sexual experience. As a result, the ninth grade boys develop an inferiority complex, feeling that they are not attractive to those girls to whom they are attracted. To compensate for these feelings of inferiority, men feel they have to prove that they are indeed worthy of the attention of girls and start a lifelong career of achievement, thinking that if they succeed others will love them. If only they are rich enough, the attractive women will want them. If they make the varsity team, women will be attracted to them. If they make enough money to buy a Corvette, they will receive nurturing. The irony of this approach to gaining approval from females, as Farrell points out, is that men spend so much time trying to achieve the things they think will make them attractive, that they never achieve emotional closeness. In addition, the skills they develop in their rush to succeed in the competitive world are opposite to the skills needed for emotional intimacy. Men carry this behavior into their families ('breadwinner' message) where they feel that if they provide support and material goods, they will be loved.

A 41-year-old professional man (Caucasian) wrote the following to describe the 'breadwinning' message:

> I grew up believing I must be the breadwinner, be strong, be educated, and must take care of my family. Things, events, actions which happen to me must be taken in stride and roll off my back. 'That's the way it is and I must take it and deal with it.'

A synonym for 'breadwinner' is 'provider'. Males feel the obligation not only to provide for themselves but also to provide for other family members. Men striving to fulfill the requirements of the 'breadwinner' message try to be the best they can, to control others, to overcome hurdles, to be successful, and to work hard.

The 'breadwinner' message was rated as the tenth most important message. Fifty-two per cent of the men indicated it was a strong to dominant influence in their lives when they were 18, but the influence of this message declined over time. This message showed the greatest variance of all the messages, which indicates the importance of providing for a family in some men's lives. For those men who never became fathers the influence of this message declined. For those men who became fathers and realized that fathering meant more than just bringing home the bacon, the influence of this message also declined. For those men whose lives were dominated by the economic responsibilities of fatherhood, the influence of this message increased dramatically. Many of the complex obligations of this message were not foreseen by men at age 18. But by the time men had spent some years raising a family, the 'breadwinner' message exerted a powerful pull within their male gender identities incorporating many classical aspects of male behavior.

The 'breadwinner' message had a negative correlation with the 'rebel' message which indicates the men who take on the role of family provider conform in order to fulfill the demands of that role. The 'breadwinner' message also had a negative correlation with 'nurturer' over time which implies that men who play the provider role in their families may not fulfill nurturing roles.

Breadwinners are task oriented, focusing their energies on work, social, and family obligations. Mike, a 51-year-old business consultant and father of four boys (Caucasian), had earlier (when his blood pressure was extremely high) quit his job as a superintendent of a rural school district so he could get his life in order. Mike felt he had to compete with other men to live up to the demands of this role. 'Part of it was satisfying mother or mother's substitute', he said. 'Part of it was satisfying my family, kids, providing for them. Yeah, fulfilling that role model image, the hero, the provider.' For many men, sacrificing for the family, leaving the home to go to jobs they may hate, and disciplining themselves to bring home a check, takes on heroic proportions. Part of the heroism is having a woman at home dependent upon them, so that being a breadwinner means not only being a provider, but also a protector.

One of the breadwinners interviewed – Virgil, a 55-year-old bus driver and ex-professional boxer (Native American) – was recovering from a back injury and had run out of savings. In spite of the financial hardships his injury had caused his family, he would not let his wife work. Virgil talked with great pride about how important it was for his wife to be home to look after his children while he was away at work. 'It's part of protecting my family', he said. 'Having their mother in the home to care for the kids when I'm not here. I feel safe and secure.'

Breadwinners do not necessarily contribute to the emotional life of a family, as was pointed out by a 23-year-old service worker (Caucasian):

I was definitely brought up believing that men should be the bread-winner. Unfortunately, I was also brought up with tough dominant male emotions. I wish I could show more sensitive feelings more easily.

Children are a key part of the 'breadwinner' message. One breadwinner said he was not even aware of this message until he had his second son, and then the responsibility for providing for his children became overwhelming. Virgil, who had 14 children by four different women, was extremely devoted to his offspring. His children provided him stability and a sense of purpose. Some of his relationships with the mothers of his children had ended with real bitterness, so that his love life, far from being satisfying, had been chaotic and unsatisfying. Through all the ups and downs of these relationships, his children had been a constant source of love.

Virgil mentioned numerous sacrifices he had undertaken in order to support his children. He had to stay in jobs he hated simply because he had to bring home a pay check to support his family. He often felt hedged in by the responsibilities and resentful because he never had any money to spend. Ed, a 57-year-old farmer in Iowa (Caucasian), talked about how hard he had worked to pay off his debts (for farm equipment) and how one of his goals in life had been to have a little extra money to spend. He felt bad for his father who had worked real hard in South Dakota during the depression but had not been able to save any money.

The average age of the men interviewed for the 'breadwinner' message was 57. Men under 30 had a significantly lower score for the influence of this message than men over 30. High rates of divorce, couples living together, reconstituted families, single parent head of household families, dual-worker families, and role-sharing families have all challenged traditional views about the fathering role for men in modern societies. The breadwinning role is no longer a heroic task taken on by fathers alone, but rather in modern life most mothers also work outside the home to support children financially. Declining incomes have made it harder for men to live up to the expectations of the 'breadwinner' role.

Nurturer

Among other things men are gentle, supportive, warm, sensitive, and concerned about others' feelings.

Every person on this planet has a father. In spite of this obvious fact, the parenting literature until the 1970s totally excluded fathers from their discussions (Parke, 1981). Distant providers, their nurturing roles were totally ignored. The 'professionals' delegated the task of raising children entirely to women. In the 1970s because of changing lifestyles, divorce, and mothers working outside the home, some fathers have started to to assume caretaking responsibilities as capable nurturers.

Nurturing seems to be something that men grow into as they mature. Fourteen per cent of the respondents to the questionnaire indicated that the 'nurturer' message had no influence upon them by the time they were 18, but this message exhibited the greatest increase in influence for respondents over time. The 'nurturer' message had negative correlations with many of the more traditional aspects of male behavior, indicating that nurturing men do not fit traditional masculine stereotypes. As might be expected, men who try to be perfect ('superman'), who do not show their feelings ('stoic') and who act tough ('tough guy') are not nurturing. The 'nurturer' message has a positive relationship with 'nature lover' and 'good samaritan'.

Nurturing implies caring for others, being helpful, assisting people in their development, concern for other's well-being, showing kindness, and being supportive. Joe, a 45-year-old ex-librarian studying to be a therapist (Caucasian), described the influence of this message:

> Nurturing men are gentle. I played football in high school, but I wasn't very good at it. I guess I got pushed into being in some sport, but I didn't have the necessary competitive edge. You're supposed to hit in football. Hitting was not my thing. You're supposed to have a sort of killer instinct. I couldn't do that.

Joe was an only child, 'the apple of his parents' eyes'. His mother was the breadwinner in the family, while his father was partially employed. Joe had learned some of his nurturing skills from his father. 'My father didn't like work', he said. 'He'd rather be with me. Take me in his cab and show me off!' Joe remembers his father as being someone who was there when he needed him. Joe, for whom the nurturing message has played an extremely important role of his life, said that he had an emotional bank account. He said his first wife drained his bank.

> I have a good sense of these accounts. You can overdraw, overspend your balance. Today I draw people to me that give as well as me giving back. I try to choreograph my life not to be in the presence of people who only draw on my bank account, the emotional one.

In relation to his current wife, Joe said he was more nurturing at age 45 because he was living with someone who returned his love:

> I don't know if all nurturers are like this, but to be nurturing is to have to find nurturing, to order your world to find it. When it wasn't coming out of marriage, I had to do something about my marriage. Work never gave it to me. I didn't perform well at work.

The 'nurturer' message spills over into men's work. Joe explained how he had had a peripatetic career as a librarian, travelling from job to job looking for a nurturing environment. If he did not find it, he would leave or get fired. Finally, he realized that he was not going to get nurtured, or be able to nurture others, as long as he worked in library settings. He decided to change careers, hoping that by being a therapist, he could develop the nurturing side of his personality. He describes his frustrations with his career in the following way:

> I was a very good librarian, very nurturing. I could make you, as a stranger, scared to death coming into my library, feel welcome. But, I found myself moving up a career ladder for some reason, and because of what society says, further away from patrons into administration with more people under me, up to 70 at one time, and I'm not good at that. How do you nurture 70 people? I had to fire people – a very hard thing to do for a nurturer, very beaten down by work.

When he was in school, Joe said he was very personable:

> I saw other people's ideas as something to help me grow. So I think I validated people. Women were attracted to me. It was very easy. I had no problem with dates. I was a good conversationalist. Both boys and girls liked that. I made people feel good. I grew up wanting to please.

This is somewhat ironic because popular myths state that women are not attracted to men like Joe but rather to men like James Bond – cool, calm, diffident, unemotional, and uninvolved.

Slim provided some insights into the 'nurturer' message which he had received from his mother. He felt an important part of this message was self-nurturing:

> I got to watch out for me, too. I can't just look for everybody else and leave me out, because I need time alone, especially now as a teenager. I spend some time thinking, you know, what am I up to? What am I doing now? Where am I at? Am I where I should be?

He saw this aspect of the 'nurturer' message as self-preservation. He said, 'It's not that you're placing yourself in front; just you shouldn't forget yourself.' Slim said he finds himself wanting to help people. He gets mad when he sees people putting others down; and he gets satisfaction out of having relationships with people where he can talk openly.

One man who made nurturing a priority in his life was Rob, a 35-year-old paramedic (Caucasian). Rob's first divorce was at 18, when he lost his daughter through a custody battle. He remarried and had two children. After that marriage broke up, he gained custody of the children. When interviewed, he was in his third marriage. He described how he learned the 'nurturer' message:

> I think after my son was born, my wife sort of got tired of doing stuff with him when he was little, and by the time my daughter came along, I was the one every night to get up and take care of her and change diapers and feed her ever since she came home. I like that. You get to feel your life actually means something. You feel like a special person when you are nurturing.

He makes time to be a nurturer. He arranges his schedule to be at home when the kids return from school.

> What more important thing can there be for a person to do in life than actually bring up children and be a family which gives people the basis for a set of values they will develop on their own?

Rob is guided by a sense of responsibility. He wants to set a decent example for his kids and does not want his children to feel they are taking a second place in his life. Being a father helps him feel important and sets his priorities. Like the faithful husbands in the next section, Rob limits his outside activities so he can spend quality time with his children. Rob said, 'I want to have nice memories when I'm old and retired. Running around with my friends and doing things won't provide good memories. Being with my family will.'

Rob's nurturing personality spills over into his job as a paramedic in the toughest part of an inner city, where he comforts people in the midst of awful crises. As a result of this message he says he is able to be:

> a little more understanding with people; being able to empathize with them a little more. Or you can say, 'What if I was in this position and this was happening to me?' If somebody has really screwed up you don't blame them as quickly. Would I have done this same thing? You really don't look down on somebody that makes mistakes in life because anybody can; and if things happen to someone, you try to help them out.

He likes his job helping people in need.

Nurturing is a pleasant part of life, but most men do not respect that aspect of masculinity. Joe felt, 'Everybody has nurturing in them. All these other messages block it.' About the condition of being male, Joe exclaimed, 'If we were left alone without all this crap, we'd be incredible nurturers!' Sexuality inhibits nurturing. The 'nurturer' message correlates negatively with the 'playboy' message. Men who practice promiscuous sexual behavior are not likely to be nurturing, while those men who are nurturing are likely to be faithful husbands.

As the following statement by a 25-year-old construction worker (Hispanic) indicates, most men fail to realize that nurturing is something they are supposed to do:

> More often than not, as a teenager, I found myself rebelling against some of the 'male messages' rather than adopting them. Some of them, like 'nurturer', I had little idea were even a possibility for an American male.

Many men become aware of their nurturing sides as a result of a divorce, a crisis that forces men to readjust their values. Carl knows a lot about divorce. Although as a lawyer he does not handle divorce cases, he is familiar with how traumatizing the process can be for the individuals involved:

> Divorces hurt everybody. Whether its voluntary divorce or mandatory. The whole process is very painful, demeaning, shakes your sense of where you've been, what you are all about, like no other ceremony in our society does.

Before his divorce, Carl was a workaholic who did not spend much time with his children. As a result of the divorce, he spends more time with them, so the divorce became an important part of how he learned to appreciate the 'nurturer' message. Prior to his divorce Carl thought that men had to be rulers in charge of everything, controlling their relationships and making all the critical decisions in a relationship. They were all-knowing, wise figures. Carl explains that he now lives under an entirely different set of rules:

> The rules are be honest; the rules are do your best; the rules are respect and appreciate the capabilities and potential of the other person; the rules are be supportive; the rules are don't gratuitously criticize. No more 'I got it figured out. This is the way we're going to do it', and 'I absolutely positively confidentially know what I'm doing, so don't question what I'm doing.'

This author feels he learned to value the 'nurturer' message on his own when he was 11 and visited a friend of his mother who was in a hospital with terminal cancer. He remembers spending over an hour with her and leaving the hospital feeling if he were floating on a cloud. He wondered at the time why he felt so happy. After all, it was depressing that this woman, whom he had know for a long time, was dying. He concluded that through the interaction he had discovered the power of his ability to nurture which was positively exhilarating. From that time, this author has gone out of his way to visit people who are sick, to serve meals at a shelter for the homeless, or to visit men in prison because he enjoys the good feelings he gets from nurturing people in need. American Indians say that if you give a gift to someone you get it back nine times over. Nurturing and loving are like gifts. They are returned because they help fill our worlds with tenderness, care, and concern.

Faithful Husband

Men give up their freedom when they get married.

Lasch (1979) has pointed out how, in the modern worlds, a man's family is a 'haven in a heartless world'. The 'faithful husband' message implies that men are devoted to members of their family, that they are loyal, that they can be counted on, and that they do not have extramarital affairs. This message differs from the 'breadwinner' message because it emphasizes interpersonal commitment and not just bringing home the bacon, although that is a part of the 'faithful husband' message. The 'faithful husband' message had a positive correlation with 'breadwinner' at age 18 and over time. The 'faithful husband' message also had positive correlations at age 18 with 'money', 'law', and 'president'. Over time it had positive correlations with 'law', 'control', 'money', 'hurdles', and 'self-reliant' which implies that men trying to fulfill the requirements of this role play by the rules, value money, stand on their own two feet, and try to control the behavior of others.

A faithful husband has serious financial and emotional commitments to his family. Walter, a 36-year-old social worker (Caucasian), said that it involves more than just earning enough money so that his family can survive at a subsistence level. It requires working hard to send his kids to college so they can achieve a middle class life style. It also implies a commitment to honesty within the marriage relationship.

Walter, who said the 'faithful husband' message did not exert much influence in his life until he became married, suggest that men grow into the requirements of this message. Seventeen per cent of the respondents to the questionnaire indicated that this message had no influence in their lives by the time they were 18. The 'faithful husband' message had the highest variance score at age 18, indicating that young men have divergent feelings about assuming the responsibilities of a devoted spouse. Getting married is a transition point in a man's life. Prior to that time many men feel they do not have many responsibilities. When men marry they have to control their desires to roam and become reliable mates for their spouses, a sentiment expressed by a 45-year-old craftsman (Caucasian):

> Marriage has definitely helped to change a lot of my so called macho views. I believe that I do not have to be so aggressive to prove myself as my deeds can do better.

Marriage takes a man out of the rough and tumble world of bachelorhood, where he has to prove himself and take risks to get his emotional needs met, and allows him to abandon many of the trappings of classical masculinity.

Neal, a 51-year-old elected state representative (Caucasian), stated that he learned this message from his mother, whom he greatly admired. For Neal this message implied respect for women:

> I don't like to see women used. When I see other men displaying disrespect, it shows a lack of strength. It was their biggest weakness. The use of women made them look like fools. I never really liked to be with a group of men who were boasting and bragging about their prowess with women, like a bunch of kids, that is so immature. Those people have no control of their lives.

Neal felt that a man who was disrespectful of women could be taken advantage of and controlled by his dependency upon women.

Neal saw that the 'faithful husband' message was a source of strength in his life, allowing him to focus on things he values:

> If things just aren't going right, I have my down points. I say, 'Why am I around?' I get tired of living. I would say in the last seven years I have gone through ... I've been in deep depression where I viewed death as a well deserved vacation. Just tired of the exhausting demands that are made by others, and myself, upon myself. And the strength and beauty of my spouse helped me survive; gave me the strength to rise above and to say, 'I'm really lucky to have a person so good and so willing to share my life.'

He also enjoys growing with his spouse to whom he has been married for 14 years:

> I think it feels very good to love. To love means to be able to find comfort in being in the presence of another person, being able to see your spouse grow, and appreciate her efforts in strengthening you.

He felt that the commitment he has built with his wife has given him security. He and she share a vision. When that vision gets challenged in Neal's life, he gains strength from his wife's support.

Religious training played an important part in learning the 'faithful husband' message for all of the four men interviewed. Walter, who is Jewish, stated that he picked it up from the Jewish culture, which contains very strong norms about appropriate family behavior.

One of the men interviewed for this message – Hank, a 24-year-old college student from Minnesota (Caucasian) who had been married for two years – was resentful at what he felt was a loss of freedom. He said he did not particularly want to play around sexually, but he was frustrated because the time he spent in his marriage with his infant daughter and wife kept him from developing close friendships:

I haven't had a chance to grow up. I haven't had a chance to experience my own feelings and how other people feel about me as a person. I never really dated much in college. When I met my wife, I cut everything else off, but I'm still in the same mind frame that I was three years ago.

Just because men get married, does not mean that the influence of the 'playboy' message upon their gender identities disappears. The tension that exists between these two messages provides a fine example of what researchers call 'sex-role strain' (Pleck, 1981; Weitzman, 1979). Men receive conflicting messages which cause tension in their lives. Even though men may be married, they still live within a culture that applauds a sexual market place, where being single, youthful, and sexually promiscuous are promoted. Heterosexual men, regardless of their marital status, are still attracted to the notion that they can achieve excitement, adventure, sexual satisfaction, and even happiness sleeping with different women.

This tension between personal honesty and sexual fidelity was the chief ingredient of the 'faithful husband' message for Jim – a 61-year-old graduate of the Naval Academy, a businessman (Caucasian) – who had been married for 35 years, and divorced within the last year. He was raised in a devout Catholic home and attended an elite private school, where he was brought up to do the right thing so he was a virgin when he married. He explained why he got married:

At 25, it was time for the next phase in my life and that phase had to be marriage. Or else I would have had to quote, sin against the church or sin against whatever I was brought up with. Black and white. There was no grey. How do you get from black to white sexually? You get married. You pick a girl with nine of the ten qualities you're looking for and you hope it works. And it worked for a while, but it really didn't work.

In retrospect, Jim thought that getting married was another step in his career, something he was supposed to do. He doubts if he ever really loved his wife. Towards the end of his marriage they were escorts for each other, pictures of a happy family, but the chemistry was missing. He felt he was unfaithful in his marriage because he was fantasizing about other women and developing deep platonic friendships. 'The grass is always greener on the other side of the fence', he said. Jim's divorce was so difficult for him because he was torn between his own sense of commitment to the law (being a faithful husband was a commandment that men followed) and his own commitment to his personal growth.

All the fathers interviewed for the 'faithful husband' message took tremendous joy in their relationships with their children. Hank would light up when he talked about his daughter, Ashley. 'Being a father is very rewarding', he said. 'Being a husband isn't.' Hank said that he would have divorced his wife a long time ago if it had not been for his relationship to his 2-year-old daughter. His wife actually threatened him that if he left her, she would not allow him to see Ashley again. Walter always liked children. He had a good relationship with his 5-year-old daughter and was extremely fond of his 2-year-old son. His father had made being with the kids a priority. Walter stated that it was an expectation of his culture that fathers would spend time with their children. 'Besides', he said, 'it's a joy. It's not a burden.'

Playboy

Men should be sexually aggressive, attractive and muscular

For thousands of years in western culture the 'playboy' message has been an important cultural norm for male behavior. In the Greek myths the male Gods were polygamous, often raping women at will. In the fourteenth century the Italian writer, Boccaccio told ribald tales in *Decameron* about male sexual exploits. Don Juan, the breaker of young women's hymens and hearts, has been an important figure in western literature. This cultural norm contains stereotyped images of adventurous male sexuality.

As Ehrenreich (1983) has pointed out, the 'playboy' message has assumed particular significance in modern times. Developed in the 1950s this message appealed to company men who were members of a faceless mass. The playboy image provides men a new arena for heroic accomplishments. It promotes a consumer industry based upon expensive clothing, cars, houses, and a lifestyle calculated to win the attention of attractive women.

Males are expected to be interested in sex, but the type of sex discussed here under the 'playboy' message is different than the type of sex involved with the 'faithful husband' message and the type of loving associated with nurturing. Playboy sex is genitally oriented with no commitment. Playboys isolate sex from other parts of their lives. Their desires for sexual conquest with many partners precludes developing nurturing relationships based upon trust and self disclosure.

A 65-year-old man expressed the essence of the playboy life style:

> The main message was hedonistic; enjoy yourself, be cautious, and don't get caught but seize every opportunity for pleasure and self gratification; consider the feelings of others but only to turn to own advantage.

The 'playboy' message has a positive correlation with many of the classical male roles – 'adventurer', 'be the best you can', 'breadwinner', 'control', 'hurdles', 'money', 'president', 'self-reliant', 'sportsman', 'stoic', 'superman', 'tough guy', and 'warrior'. This list of roles typifies the modern playboy who is success oriented, unemotional, adventurous, aloof, aggressive, and tough. Over 9 per cent of the men who responded to the questionnaire saw a relationship between the 'playboy' message and 'tough guy' and 'warrior', both of which contribute to male aggression. Social critics have for a long time complained that men see a relationship between sex and violence (Bradbury, 1972). These high correlations suggest that aggressive, warrior-like behavior is associated with sexual conquests. Although this message did correlate with many other classical male roles, less than 1 per cent of the respondents to the questionnaire said the 'playboy' message was the most important message in their lives.

For Chuck, a 33-year-old student (Caucasian), the 'playboy' message was a crucial part of his masculine gender identity. As a young boy he wanted to be a sexually attractive man. With no emotional component he lost his virginity at age 15 as a result of a competition with his brother. He used to feel he was fat and unattractive. When he started becoming sexually active, he worked out with weights and enjoyed it when other people would find him attractive.

Leroy, a 41-year-old counselor (African–American) in a program that counsels violent men, felt peer pressure to be a playboy. A light skinned black, he was in much demand among the women where he attended college. He enjoyed the praise he received for his sexual exploits. He would feel great about himself when someone would say, 'Man, you got so many women after you.' He said, 'It helped give me a kind of power or charisma.' Because of his sexual exploits, he said he was always in the limelight.

A playboy is a stud who tries to pick up as many sexual partners as he can. 'Find 'em, fuck 'em, and forget 'em' is his motto. Other people are sexual objects to conquer. He is a smooth operator – quick talking and quick thinking. He is charming and has a line to say in order to get somebody to feel a particular way. Intent on what he wants, he is not considerate of other people's feelings.

James – a 29-year-old unemployed man (African–American), who was a consummate playboy – expressed these aspects of the 'playboy' message. He liked women. James had spent 10 years on the streets living the life of a modern Don Juan. He described the kinds of playboy standards that he used to try to live up to by first quoting a Jackie Wilson song:

> 'I know the secret now, Since I fell in love and my heart was broken, from now on I'll just play them all.' That way I don't have to risk being hurt by any one of them. Because if one leaves me there's another one there. Pair on the spare is the first rule of being a playboy. You got to have a pair on the spare. And then there are different levels of it. I mean a pair on the spare is basic. Then you're basically equipped, but if you really get deep, you gonna need four holes, a bull dagger, and a cock in the trunk. (Translation, four ladies, a lesbian, and a gay.)

Having many women meant that if one lets you down, you have no need to worry, because you have many others. Quantity was more important than quality. James has paid a price for his promiscuous behavior. He is HIV positive.

James explained that some guys are just horny, which is why they like so many women, but playboy behavior on the part of men goes beyond sexual need gratification:

> For some men it becomes a status symbol. A lot of times the guys do

it for the fellas. So they can show the guys how many ladies they can come up with. Some guys feel they have to have the finest. Other guys just like multitudes.

James went on to explain the deeper psychological meaning of the 'playboy' message.

It really is an inward battle. You're trying to get the approval of yourself, a way of letting yourself know you are cared for. Somebody gives a damn for you. Even though all these relationships are shallow, but at the same time you can protect your feelings, not really caring about the women as individuals.

James said that being a playboy was basically an ego trip, being enchanted with your ability to have sexual conquests. Playboys are in love with themselves.

Earl agreed. He had spent 30 years being a playboy. The 'playboy' message urged him to seduce women, sleeping with them, talking about women all the time, and waking up in the morning thinking about getting laid. He used to have a bag of tricks he would play, 'guilt numbers, suggestions, subtle coercions, and invitations. I could really play the whole playboy number in spades.' Seducing women provided him with status and self esteem:

Some guys are really good at baseball. Some guys became superstars as ends or quarterbacks for the football team, or scholars, or class presidents. For me, my status became my ability to hustle women.

Earl wanted to get into the playboy fraternity at college, a real animal house. He was proud when his animal brothers at the fraternity would say of him 'He's gets more ass than a toilet seat!'

Earl described the sources of his playboy behavior from his youth when he was smothered by his mother. Of the puer-mother relationship he said, 'She needed us but her needs were overwhelming, psychologically destructive. We get our attention from women, but we damn well better not get real close or they will devour us.' So he needed to walk a fine line between having women around and not giving them what they need, which is an essential contradiction, needing to have females take care of him, but also needing not to be tied down. 'I have only been committed once', he said, 'and that was terrifying!' He was aware that as a puer, he would act out his anger towards his mother by leaving sexual partners.

Earl understood that the playboy life style meant more than simply conquering women. It was an easy way of living full of adventure that implied freedom, being your own boss, and not having to answer to others. 'My entrepreneurial spirit is real high,' he said, 'I haven't worked for wages for 14 years.' Earl also acknowledged that beyond sexual gratification, the 'playboy' message was a great adventure:

The game has to do with the addiction. It was always a rush. It was being addicted to that romantic buzz. It was another high – shooting up with the excitement of being with this new woman – all that romantic junk. Once it would fade, I was out of there.

James also said he found it real exciting at first but after ten years he tired of being a playboy, of the trickery and deceit. 'The part that's really a shame', he said, 'is that most of the victims are innocent, just looking for a little intimacy.' He expected to be nurtured by having contacts with women, but as he explained, 'The reality of the situation was, I wasn't. Not by the women, not by the guys that I was trying to impress, not by anybody except myself. I wasn't getting what I wanted out of it.'

All four of these men interviewed for the 'playboy' message have stopped being sexually promiscuous, Earl because he finally stopped giving all his power to women and has developed a close circle of intimate male friends, James because he is tired of all the mind-fucking, and Chuck because the 'playboy' message has created a lot of confusion in his life. He thought he was supposed to have sex with women but slowly discovered he was not attracted to women and was gay. He became very sexually active because that is what he thought gay men did, hang out in bars and pick up other men:

I noticed that there was little difference between the bar situation in the heterosexual and homosexual environments. I noticed that there probably was much more promiscuity in gay relationships because they were much easier and because it was easier to be anonymous; let's get this over with seems to be the predominant way of doing things.

He felt that his playboy behavior had been detrimental because he became distanced from himself and it was hard to get close to people. He was looking for validation from relationships, but the casual sexual relations he was having through the gay bar scene were not validating. He resented the 'playboy' message because it placed such an emphasis on sexuality which 'is such a small, tiny, minute part of an individual's life'. He has since found other ways of validating himself by spending time alone and looking for in depth relationships. 'At this point in my life', he said, 'I am more apt to look for a relationship. Someone that I can respect, someone that I will take home and love.'

Leroy mentioned that his notions of sexuality had evolved. Originally it was mostly a physical thing, but early in his twenties he tired of being a playboy:

A lot of times I'd be involved with sex, and it wasn't what I wanted to do. I found myself stressed out by the demands of having a lot of female friends, and not knowing how to say no, when to say no, not feeling comfortable with saying no, believing that it somehow threatened my image. To me getting married meant this is a monogamous thing. I didn't have to spread myself out. It could be one-dimensional. It was going to be safe and secure and a relief, not having to be a playboy.

Leroy has been through a couple of divorces and has had three children by three different women. He is extremely critical of the pressures that exist in the black community that compel young boys to be sexually active to prove their virility:

I'll just sort of reemphasize that I think the idea or the notion of Playboyism or baby-making-ism that bombards Afro–American males is probably one of the most devastating, and it's one of the misconceived attitudes. It is one of those items that needs definitely to be dealt with. It's not an expression of manhood; it's not an expression of maturity; it's definitely not an expression of constructiveness to believe that you are compelled to have as many women, like a harem or something, as possible; to make as many babies as possible; because if you do, you act it out and you make babies. You are not in a financial position to be able to provide for them. If you are not in an emotional position to be able to provide for them, then what winds up happening is these young kids grow up and they start feeding on you. It's a negative image and a stereotype because the larger culture also says that about men of color, that's all we want to do. So people begin to play out those stereotypical roles. But I think that's one of the most devastating and destructive attitudes or/and behaviors that we have facing the Afro–American community.

Leroy, who is now in his middle adult years, has noticed a change in his own sexuality. He used to think that sex was simply a physical act that he carried out with a woman. In his middle adult years he has discovered that sex has a kind of sensuality to it, that includes emotions:

Sensuality, to me, implies a much broader approach than just fucking. I mean, I can be sensual through my emotional sensitivity. Whereas before, sexuality was almost a bang, bang, bang thing – I mean it's strictly physical; we touch for a minute or two, or maybe even we may touch longer than that, but the goal of the touching is to reach some kind of a height so that there's some kind of climax physical, sexual coitus or whatever.

Sensuality has more to do with that. There's an emotional part to it, which I think a lot of times was left out; and I equated, again, physicalness for intimacy and thought that somehow I was going to develop some kind of an emotional growth out of how many times I climaxed. And that's not the case. Sometimes I can get some of the greatest thrills out of maybe doing no more than holding hands. I'm recognizing how to have an emotional interchange with a person.

Men are attracted to the playboy image for a variety of reasons. Many men, as young boys, are sexually titillated by pictures of nude women, which constitute their first sexual experience. They objectify these women and learn to fixate upon parts of the female body – breasts, buttocks, legs – which become associated with pleasure. They masturbate to these images, so that sexual pleasure does not so much come from intimate contact with another human being but with ejaculation at an idealized portrait.

Men are misled by playboy images. They want intimacy but, as a 33-year-old professional man put it, 'I was taught to sexualize my desires for closeness or intimacy.' Playboy behavior grows out of insecurity. Being horny is related to anxiety. Lonely men conquer women sexually (or men if they are gay) because they believe they will fulfill their needs for closeness by fucking another human being. Some men have been deeply wounded by sexual abuse which makes them angry and confused about their own sexual behavior. (Over 60 per cent of male rapists were themselves sexually abused (Petrovich and Templer, 1984).) For many of these victims sex becomes a kind of revenge for previous injustices and not a sacred act. For many men the ability to exercise power through sexual contact becomes more important than satisfying mutual needs.

Conclusion

The above discussion of what men learn about relating to others from male messages presents a picture of emotional tragedy. The stories told in this chapter are not particularly happy. Men value family life as an arena for emotional expression, but even that 'haven in a heartless world' contains great pain. Men traditionally turn to women for nurturing, but the relationships they have with their female partners do not always provide stability. Of the 15 men interviewed for this chapter who had been married, ten had been divorced (three had been divorced twice); one had been married for two years but already admitted he was unhappy with his marriage and was trying to separate from his wife; only four of these men had experienced long term, committed relationships that had been a source of satisfaction in their lives. Even Jim, the pillar of the community who had lived what many people probably would describe a picture perfect marriage, admitted about his married life, 'I have always been alone.'

The alternative to getting married, the life of a bachelor, does not hold much promise. As the stories of three committed bachelors – James, Chuck, and Earl – illustrate, it is a lonely life of shallow relationships. In contrast to the glamorous image of the successful playboy broadcast in television, on movies, and in magazines like *Playboy* and *Hustler*, single men have the highest suicide rate of any group in the United States.

> All the studies I've read on the subject, in fact, suggest that, of the four possible heterosexual categories (married men, single men, married women, single women) single women and married men tend to fare psychologically the best, married women and single men worst. What this might say about who 'needs' whom the most I leave for you, gentle reader, to decide. (Blumenthal, 1987, p. 136)

The good news about men as lovers is that many men care deeply for their children. Fatherhood can be a source of stability, play, joy, and emotional intimacy in a man's life. Unfortunately, here again divorce raises its ugly head. Over half the marriages in the United States end in divorce and statistics show that most children of divorce rarely see their fathers (Furstenberg and Spanier, 1984). Men get custody of children in only ten per cent of divorces.

This chapter that describes men as lovers does not describe male friendships with other men. This is missing because in the seven years that this researcher explored the impact of male messages upon men's lives, the issue of men's friendships with other men did not arise. Only three of the men interviewed for this chapter mentioned that friendships with other men were an important part of their lives. Two of these were leaders in the emerging men's movement, where they had, for years in supportive environments, been taking risks experimenting with more emotional ways to relate to other men. It can be assumed that gay men like Chuck value friendships with males. However, his attempts to grow closer to men have been made difficult because of the emphasis upon anonymous and promiscuous sexuality.

Why do men not have closer relationships with other men? There are at least five possible answers to this troubling aspect of men's lives:

1. Men are so busy doing other things that they do not make male friendship a priority in their lives;
2. tortured relationships with their own fathers do not provide a basis of intimacy with the male species that could motivate them to seek male friendships;
3. men tend to be homophobic, which means they fear sexual contact with other men, do not want to be considered gay, and as a result are terrified about establishing close ties with men;
4. intimacy patterns established in their home when they are young, where their mothers are their primary caretakers, teach adult men to turn to women for emotional support; and
5. men live in a competitive world.

Earl told a devastating story about how competition between men makes it impossible for them to grow close:

> So one of the ways I would relate to men would be through a pure, competitive model. I didn't know how to be vulnerable at that time with men, so I would get pseudo-friends, guys who were willing to go out and party with me, and then what I would do was wait until we were either drunk enough or until he was vulnerable enough, and then I would bring out my whole war chest of stories, all the women I had seduced and just dump it all; and I could never understand why this guy would never party with me any more, so I'd wipe him out in my competitive way. I'd just destroy the sucker. I was so far from being conscious that I didn't recognize how destructive that behavior was.

Lovers

A gay man once explained to this author that his goal in life was to establish caring networks of men upon whom he could call when he needed support. Out of this network he would upon occasion couple intimately with another man. It was his network of friends that provided stability in his life, not his intimate relations with lovers. Men can develop the 'lovers' aspect of their identity through nonsexual relations but have little understanding of how to maintain close friendships.

Earl and Joe have learned through the men's movement just how supportive such networks can be. Earl commented that he had been celibate for six months, because he no longer wanted to give his power to women. He lives alone with his 17-year-old son. To his surprise and joy he has found that he is well-loved, nurtured, and cared for by his male friends. He no longer needs to turn desperately to women to get his nurturing needs met.

Chapter 7

Bosses

I've always wanted to climb to the top. Being second best never has been good enough. When I was young I used to compete in every sport. I still want to win.

43-year-old college professor

Male dominance is embedded in most societies and rewarded through institutionalized relations of gender and power. The social norms promoting patriarchal social arrangements are embedded in the 'Bosses' aspect of masculinity. Modern societies with hierarchical social institutions promote competitive behavior among men. Successful men aspire to be leaders. Not happy when others control them, ambitious males climb to the top of bureaucratic structures, dominate sports teams, head corporations, and direct boards of organizations. This aspect of male behavior, captured by the title 'lord', connotes an exalted position of dominance. Throughout history great lords have become warrior kings. This dominator paradigm in modern times urges men to rule, by heading social institutions and lording over family members.

Men are groomed for power through an elaborate competition that permeates all aspects of a boy's life – from getting good grades to starring on athletic teams. Boy scouts provide a training ground for some young boys to learn leadership skills. Others learn the ropes of competing for status through teenage gangs, where young men struggle to prove their manliness. Men who join the armed services are rigorously inducted into hierarchically structured organizations which train them to conform to the dominator paradigm. Annual sports rituals allow millions of male spectators to relish vicariously the thrill of being number one, heroes in a competitive world, looked up to because they are winners.

In Genesis men are given dominion over all things. An archetype for a male ruler is Zeus, the Olympian God who held an exalted position of power. Heads of most states and religions are males. Historic figures like Moses, Napoleon, George Washington, Winston Churchill, and Ronald Reagan provide models for male leadership. Male supervisors boss their workers, while male chief executive officers (CEOs) make decisions that affect the lives of millions of people. Male generals and heads of state send soldiers to battle. War allows men to demonstrate their manliness while a macho militaristic ideology in modern states promotes a cultural milieu that rewards bosses.

Bosses

Being the boss is crucial to a man's self-esteem. As Marc Feigen Fasteau (1974, p. 98) has pointed out:

> The male stereotype pushes men into seeking their sense of self-esteem almost exclusively in achievement measured by objective, usually competitive, standards.

In a competitive world, men who feel inadequate often resort to violence and distorted images of power in order to express their mastery upon a world that expects them to lord over others, using force and guns to assert themselves. Some men with low self-esteem bully others to express this aspect of masculinity. Such behavior is accepted in a dog-eat-dog masculine world which encourages men to do anything they can to advance their own interests.

The category of 'Bosses' is defined by seven messages – 'control', 'president', 'hurdles', 'adventurer', 'sportsman', 'be like your father', and 'warrior' (29 per cent of those used in this study). Although these messages are not identified by respondents as being the most influential in their lives, 'Bosses' is the largest factor used in this study. The size of this factor indicates the importance of the dominator paradigm to masculinity. The behaviors implied by this factor orient men to go for the gold. Even though not all men can be quarterbacks on a football team, many men desire that position and envy those who have it.

Control

Men are in control of their relationships, emotions, and job.

The 'control' message has dual implications – self-control and control of others. Having been taught to strive for perfection, to work hard, and to succeed in life, men think they can get what they want by controlling others. Men in control have power. This desire to control is so widespread among the male population that only 6 per cent of the respondents at age 18 indicated that the 'control' message had no influence on them. At age 18 this message correlated positively with more other messages than any other male message. Over time this message had a positive correlation with 'be the best you can', 'breadwinner', 'faithful husband', 'good samaritan', 'money', 'hurdles', 'law', 'playboy', 'president', 'self-reliant', 'sportsman', 'stoic', 'tough guy', and 'work ethic'. Seventeen per cent of the respondents at age 18 felt there was a relationship between 'control' and 'breadwinner', while 24 per cent felt a relationship between these two messages over time. Men who provide for their families expect to be obeyed. Over time the 'control' message has a negative correlation with 'nurturer', which suggests that the male desire for power keeps them from achieving intimacy.

Young boys are taught at an early age to control their emotions. Men involved in the competitive struggle to be number one project identities in the public realm with a tough exterior, denying doubts and fears. Men climbing to the top hide behind a wall of inexpressiveness, placing a high value on self-control. Neal felt it was important for men to exhibit self-control. Men who do not have self-control lack discipline, a manly virtue, and are seen to dissipate their energies.

Guy, a 37-year-old business man (Caucasian), described the control message in the following terms:

> The message I received at home from as early on as I can remember is that your life is lived in your head not your heart; that it was very important to project a solid image to your peer group, teachers, and parents; and that the single most important thing to a successful life was self-control.

Guy said that he attended a parochial school that was run like a concentration camp. His masculine ideal was a successful man, good at athletics, in control of his emotions. Leo mentioned that in his home, where both his parents were very controlling (his father overtly and his mother indirectly through manipulation), that the only emotion ever expressed was anger. He did not learn the 'control' message by having his parents directly teach it to him but rather by watching the behavior of two very controlling parents.

Men who value this message lead patterned lives because they cannot stand uncertainty. They gain power by 'cracking the whip' and are extremely clever at manipulating situations so they can be in control. Men who value control do not make themselves vulnerable and have a hard time letting others help them. These types of men try to climb to the top of any hierarchy, not so much for the prestige of being at the top, but because they want to be in control. Men who exhibited these characteristics are looked up to because they have everything in hand and showed no signs of stress – no problems.

Steve, a 41-year-old Baptist minister (African–American) mentioned that from fifth or sixth grade he became very adroit at psyching out people so he could get what he wanted. He would not associate with guys stronger or faster. Steve said he wanted power, so he, himself would not be dominated. All four of the men interviewed for this message said that they became obsessed with it. If they were in a situation they could not control, they would withdraw. They thought it was catastrophic when events did not turn out the way they wanted and would worry all the time about things in their environment. One man stated, 'I unnecessarily worried about things I had little control over.' Another man stated that he looked up to powerful men with big muscles. Being strong in a man's world implies being in control, not letting others push you around.

This message can create emotional chaos for men. A 38-year-old manager (Caucasian), said the following about the 'control' message:

> The strongest message was emotional control with others. This primary message was obtained at the cost of emotional awareness. The internal controls were so strong by adulthood that my own knowledge of emotions consisted of only knowing the fear of being out of control, i.e. showing any emotion at all.

Two of the men said that this message had driven them to the point of emotional breakdown. Guy mentioned that he had paid a huge price for monetary success, a couple of breakdowns in his thirties, serious problems with drugs and alcohol, and had become so stressed trying to control everything in his environment that he became suicidal. When he lost control of the externals, which after many years in therapy he was able to admit he never had control of anyway, he thought his world was collapsing around him.

Bruce, an 18-year-old high school student (Caucasian), was living in a world of emotional chaos completely out of control. Having already spent time in drug and chemical treatment programs, he was trying to gain some stability. The positive side of the 'control' message helped him become a 'self-policeman' so he could manage his affairs in order to survive. Bruce said that he does not like unpredictability and is afraid of change. 'I have all I can do to maintain my autonomy and my own safe place in the world.' He said he was terrified every time he went to school. Bruce did not like to see controlling behavior in other people, because that reminded him of an aspect of his own behavior which he did not particularly like.

Men indicated they did not like being controlled. One man stated 'I don't like to be told what to do and try not to tell others what to do.' Leo said that for a long time he hated his extremely controlling mother and that his ex-wife became mean because of his attempts to control her. One man mentioned that he saw the whole issue of male control as being a facade for impotence:

> The myths of male control: Mom ran the show from a point of weakness and helplessness, but that was never acknowledged; therefore I lived a lie about the myth of male control.

Some men want to feel they are in control, because they feel that it is manly to be in charge, but the truth is you can never control another's behavior.

President

Men pursue power and success. They strive for success.

The 'president' message has a wide variety of meanings for men. Fourteen per cent of the men responding to this questionnaire saw a correlation between the 'president' and the 'money' message at age 18, while 18 per cent saw a correlation over time. The desire to be top dog can be translated into different levels of affluence – owning a house and two cars, sailing your own yacht, having a vacation home, joining a particular club, or no longer worrying about money. The relationship of 'president' to other components of classic masculinity ('be the best you can', 'breadwinner', 'money', 'hurdles', 'law', 'playboy', 'sportsman', 'stoic', and 'tough guy') increases as men grow older. Winners take on the standard attributes of masculinity. The correlation between the 'president' message and the 'playboy' message increases over time, which supports the popular notion of playboy promoted through the media, e.g. successful men seduce women. Men who strive hard to be number one pay the price of being emotionally distant, as emphasized with a negative correlation between the 'president' message and the 'nurturer' message over time.

For some men, like Malcolm, this 'president' message motivated them to be leaders. At age 42, Malcolm (Caucasian) was the president of a steel tubing firm with 40 employees. He recalled that as a young child the 'president' message influenced him strongly. He did not want to follow other boys as a matter of convenience. He got his friends to do what he wanted, as opposed to following. At the top of his pecking order, Malcolm had to be prepared to defend his leadership position. 'When someone else tried to lead the group we hung around with there was always a confrontation.' Malcolm explained that he would fight other boys who challenged his position as top dog. Malcolm likes to feel powerful and wants to be respected. He never wanted to be a follower, dependent on others. At a young age Malcolm decided he did not want to be part of a corporate ladder 'running around like a chicken trying to make other people rich.' When he got out of the Army he bought his first small business, and by taking great risks was able to trade various investments into his current position. Being president of his own company gave him a certain independence which he valued:

> I guess the only way to do this is to be the boss myself and not have to answer to anybody but my customers, or the people I choose to answer to. And if I don't choose to answer to those people I don't have to. I guess not taking shit from anybody. I saw too many people when I was a kid working in jobs they didn't like because they had to keep their jobs.

Malcolm said the 'adventurer' message was also important, but as the leader he gets to cause the adventure as opposed to being in the position of a private ordered into combat.

Malcolm understands that as a leader he is in a precarious position. Many people depend upon Malcolm for their livelihood. If he makes mistakes, they may suffer. He enjoys the intellectual challenges, the satisfaction of having customers depend upon him for a high quality product, the thrill of beating out the competition, the various political games required to build up his business, and the respect he earns from being a leader. Malcolm defines success as having smart men follow his directions, as not feeling intimidated by others, as dealing from a position of strength, and as not being concerned with material things. His main goal is to do right, not to conquer the world.

Dave, on the other hand, had more worldly ambitions. A 45-year-old university professor (Caucasian), Dave had always been an overachiever. He grew up in an affluent suburb of New York surrounded by famous people. Adults in his community, including his parents, expected him to strive for high achievements:

> My father was English, and I'll never forget when I graduated from 8th

grade, my father and some friends sat around talking about whether I would be President of the United States or Prime Minister of England. I thought that was very cute at the time, but in retrospect I'm pretty angry about it. That really lit a fuse under my butt. It was hard for me to be happy with anything I was doing unless I was reaching these lofty goals of success.

Dave described the influence of the 'president' message as a thirst, a craving he could occasionally satisfy but it kept returning, demanding that he achieve more. Dave had a famous uncle who was on the cover of *Life* and *Time*. Because his family expected him to achieve at a similar level, Dave had been involved in politics (student councils in high school and college). He also pursued leadership positions on the sports field like quarterback on the football team, pitcher in baseball, and center half on the college soccer team.

The 'president' message has made it difficult for Dave to deal with failure:

So there has been a sense that when I've made mistakes in life – and we all make mistakes – that this is really disastrous because I'm supposed to be such a successful person, and I've got these failures. For instance, you get a ticket and you have to go see a judge – you say, 'Oh, my God, I've failed! I've let my father down; I'm not this wonderful Golden Boy that he expected me to be.'

He now feels that the recognition that goes along with the fame he has always sought is a bother. He finds he has many responsibilities associated with his position of leadership as the head of an academic department, and his duties make it hard for him to pursue his own scholarly agenda. He also feels lonely. He has earned the respect of many but works so hard that he has few close personal friends.

Harry, a 29-year-old business consultant (Caucasian), felt that the 'president' message was almost instinctual, something which his father and grandfather conveyed to him in an implicit way. Harry's father was so consumed with his career that he could not hold his family together. His mother divorced this hard working breadwinner in order to have a life of her own. At the age of 18, Harry decided he did not want to follow his father's script. Instead of going to the college Dad had picked out for him he joined the Navy. At age 29, Harry still had not completed his college degree and was contemplating leaving his business to become an artist. Feeling the pull of the 'president' message, he wants to be a great artist but not a corporate success which was his father's wish.

If I want to be a good person, I want to be a success as a person. So I think that the presidential message as it applies to success doesn't necessarily apply to a business success; but to me, I would define success in the presidential message as it affects me, as being a success in everything that I do. And I think maybe that's the way I've translated my own father's success.

Harry will not be satisfied 'being on the bottom of the heap'. Harry said that the most important thing in his life was being a good person:

> I want to be great in a number of things. I don't just want to be a success at work. I would rather have a lot of areas of expertise, and just be a good person all the way around. I would define a good person as somebody that has a strong set of values, and isn't selfish; but somebody that is benevolent and wants to do good for the other person. You want to put something back into the world where you live.

In this regard Harry resembles Ben, a 43-year-old massage therapist (Caucasian). Ben felt that the 'president' message was very similar to the 'be the best you can' message, a feeling shared by 11 per cent of the respondents at age 18 and 14 per cent of the respondents over time. He remarked that social pressures drove men to be successful:

> I think that society as a whole, is very success oriented. And success is usually judged or approval is given to people who are financially successful. If you own your own home; if you pay your bills and drive a new car, you are seen as a success.

Ben described his parents as real go-getters. Everything he did had to be perfect. He saw that men who valued this message, like his father, were role models. Fair and honest, they provided for their families, and were responsible citizens who behaved kindly towards others.

The 'president' message had motivated Ben to change his career on numerous occasions. He used to be a teacher, but left that profession because it did not have enough status to satisfy his presidential ambitions:

> Teaching was not something that my father thought was an O.K. profession for a man. His idea – where he came from – was that teachers did not have a very high standing because of not having a lot of financial buying power. And, so for me, teaching was quite a departure. And I don't know that I left teaching because of the money, although that was a factor. Another factor was that there was very little respect for teachers. And what I used to hear a lot was: 'Those who can, do; and those who can't teach.' I wanted to do something that felt like it was more important; although when I think about it, I can't think of anything that's more important.

Other men suggested that the 'president' message contained a similar moral or ethical dimension. Malcolm stated that this message gave him a mission in life, to do right by the people who count on him. He stated that he wanted to be a leader not only for himself but to better humanity. Malcolm said the power of the president is to improve the world, promote harmony, and maintain prosperity. Dave saw that the 'president' message motivated him to work for justice. Men may start out trying to be presidents because they have a selfish desire to dominate, but they soon realize they have to work with others, that they get promoted for supporting the general good of an organization, and taking other people's interests to heart. Men gain trust and admiration by their dedication to the good of the cause. The 'president' message has an egotistic aspect, beating the competition, but also contains an altruistic component, being a good team player.

Hurdles

To be a man is to pass a series of tests. Accomplishment is central to the male style.

For men life has the following hurdles: Young boys have to gain approval from others for having manly characteristics. At first in school they literally have to pass a series of tests, which lead to a big reward, getting into college. If they do not do well in school, they soon learn the value of those hurdles they failed to navigate successfully, because men without high school diplomas have difficulty earning money legitimately. As they grow into maturity, they seek areas where they can distinguish themselves by demonstrating competence. After school the next hurdle is getting a good job. Within that job there are various promotions that mark the watersheds of a man's career. On a personal level men leave home at about age 18 to become self-reliant. This involves making enough money to live without parental support as well as building a nest of supportive relationships with friends, including significant intimate relationships with sexual partners. For some men the financial responsibilities of being a father represent an enormous challenge as indicated by high correlations between 'hurdles' and 'breadwinner'. As men grow older they face the challenge of self acceptance and have to learn how to live within deteriorating bodies. For all men perhaps the most difficult challenge is their last, coming to grips with the grim reaper, death.

Overcoming hurdles implies getting ahead, receiving promotions and being rewarded for accomplishments. Larry, a former high school track hurdler, typified this approach to life:

My vision of life when I was younger was like a sprinter. I saw a never ending line of hoops going on to infinity. Let's say I jump through a hoop and now I see maybe three of four hoops in front of me, all with different things. One might be work-related; one might be relationship-related; one might be play; one might be recreation, whatever.

In terms of how he learned the 'hurdles' message, Larry remembers his father saying, 'Do your best; there'll be all these challenges that you will have to meet, but you will succeed as long as you do your best.'

The list of male messages that correlate with the 'hurdles' message reads like a Dale Carnegie list of behaviors men ought to demonstrate in order to be successful. They should be the best they can; support their families ('breadwin-ner' and 'faithful husband'); be involved in civic affairs ('good samaritan'); work hard and be self-reliant; value money; not show their feelings ('stoic'); strive to get ahead ('president'); present a tough exterior to the world ('tough guy') and conform ('law').

A man who sees life as a series of hurdles tries to be a winner so he will be first at the finish line (become the boss). This aspect of hurdles behavior was highlighted by Larry who feared failure:

> That was a clear message – not rocking the boat. Whatever you do, do things that are fairly safe that you know you can do well in, and just don't risk, because risking may mean that you won't be at the top of the class or you might not get a gold star. You might not make it over the hurdle.

The relationship between 'hurdles' and conformity was further exemplified by the 14 per cent of the male respondents to this survey who sensed a correlation between 'hurdles' and 'law' over time.

Gregg, a 25-year-old assistant manager of a fast food restaurant (Caucasian), learned the 'hurdles' message from his father who rose through the ranks of a fortune 500 corporation. He remembered his family going out to dinner to celebrate his father's promotions. Passing various tests had provided Gregg a sense of responsibility and built his confidence as he improved himself by doing things better. He admired men who climbed the corporate ladder and wanted to be like them.

Jesse, a 57-year-old Baptist minister from the South (African–American), felt that he was born in a caste system which had a whole series of obstacles to conquer because of racism. His father only finished the third grade and overcame illiteracy to become a minister. Even though he was the valedictorian in his high school, Jesse felt that he had to overcome enormous hurdles in order to succeed:

> The hurdle is higher for minorities than for the majority, because the majority have access to better schools. So if a minority gets an opportunity to go to college, he has to overcome the deficiencies based upon the inferior schools he has attended. Many black high schools did not teach physics and chemistry, English literature, and other subjects which whites were taught and were expected of you in college.

Jesse felt that the 'hurdles' message had taught him to demand the respect of others and not to avoid difficult situations.

Jesse stated that the 'hurdles' message had given him a healthy outlook to life's obstacles and taught him not to be bitter or vengeful:

> I don't go around trying to harm people, spending my energy in a negative way, trying to manipulate people. If a person, for whatever reason is against you, fine. You gotta overcome it. So I'm accused of

being astute at going around a problem, finding another way. To me, that's overcoming hurdles.

Jesse stated that it is important to achieve your objectives in life and not dwell on difficulties. He has a faith in himself and a faith in God that hurdles can be overcome.

Geoffrey, a 35-year-old alcohol and drug counselor (Caucasian), said he had learned the 'hurdles' message from his mother, most specifically from his mother's criticisms of him, which he felt he had to overcome in order to feel good about himself. For Geoffrey this message provided a way to view life – every encounter was a hurdle. He was insecure and felt he had to prove himself to gain acceptance:

> Life has been a series of hurdles. Every time I meet another person I feel
> I am going to be put down and that I have to earn that person's respect.
> I was always scared that people would feel poorly about me and had to
> overcome my fear to venture out into the world.

The 'hurdles' message can form an integral part of a male's identity for a man sees himself in terms of his accomplishments. Each achievement represents a challenge which makes life dynamic, but some men get so overwhelmed by achieving these external standards that they ignore their own internal development. They see themselves entirely in terms of how well they finish in a competitive race and not in terms of emotional growth and relationships they have with others. Running over hurdles becomes the exclusive goal of life for many male overachievers.

Adventurer

Men take risks and have adventures. They are brave and courageous.

The 'adventurer' message, by expecting men to be both brave and bold, helps define the behaviors imbedded within the factor 'Bosses'. The 'adventurer' message correlates with six of the seven messages in the category 'Bosses', which indicates that risk taking is an important characteristic for those males who want to get ahead. Masculinity has always been associated with adventure. From the novels of Mark Twain, to westerns, to popular cop shows on contemporary television, men prove their masculinity by being brave, bold, and reckless. Adventurers take risks, seek thrills and search for excitement. Through their ability to master various adventures men prove they are strong, smart, and cunning. Their adventurous spirits are stimulated by brave media star heroes. As men grow older they decrease their risk taking behavior.

Alan, a 19-year-old college student (Caucasian), defined the 'adventurer' message in the following way:

Men are known as having an understanding that they're the ones who should readily risk their lives to help others, and that if the situation should come where you might have to give your life to save some else, it's part of being a guy.

Alan associated the 'adventurer' message with facing death, something men do to test their courage. Adventurers serve in armed forces, die in battle, and risk their lives to rescue others.

For Alan life is full of risks. 'In today's society,' he said, 'breathing the air is taking a risk.' Alan had on three separate occasions almost lost his life: Once when he was climbing a tree, he fell 20 feet onto his head on a metal bar; another time he was hit in the neck by a pellet from a gun shot by a friend; the third was in a bike accident on a road clearly marked 'No bikers allowed'. He tried the hill anyway and wiped out in the last turn, skidding 30 feet on his side and receiving a concussion. Men often take such risks during their adolescent years to prove their manliness.

Real men accept danger and confront trouble. Part of becoming a man requires overcoming fears. An adventurer accepts challenges with a sense of *joie de vivre*, rather than a sense of dread. Alan explained, 'If you're not brave, then what kind of man are you?' The 'adventurer' message implies that men prove their worth by gambling against fate. Jacob, a 33-year-old architect from New Jersey (Caucasian), stated that men take calculated risks:

I think being adventurous gives one the freedom and mobility to try new things. And in this way we enrich our lives by higher exposure, and we can pick and choose different things we've seen in our world travels to adopt and incorporate into our lives.

Jacob had attended the Coast Guard Academy where he experienced many adventures. He felt that the human brain abhors boredom and seeks stimulation. He associated the 'adventurer' message with creativity, an intellectual journey, looking at things in a different way, gaining a new perspective, discovering better ways to do things. This message means accepting a challenge and coping with it as best as possible.

Jacob races competitively with bicycles. He likes the thrill and challenge of pushing his body to its limits. Many men who jog describe breaking through 'the wall', a point of pain at which a body wants to give up. A true adventurer reaches that wall and goes inside to find the reserves to keep on racing, pushing himself to the limits. This same process of discovering new limits applies to intellectual as well as physical pursuits.

Intellectual adventurers, like Ralph, discover new frontiers. Ralph, a 43-year-old visionary thinker from the Washington DC area (Caucasian), said that as a young boy he used to have fantasies about being a hero in battle, rescuing women and being rewarded for his exploits. He learned the 'adventurer' message from pioneer imagery, white male role models who conquered the west. Ralph explained. 'My highest value is to take a path of integrity; to follow the flow of energy.' A *summa cum laude* graduate from Harvard, Ralph has been a nonconformist, pursuing his own vision and not developing a traditional career. Ralph is painfully aware that he has paid a price for his adventurous life style. He does not make much money and has no job security, but still he follows his spirit writing books that point to new ways for human beings to live on this planet.

Ricardo represented a different type of adventurer. His restless life has been a search for adventure. As a young man he joined a street gang, where he distinguished himself by fighting, womanizing, stealing cars, dropping out of high school and signing up for the Marines in Vietnam where he served as a grunt on a mortar team:

> The ammo carriers carried anywhere from 80 to 100 pounds besides their own gear up and down hills in the jungle. I volunteered just to prove I could do it. A lot of guys in the company used to say I was crazy. I used to find the highest part of the area and go there with a white T-shirt in a green jungle. When I think back about it I must have been really crazy to do that.

Having been honorably discharged from the Marines, Ricardo got a job with the Post Office, married and settled down for about 15 months, when American Indians, including some of his friends, seized the town at Wounded Knee at South Dakota. Ricardo left his family and job to participate in that adventure. Upon return he made a living selling drugs and ultimately got caught, spending four years in prison. He became a leader in prison, helping inmates set up self-help groups. He thinks that being an adventurer means earning others' respect. Carrying a gun is an adventure. Ricardo likes the adrenaline rush he gets in risky situations, although at age 31 he understands that there is a down side to the 'adventurer' message:

> Living by the gun, I've had guns put at my head. As I think back about it, I could've been dead already. Ending up in prison was another bad aspect of the 'adventurer' message, and not being able to form a long-lasting relationship with one woman, breaking up a marriage and leaving several kids.

Ricardo felt that society exacts a price for conformity, a lackluster, humdrum existence. Being adventurers, men like Ralph and Ricardo want to live on the cutting edge. They are wary of routine and embrace opportunities to demonstrate their bravery and courage. Why do men climb mountains and take such risks? Ralph implied that men take these risks because they want to prove themselves to their fathers:

> I have a need up to a certain point to appease the Gods; and I think God in this case may be my father more than anybody else. Appeasing him meant to perform up to his standards and to satisfy him that I had passed

his course. And he had very high standards. The course was a rigorous one.

In a corporate world men also take risks in order to get ahead. Those men who are the most adventursome, who take on the most difficult tasks and accomplish them, will get recognized. The 'adventurer' message defines the kind of behaviors men must exhibit if they are to have power. Meek males do not get promoted. Bold boys become bosses.

Sportsman

Men enjoy playing sports, where they learn the thrill of victory and how to compete.

Boys learn through sports to achieve a successful male identity by competing. Organized sports have become a primary masculinity validating experience where men learn that they must constantly prove themselves in order to gain acceptance (Dubbert 1979, p. 164). Through sports men learn the rules of competitive behavior required to be the boss. Becoming an athlete can be a crucial masculinizing experience, engendering self-confidence that generalizes to all aspects of a man's life.

Danny, an 18-year-old high school graduate (Caucasian), described the influence of this message:

> I guess I've always had sports figures I wanted to be. In each sport I have a particular favorite sports person. I don't really remember how I got into playing sports but I realized early on, when I lived on 40th St., there was like 8 to 10 guys and all of us every single day played some kind of sport. When you have that many guys it's fun to do. Everybody considered me the best, and I guess it started like that when I was little. I realized it's fun to compete. I love a challenge. It's cool to have people look up to you and consider you good at something. I guess it's just the thrill of always having the opportunity no matter what happens to have this thing inside of you that says, 'You can at least try it.' So now when something comes along I have this inner force inside of me that says 'go for it' or 'compete' or 'go for victory'.

Because he was a star basketball player in his inner city community, people looked to Danny for leadership. He enjoyed the status he earned through his success on the basketball court.

Through his participation in sports Danny learned how to be a winner, an attitude that he feels has been helpful in many different aspects of his life, including his relationships with women:

> From the sports background I've had, I know I'm going to lose again.

I'm not saying I've been a winner every time, but it helps coming from a competing background to understand that winning as well as losing comes with the competitive turf. Sometimes when I first meet a girl – real quick in my mind I go through 'how should I act?' real quickly as though I was playing a sport, 'How should I do this? How should I do that?' It's just been real helpful and inspirational to my life to know that if I get rebuffed that there will always be other opportunities.

Young men often get rejected playing the dating game which can be psychologically destructive. For Danny, dating was like any other sport – a challenge. You do your best, but if you lose, you wake up the next day, try to improve your performance and go out for another 'touchdown'.

The 'sportsman' message teaches men how to compete so they can become bosses. Danny felt that his love of competition had helped him earn good grades in school. Danny wants to be a lawyer, a career that will draw on the skills he has learned as a sportsman. He approaches life with a certain gusto:

I have this overall look that I'm going to try to get the most out of my life, now that I'm here on the Earth; and I also have this feeling that when you're young and you're energetic and you have the willpower and the energy to do stuff, you should do as much as you can. Often I find sleep stupid; it's such a waste of time. I know it energizes you and you need sleep, but if I had a choice I wouldn't sleep. You're wasting a third of your life. This sportsman attitude, the competing in me, has brought me to realize that I want to try to do different things; and in order to try different things you need time to do it. And it just made me realize that there's not much time in a lifetime to do everything you want, and I'm trying to do as much as I can.

Such an attitude will serve Danny well in the corporate world where he will be an enthusiastic team player, not afraid of taking on challenges.

Ray had a similar attitude about sports. A 34-year-old electrician at a large firm (Caucasian), he had played football, baseball, track, and wrestling in high school. Ray has met his best friends through athletic activities and feels that sports provide men with opportunities to make friends because of the common interests they share. Currently he plays basketball in a recreational league, where he gets to know his fellow workers better through the camaraderie they experience. Such leagues allow adult men to pursue sports interests and to be stars they may not be in dull routine jobs. By bowling 200, hitting a homerun, making a slam dunk, or winning a championship, men in recreational leagues get an opportunity to earn the respect of others.

Ray has learned through sports an attitude that has helped him survive on his job:

If you expect to make a living on a regular basis, you're going to have days where you don't feel very good, and you just don't feel like working, and it's just too bad. Because if you don't go, you don't get paid, and if you don't get paid, you don't eat.

The harder men work, the more they get rewarded. Part of the 'sportsman' message means pushing your body to its limits. Ray has found out at his job that the people who get promoted perform like star athletes:

There's 33 players on a football team, and only 11 are going to play at one time. If you want to be one of the 11, you have to do a little better than the others. The same goes for work.

The 'sportsman' message has helped Ray appreciate the importance of sticking to a task. He said, 'It just made me realize that if there's something to do, you have to do it.'

Sports have enriched Ray's life. The emphasis upon physical fitness has improved his mental attitude. He works out his tensions on the playing field, although if he loses and does not play well, that can add to his frustrations. Ray also feels that this message has taught him not to hold grudges. 'If you get beat', he said, 'give your opponent credit. Learn how to do a little better next time.' Although all sportsmen hate to lose, they can admire a competitor who beats them fair and square.

As he has grown older, Ray has discovered some disadvantages to the 'sportsman' message. Over the years his body has taken a beating. He has broken various bones and has weak ankles. He would love to spend all day in the gym and the evening with his family, but his job does not make that possible. This feeling must be shared by other men, because the influence of this message decreased over time.

Roger sees that the 'sportsman' message inculcates a competitive spirit that influences many aspects of his life. An 18-year-old high school graduate, he defines a sportsman as a talented, well-built, muscular man, popular with his peers. Healthy, with a good physique he always wants to win and competes fiercely to prove he is better than others. Roger has learned that sports promote a tough attitude in men:

In athletics you have to be an extremely competitive guy. A sportsman can make a sport out of anything; because I define sport as competition. So you can turn anything into competition: how fast somebody eats their food. Go to the table and eat my food fast; I'll get a higher grade on this test than you will. A sportsman can find competition in anything.

The 'sportsman' message has both a social component where men compete with others to establish their dominance, and an internal component where men strive to improve themselves. This internal aspect was most important to Pete, an unemployed 34-year-old auto body worker from Iowa (Caucasian) who used to drag race. This message implied doing his best to win at the drag strip as well as other aspects of his life. The 'sportsman' message meant pushing himself to be the best he could. Over time 9 per cent of the participants in this research also saw a correlation between the 'be the best you can' message and 'sportsman'. As did other respondents, Pete felt there was a relationship between 'sportsman' and 'hurdles'. He feels that he enjoys the challenge of pushing himself to new limits. In his current sports, fishing and hunting, he sets standards of achievement – catching a large bass, shooting a 12-point buck – and gets a sense of accomplishment from achieving those standards. Each standard becomes a new hurdle, a challenge to be met and overcome.

Pete felt that being a sportsman meant playing by certain rules of fair play:

> It means giving the other person a fair chance. It doesn't do any good to beat the other person if you beat the gun. In drag racing if you get an unfair jump on the competition a red light goes off and you automatically lose. Sportsmanship is not lying to your competition so you can get an advantage. It's telling the truth and playing a game fairly, so both of you have an even chance to win.

Sports provide an important proving ground where men can earn praise for their prowess. However, not all men enjoy the experiences they have playing sports. In spite of the popularity of sports, this message was ranked 18th out of 24 when men were asked to indicate the most important message in their lives. Ten per cent of this sample indicated that this message had no influence on them at age 18. Competitive sports can be painful for those men who feel inferior because they cannot perform to the standards expected of them (Stein and Hoffman, 1978). The demands to produce at such high levels creates anxiety, as indicated by a 35-year-old salesman (Caucasian) who said, 'I found myself influenced negatively by some of the messages (such as sports, which I detested and made me feel very bad about myself).' Not being chosen for a team or not being one of the dominant male group of sports stars can make men feel bad about their masculinity. Rather than feeling inadequate, many men withdraw from the playing field. The 'sportsman' message may motivate men like Ray, Roger, and Danny who were successful athletes, but for other men who do not succeed, the 'sportsman' message can cause them to doubt their worth as men.

Be Like Your Father

Dad is your role model. Males express feelings in ways similar to their fathers.

Joseph, the father of Jesus, provides a significant metaphor for fathers. Joseph of Nazarath was a carpenter. He provided for nine children. He has been removed from history books and religious texts, so we know almost nothing about him. Jesus' mother, Mary, gets all the credit for raising him. Joseph is not unlike modern fathers who are relegated to a subsidiary, insignificant role in children's lives.

In previous times, fathers were powerful patriarchs who played important breadwinning roles in the family. Father's judgement on moral and social questions made him priest as well as king within his home. As adults appropriately involved in the care of children, fathers in advanced industrial societies are becoming a luxury item, an optional extra that an increasingly small number of privileged children enjoy. Evidence of father absence in this research appeared when 15 per cent of the respondents indicated the 'be like your father' message had no influence in their lives at age 18. Only four other messages had greater scores for no influence.

The traditional family has always been male dominated (Demos, 1982). One hundred years ago men were patriarchs who ruled over the family. Because they provided for family members, fathers were allotted special status and prestige. The placement of the 'be like your father' message within the 'Be the Boss' factor hints at the power of this traditional patriarchal family, where fathers are lords in positions of authority. These fathers are stern disciplinarians. A description of such a traditional father appears in the book, *The Intimate Connection* (Nelson, 1988, p. 120):

> My own childhood came during the Depression years, and like many of my generation I experienced my father as having a mysterious, remote quality. I knew little of his inner life, what he thought and felt as a man. He was a large, strong figure to me, one whom I could neither approach nor avoid. His expectations were high, and he held his sons to them. I felt his pride in my achievements, his judgment on my failures. Like many men, he showed his love more symbolically than through his words: working hard, providing well, being a responsible and respected community leader, occasionally showing a rough tenderness. His love was expressed from a distance. Even then, he could withdraw his love, and when it was withdrawn it sometimes felt as though he might never come back. One part of me wished desperately to be a good son, while another part deeply rebelled.

Fathers were the moral overseers of traditional families, providing ethical teachings and sharing their wordly perspectives with family members (Pleck, 1987), but today children get their information from the media and mistrust their fathers' interpretation of reality.

These traditional views were reflected in this study by comparing fathers' responses to the different male messages to the response of men who were not fathers.

Table 7.1 indicates how modern fathers see their role. They have to work hard to support their families (Breadwinner* and Work Ethic). The higher influence of 'warrior' message implies that fathers are willing to take risks, so that those men at age 18 influenced by this message were more likely actually to become fathers. (Being a father is one of life's great missions!) The decrease in average score for the influence of 'playboy' message indicates that over time fathers are less likely to pursue promiscuous sex.

Table 7.1 *Significant differences between fathers and nonfathers*[1]

	Fathers' average	Nonfathers' average
Number	283	272
Breadwinner*	1.850	1.494
Playboy*	1.326	1.565
Warrior	1.747	1.413
Work Ethic	3.213	2.768

* implies response over time (average age 37). Those messages without * indicate responses at age 18.

The ambiguous feelings that men have about their fathers were reflected in the variance scores for this message. At age 18, the 'be like your father' message was rated seventh highest in variance, while over time it had the third highest variance score, indicating that men have widely diverse feelings about their fathers. Such diversity was reflected in the four men interviewed for this message, two of whom hated their fathers, while two deeply respected their dads.

Keith, a 32-year-old itinerant seaman from Maine (Caucasian), admired his father who was a merchant marine captain. Keith grew up wanting to be just like his father:

> For years I thought I had no hero and then I realized it was someone like my father. All the things I did in my life I did because I thought those were things I thought men should do. They were the same things he did, go to Alaska, ship out to sea. I even wanted to go gold prospecting, which was a dream of my father's.

Keith said there was no pressure to be like his father. Keith worked outdoors with his father and had an unusually secure male identity: 'I never felt any pressure to prove myself even in high school as far as being manly or anything.' He was very close to his father, who had a masculine job as a lumberjack, and assumed the same confidence in his male identity that his father exuded. In his thirties he is starting to develop an identity separate from his father:

> I think it was a good message to have, because I still admire a lot of his qualities and feelings, and morals. So I feel I've done right and wrong. But I think possibly I haven't always done what I wanted to do.

Aaron, a 34-year-old salesman from the Midwest (Caucasian), had a very different relationship with his father. Whereas Keith's father was the patriarch of the family, Aaron described his Dad as a wimp who was pushed around by his mother and did not stand up for himself. Aaron was constantly told by all his relatives that he should be like his father, who was a tremendously crafty handyman:

To be very honest with you, I hate my father. When he died, it didn't bother me one bit. In fact I was waiting for it. I always wanted to do the things he was capable of doing.

Aaron felt he could never live up to his father; therefore the 'be like your father' message was a put-down. He has rebelled against this message: 'I wanted to get away from my father, let people know I am not my father. I am someone different and I have a life of my own.' Aaron who was very distant from his father, had been shipped out to foster homes because of violent struggles within his family. He does not want to repeat the same mistakes his father made. Aaron has become divorced from the mother of his children and is fighting hard through a father's rights organization to gain custody of his children. He wants to raise his kids 'in a good old fashioned home environment with a lots of love and attention'.

Rusty also hated his father. Like Keith, he learned the 'be like your father' message passively by living around his father. Rusty was a 47-year-old salesman who had completed 20 years in the Air Force and taken an early retirement (Caucasian). Unlike Aaron's father, who was passive, Rusty's father was a domineering patriarch. Rusty's father, who comes from a blue collar background, still will not let his wife drive a car and controls all of the money. Rusty described his father's life in the following way:

> ... working in a factory 40, 50, 60 hours a week, same routine day after day, driving to work on the same streets every day and coming home on Friday, stop at the corner bar with his pal, Eddy, have a beer, cash his check and come home. I didn't want to do that. I wanted variety in my life.

As soon as Rusty graduated from high school he joined the Air Force and travelled around the world. Rusty has made a conscious effort to not be like father. Both he and Aaron have counterdependent relationships to the 'be like your father' messages.

Scott, a 29-year-old manager of a rock and roll band (Caucasian), has an entirely different view of his father. Scott said he felt no pressure to be like his father and did not start to appreciate him until he was 22 and went backpacking with his dad in the Rockies. Up to that point Scott said:

> I guess like every other 16-year-old I didn't like my parents. You think they are the greatest people in the world, and you're supposed to like them but you don't. When I was younger in grade school and high school I didn't want to be like him. I knew everything. My parents knew nothing; they were old and out of it. They didn't know what was going on. Then in my late teens I started to feel they are OK, and in my present life I feel they are real special people.

Scott's father was not an overbearing influence upon him, like Keith's father.

The influence of the 'be like your father' message was very subtle. According to Scott, his father had the attitude, 'You gotta learn on your own. I'm not going to tell you what to do.'

Scott said that this message makes him want to be a better person. His father was a good samaritan who believed in 'leaving the world a better place than you found it'. Scott feels that his father never really thought making money was extremely important and consequently he has never felt a great deal of pressure to make money:

> He often stated that his main goal in life was to get to heaven. This message has become more important to me as I grow older. I used to think of my dad as some kind of weirdo, but now I respect his values, his love of nature and his spiritual sense; not being focused on money.

Scott said he has learned how to be a sensitive man from his father's example.

In the modern industrial world the family is no longer a stable institution, and father may no longer be boss. Fathers need to find out how to contribute as equal partners in modern family arrangements or lose their influence altogether. If fathers do not figure out appropriate ways to get involved, the future is weak both for the family and for them. Children will learn there is something untrustworthy about dads, and consequently men, because their fathers are not there for them. Fathers will lose out on developing their capacities to love. Fathers who do choose to nurture their children can experience tender aspects of their own beings. Life will be more satisfying for both fathers and children, partly because the social order will be less full of the severe pathologies created by father deprivation.[2]

The goal of modern parenting is to create a flexible, tolerant, and democratic family where everybody's views are listened to and respected. A good father is alert, aware, responsive, giving, and patient. Rather than being a domineering boss, he is a good listener. In the Old Testament God, the Father, was punishing, vengeful, and demanding. The old stereotype of father as a terrible father figure, like the Divine Right of Kings, is fading away, or, as in Rusty's case, points to ineffectual fathering that creates animosity rather than strong bonds of love. A modern father serves members of his family. He realizes that children have minds of their own. A good father is a blessing. An inadequate father may be worse than no father at all.

Warrior

Men take death defying risks to prove themselves and identify with war heroes.

The final message in this section, 'warrior', implies that men fight. Young boys learn about warriorhood from action oriented figures like GI Joe and other war heroes in the popular media. The 'warrior' message ranked the lowest of all the

24 male messages at age 18. Twenty-six per cent of the respondents said it had no influence upon them at that age. Even though popular culture glorifies the role of warrior, men do not seem to be as influenced by this message as they are by other gender role expectations. Some men do commit acts of violence, acting like warriors in civilian society, but the low influence of this message suggests that the reasons why men are so violent and warlike may not be because of their social conditioning but rather because of other factors such as the way they are taught to express their anger and the amount of rage they have inside them.[3]

The 'warrior' message represents the violent side of men, where males use force to impose their wills upon the world. Brave, strong, and well-coordinated, warriors who know how to fight take on heroic adventures. They force to get their way and push themselves to their limits to pursue their mission. War heroes are looked up to because of their courage in battle and serve as role models for other men.

Military traditions play a powerful role in modern concepts of masculinity. Boys first learn these traditions playing with toy soldiers. One out of every five adult men in the United States has served in the armed forces (Arkin and Debrofsky, 1978). Boys, lured into the military with the promise of becoming men, go through a rite of passage during basic training. Being in the military allows young men to achieve status. Young men join the armed services because they feel patriotic, want to contribute to their country, and seek adventure. In the armed forces they are taught to obey. Military discipline, shaving of heads, and following orders gets young recruits all moving in the same direction at the same time so that the system works smoothly. Men trained to do their duty are discouraged from thinking about whether it is right or wrong. Being in the military has a profound effect upon the construction of a male gender identity as indicated by Table 7.2.

Table 7.2 indicates that those young men who join the military are more influenced by classical male messages. At age 18 they are more likely to be adventurous, stoical, tough, and aggressive. Like Dick, the retired Navy

Table 7.2   *Significant differences between veterans and nonveterans*

	Veterans	Nonveterans
Number	166	363
Adventurer	2.518	2.325
Breadwinner	2.613	2.321
Control	2.599	2.383
Law	2.371	2.075
Nurturer	1.744	2.047
Playboy	2.398	2.182
Scholar	2.400	2.801
Stoic	2.464	2.209
Technician	2.544	2.069
Tough Guy	2.403	1.989
Warrior	1.964	1.413
Work Ethic	3.229	2.876

Commander, men in the military obey the law. Young men who do not join the military do better in school as evidenced by the higher score for the 'scholar' message.

Jeff, a 41-year-old director of a men's center (Caucasian), had been inundated by the warrior culture as a young man growing up in Northern Minnesota. His father, a veteran of World War II, told him war stories about combat. Jeff used to watch war movies on television and identified with war heroes. He defined warrior as 'somebody who has devoted his life to military service, and someone who is very courageous and very stoic.' Jeff remembers as a young man playing with his friends daredevil games that were very dangerous, where some boys got badly hurt. Young men were expected to take risks to prove they were warriors.

Other men agreed with Jeff about the 'warrior' message being like the 'stoic' message. At age 18, the 'warrior' message correlated with 'breadwinner', 'president', 'sportsman', and 'technician'. As men gew older they felt less correlations with the warrior message. 'Adventurer', 'playboy', 'stoic', and 'tough guy' had significant correlations with the 'warrior' message both at age 18 and over time, although every one of these correlations declined over time, except the correlation with 'stoic', which remained the same. Over time men felt a negative relationship between the 'warrior' and the 'nurturer' message. Jeff also felt there was a strong correlation between 'warrior' and 'tough guy' (at age 18, 23 per cent of the men felt a relationship between these two messages). Jeff expressed it this way:

> You stand up for yourself; you don't let anybody walk on you. And if you have to beat somebody up or fight to do that, then that's something that you should do.

Phillippo used to watch war movies as a young boy and was raised in a culture that worshipped warriors. A 60-year-old professor (Hispanic), Phillippo grew up in Kansas, the son of refugees who had fled from the Mexican revolution:

> Both of my parents were caught up in the struggle of the Revolution of 1910 as young adults and they would always be talking about their personal experiences. They talked about these revolutionary heroes as real live people and there was a certain amount of admiration, so I grew up admiring soldiers and soldiering, thinking it was an honorable profession, and looking forward to the day when I could be a soldier myself. These soldiers fought for social justice. They were the protectors of the people.

Phillippo was drafted during the Korean war and was glad to serve his country:

> I feel very strong about supporting this country, right or wrong; those two years I gave impressed me for the rest of my life. It convinced me

that military might is a necessary deterrent to aggressors who want to destroy your way of life. Thank God we have people like that, you know; while we're back here enjoying a nice quiet discussion here without threat of somebody coming in and saying 'You can't do this because it's against the police state' or whatever.

Phillippo feels that human beings will always need warriors to protect against the evil that exists in human communities. He wants to reserve for himself the right to defend himself and his family should they be attacked. He also feels that as a minority that he has to be prepared to use force to get ahead in this violent world:

When you're a minority you're always a warrior of some type because you can never forget that the dominant culture is out there and that it doesn't necessarily have the welcome mat for you and, therefore, you go out there every day looking over your shoulder just a little bit, and being on guard and watching what you do. And yet hoping for the best.

Phillippo feels that violence is a necessary deterrent, the last resort used to settle disagreements when everything else fails. He believes in peace through strength.

Dennis (Caucasian) at age 46 declares himself a new age warrior. The head of a foundation trying to improve relationships between the United States and the Soviet Union, Dennis thinks that a warrior has a mission to improve the world. As a young man he used to have the following fantasy:

I'm standing on a cliff and I'm looking down at the tribe in the valley below. It's my tribe but I'm the guardian of that tribe, one of the sentries. I've got a spear and a robe wrapped around me, and I'm watching them and watching the campfire. There is this dual feeling of loneliness, of wanting to be part of that circle of people, to be warm by the fire, and at the same time acknowledging a bittersweet feeling of rightness that this is my place.

For Dennis warriors have sacred duties. They are the guardians who both protect the weak and lead them to a more hallowed ground.

Dennis stated that the word 'warrior' is older than the word 'war'. He is critical of the notion of a warrior as a violent man who kills others:

My feeling is that the whole idea of warrior has gotten blasphemed, turned around so it's negative – hacking, slashing, burning, raping, and pillaging. We have to transform it back to its original definition, which I feel is the primal nature of being male, using your sword not as an implement of destruction, but as an implement of creativity – sweeping away the crowds, cutting through the jungle to see what's on the other side – a kind of magical connotation of what warriors are all about.

Warriors are willing to take chances.

Dennis quit school and joined the Coast Guard where he enjoyed the companionship of other men:

> The most enjoyable memories I have are of being captain of a crash boat in New York harbor, which required us to take risks every day – life and death risks, dragging people out of burning airplanes and things like that, loving not only the adventure of it but also the camaraderie that it creates among men. We were a team of men working together very beautifully. I long for those kind of connections again. They're not easy to get in life.

Many veterans talk in similar terms about their experiences in combat (Broyles, 1986). They may have been terrified by war but they loved the experience of warriorship with other men.

Harvey became a traditional American Indian warrior, someone who might accurately be called a 'brave'. He was a leader of the American Indian Movement (AIM), Harvey, a 40-year-old unemployed American Indian, hardly knew his alcoholic father. As a result, Harvey hung out on the streets with gang members who provided a sort of family for him. He was a leader of his gang and had been in lots of fights. Harvey said he would not start fights but he had no choice. Other kids were challenging him and he had to stand up to them. In his early years on the streets and in the prison, the 'warrior' message meant that he had to stand up for himself to prove he was a man.

After his first six-year stint in prison (Harvey has spent one quarter of his life behind bars), he went to Wounded Knee where he was involved in the occupation and discovered through many dramatic events what kind of warrior he was. American Indians think that power comes from being in touch with the spirits and praying. Harvey learned about this spiritual warriorship on numerous occasions at Wounded Knee where he was miraculously saved from situations which he considered hopeless:

> I never think I can do something without praying to the Spirit, the Great Spirit. I never did anything heroic alone; or I did that myself with my brain power. I never think like that; I do it with the Spirit's help and with the pipe that was given to me. All power was shown to me.

Harvey discovered in battle that men bluff at being warriors. He saw men he respected shirk dangerous missions and told the following story about a man whose life he saved:

> It's hard to trust many people, even if they seem nice. Can I trust this guy if they start shooting at us and all that? You know, is he gonna be scared or cowardly or what? In fact, I got caught right out in the open, like here's the Wounded Knee town, and here's this stretch of open land with a few hills, and then our bunker. They opened fire on our bunker

while we were eating over in Wounded Knee. So me and this guy started running to help them guys; and they're in the open with machine guns on 'em. So there we're running out there; all of a sudden we start to get pinned down by a sniper. I didn't know where in the hell this guy was, but he was – I was on a side of a ditch, on a hill partly, and I had a rifle; and every time I'd point that rifle up to try to get to shoot, he'd shoot, and I said, Damn, this guy must have a scope on his rifle. And I'd move my other arm; and he'd (score) a hit you know, and he (chased) me. Damn. And then a bullet would come right by my head. I'm getting shot at, and the guy I'm with jumps up to surrender. And he starts saying, 'I quit, I quit.' Whoever was shooting at me, shot him four times, and when they shot at him I got down in the hole more. He fell down. He was shot three times in the arm, and as he was going down they shot him through the foot. No major hits, but he was bleeding. He started to go into shock, started screaming and all that, so I had to – I seen it in a movie – I slapped him up. I told him to shut up, and while I was over there shutting him up, they shot me. And the bullet went right through my foot, right through the heel of my boot, and entered the ground. So here, I had to get him back, all the way back to Wounded Knee, and he was a big, fat guy. He was hard to drag I'll tell you. But when we got back there, the newspaper started interviewing him 'cause he was wounded and stuff. And I was in the bed across. I hear him saying how he was running and the bullets were whizzing past his head. It didn't scare him but he was still going to save his brother, and I thought, 'Shit, he was surrendering.' So that taught me another lesson.

Harvey received a sense of belonging from being a warrior. People treated him and other Indian warriors in the struggle for Indian rights with a great deal of respect as they travelled around the country, even providing them with women, which is perhaps a warrior's ultimate reward. Harvey is very respectful of women and hates to see a man acting tough on women. 'He's a mouse,' he said. 'I'd like to see him try that with a man!'

Harvey does not feel that all people in the United States have free speech. He has spent most of his life being hounded by authorities because of his advocacy for American Indian causes. Being a warrior is both hazardous and full of adventure.

Harvey described one time when he and other warriors felt they had to take the law into their own hands:

The authorities never respect our rights or give us justice. Just let me tell you one story: we were called to South Dakota by this Indian woman; she was in the hospital. She and her 7-year-old boy were walking past a red neck cowboy bar. Here the door was open 'cause it was summer, and they were all drunk in there; and they seen her walk by. They went out there and they beat the woman unconscious, and she come to. Her son was in there – they castrated him 'cause they said they didn't want him to make any Indian kids. Seven years old. So we got some Indian lawyers and we took the bartender to court. Here he'd bring those guys into court, and here they come walking in laughing and everything. The judge comes in. He starts yelling to these cowboy guys, 'Hey guys; do you want to go coon hunting this weekend?' I said, 'Man, that judge is racist.' First the lawyer got up, and the judge said, 'Are you from this state?' He said, 'No, I'm from California.' He said, 'I'm an attorney.' The judge said, 'You're not a member of this bar; sit down and shut up.' He asked that lady, 'Which one of these guys castrated your boy?' And she said, 'Well, I don't know 'cause they beat me unconscious – I woke up in a hospital – and when I woke up they, my boy was in there, and he was castrated.' And then he said, 'Well, then you don't know which one of these guys did it, do you?' She said, 'Well, no; but they did it. My boy can't have sex or anything, ever again. They ruined his life.' He said, 'I can't be sending those seven guys 'cause you don't know which one did it. Case dismissed. You guys go home.' So they started laughing right in the damn courtroom. Our lawyer jumped up and said, 'This is an outrageous monkey trial!' And the judge said, 'You're out of line. Do you want to see how our jails are here?' So we all left. The mother was crying; we were pissed off. So we went to that bar where them guys went to celebrate. We had a lot of veterans with us who knew about explosives. They fixed one up with a short fuse, and we went and threw it in that damn bar. That place blew, and we didn't stick around to see who in the Hell got hurt. We all split to a different state.

Harvey has recently had experiences with nonviolence on boat landings in northern Wisconsin where Indians have been exercising their treaty rights. He feels that nonviolence takes special bravery because he did not have weapons to protect himself. Harvey often feels called to get involved with certain causes. In his neighborhood he is captain of an anti-crime block club.

From his experiences Harvey has developed a code of warriorship that involves the following principles: A warrior is selfless and puts himself in service to others. A warrior takes responsibility and the role of boss if necessary. A warrior has a sense of right and is called to make that right come into being. A warrior sticks to his commitments. He is loyal. His word is important. A warrior respects his elders and is involved in spirituality. A warrior has to be on guard, because trust is a big issue, who is on his side and who can be trusted to carry out a mission. A warrior fights for justice, respects women, and is trustworthy.

Conclusion

Men need to feel important. Many males do not achieve a sense of belonging from their families because they are so distant from them, striving to 'Bosses', and gaining recogniton in the real world outside the family. Women have an all important task upon which the very survival of the human species depends. They reproduce the human race both by giving birth to the next generation and by raising children. Men compensate for this lack of a meaningful role in the family by becoming important in the world outside the family (Brenton, 1966). Men construct patriarchal realms of significance – businesses, volunteer groups, unions, athletic teams, clubs, and military organizations – where they can be somebody by achieving power to make decisions that affect other people's lives. Bosses have prestige. Popular men's magazines reinforce this aspect of masculinity by providing cultural models for how men should look and behave in order to become bosses.

Men feel important when they are in positions of power. This chapter indicates the kinds of things men do to be bosses. They attempt to control the behavior of others as well as discipline themselves. They jump over hurdles. They compete. They take risks. They spend hours at athletic events honing their skills. And they assume positions of leadership. Men achieve their identities in the world outside the home and are judged by their performance in this 'real' world. The more power they have, the more they are thought to be 'real men', so that being the boss enables men to feel good about their masculine identities.

As Perry Garfinkle (1985) has pointed out, a man's world is an unending series of competitions to prove his worth. In this competitive world there is little trust, because the fellow next to you might get the promotion you want so much, or you may have to fire him, if you get that promotion. In a zero sum world one man's success comes from the failure of others. In order to be a boss men learn from early childhood to succeed at others' expense. The pressure to a boss alienates men from each other (Tennis, 1985, p. 15):

> Traditional male behavior is solitary – solitary research, solitary speaking, solitary writing. All that solitariness has little to do with the virtues of solitude: It is just aloneness, because solitary behavior is often the consequence of competition between individuals for the best grade, job, or salary.

Competition for power permeates all aspects of men's lives. Businesses, which in most cases are owned and controlled by men, have a pecking order of importance. The worlds that men inhabit and construct reflect their deep desires for status.

The influence of none of the seven messages included in 'Be the Boss' increases over time. When men are young it seems they are eager to prove themselves by becoming bosses. But older men, who have been involved in the rat race, seem to devalue the strains involved in becoming a boss. They understand how hollow are the rewards of status when not accompanied by love. Love is an act of will. Generals cannot command their soldiers to love them, nor can distant fathers order their children's love. Love is something that is gained by trust, understanding, and spending time with people listening to their concerns. A busy boss who has little time for such frivolous pursuits can be a lonely man.

Notes

1 A conventional level of 0.05 is used for determining significance, though tests of significance are not entirely appropriate for this study, since the sample is not random. They still serve as a technique for eliminating arbitrariness in the process of deciding which findings are noteworthy and which are not.

2 Children without fathers turn up more often in juvenile courts and other public institutions. If fathers leave before a son is six years old, his sons will be more dependent upon peers and less assertive. Research studies indicate that a fatherless child has less self-esteem and is treated as less likable by his peers. Children with absent fathers also experience a host of gender role and social adjustment problems in adolescence (Parke, 1981).

3 For a discussion of the various factors that promote male violence see: Ian M. Harris (1991), *The Role of Social Conditioning in Male Violence.*

Chapter 8

Rugged Individuals

I was taught to stand on my own two feet and not trust anybody. Depending upon others is a sign of weakness.

31-year-old laborer (African–American)

Men learn to look out for themselves, relying on their own wits and brawn. They do not want to answer to any boss. Rugged individualistic males aggressively defend their own turf. Hiding their emotions, they ride tall in the saddle. This pioneering aspect of masculinity, which Marc Gerzon labelled 'frontiersman' (1982), is deeply embedded in cultural norms in the United States, a country developed by European immigrants who carved their homes out of the wilderness. Early settlers in this country foraged for themselves in the rich natural environments of this continent. Male farmers, craftsmen and hunters relied on their own brute strength and ingenuity to make a living. This aspect of the male psyche emulates fictional heroes who bear pain through battles and do not complain about wounds. Rugged individuals, like Hercules, they accomplish enormous tasks with ease. Film stars like John Wayne, Charles Bronson, and Clint Eastwood portray this aspect of masculinity and like the fictional character, Shane, ride off into the horizon after they have accomplished their missions.

David and Brannon (1976, p. 12), in a classical article on male gender roles, identified four different themes for masculinity in the United States:

1. *No Sissy Stuff:* The stigma of all stereotyped feminine characteristics and qualities, including openness and vulnerability.

2. *The Big Wheel:* Success, status, and the need to be looked up to.

3. *The Sturdy Oak:* A manly air of toughness, confidence, and self-reliance.

4. *Give 'Em Hell:* The aura of aggression, violence, and daring.

Three of these four themes – no sissy stuff, the sturdy oak, and give 'em hell – belong to this factor, 'Rugged Individuals'. The other theme, the big wheel, more properly belongs within the previous chapter, 'Bosses'.

'No Sissy Stuff' states that men ought not to display emotions like women, who are often portrayed as valuing relationships with others (Baker, 1966). This factor, 'Rugged Individuals', contains gender-role norms that urge men not to be like women. G. Gordon Liddy, one of the convicted Watergate conspirators, encourages men to preserve their autonomy from the 'female' world of feeling by stating that any emotion whatsoever that competes with reason is troublesome (1980). Many men feel that they should be cold, calculating, unemotional, inscrutable, and in control of all their faculties. A man who shows his feelings of vulnerability is seen as a sissy in a male world, not worthy of being called a man.

'The Sturdy Oak' encourages young boys to be self-reliant and tough. Impressionable boys learn this role by watching male heroes on television and in the movies – the stars who show a quiet strength, independence, and a cool confidence – righting wrongs in the world, while not admitting any weaknesses. Men who emulate this bravado promote their own unique style of masculinity – cowboy boots, blue jeans, leather jackets, tattoos, or pickup trucks. A sturdy oak is a courageous man who endures. A survivor, his roots go deep into the subconscious minds of men.

'Give 'Em Hell' encourages men to fight. Real men have clenched fists and flexed biceps. A man who avoids a fight is cowardly. Male aggression is still strongly rewarded (Doyle, 1983, p. 181):

> Many young American boys are actively encouraged to go out there and aggressively show 'what they're made of' against other boys. Consequently, in some groups, an aggressive boy is thought of as more masculine than one who shuns aggressive behaviors. Second, most people think males rather than females are prone toward aggressive and even violent behaviors. Physical aggression is one of the few social behaviors in which scientists see a distinct sex difference.

'Give 'Em Hell' contributes greatly to misery in the United States where a human being is assaulted, raped, robbed, or murdered every thirty-one seconds, mostly by men (FBI, 1978). The United States, run by a bunch of rugged individuals, is one of the most violent countries in the world. The country that first developed and then used nuclear weapons is willing to destroy the world in order to demonstrate its masculinity.

The factor, 'Rugged Individuals', contains five different male messages – 'self-reliant', 'stoic', 'rebel', 'tough guy' and 'superman'. These crude male features are often cited when men are stereotyped as brutes.

Self-Reliant

Asking for help is a sign of weakness. Go it alone. Be self-sufficient and don't depend on others.

A comic strip character, the Lone Ranger, provides an excellent metaphor for a self-reliant man in the US culture. A stranger who literally hides his emotions behind a mask charges onto the scene, handles difficult situations well, and then leaves before anybody can get to know him. He is strong, competent, bold, and inscrutable. A self-reliant man is hard working, does not take charity, supports himself, takes pride in his accomplishments, does not need advice, and does not let others tell him what to do. An independent survivor, he does not trust others.

Curtis, a 36-year-old bartender (African–American), was such a man who had learned this message:

> I guess I got it from my parents as I was growing up. To be able to take care of yourself was very important because in this cold world nobody really cares about you outside of the family. When it comes down to the nitty gritty you only really have yourself to depend on. I live in a city that gets like a jungle. Either you take care of yourself or you get spit up and chewed up. It's a survival mechanism.

Curtis' life quest has been to make it on his own. 'I don't want to ask anybody for anything and don't want anybody to think I need him.' He wants to enjoy other people but not depend upon them.

Curtis sees some drawbacks to the 'self-reliant' message:

> I don't see that it's all positive because you have to live in the world with other people. Maybe it's made me kind of bullheaded at times. I'm not quite sensitive to other people as I should have been, but I'm trying to work on that.

Curtis said he had many positive role models in his life, adults who encouraged him to take school seriously. As a young man learning the skills of self-reliance, he had no patience for adults who tried to set him straight. An athlete who earned letters in three varsity sports, Curtis attended school just enough to keep his eligibility. He was not interested in academics. There were much more challenging things to be accomplished on the streets outside school. As a self-reliant adult, he knew what was right and was not going to listen to any adult.

Curtis learned in the tough inner city environment where he was raised that a man was supposed to be a warrior and dropped out of school at age 17 to join the Marines. One of his role models was Audie Murphy, the most decorated soldier in World War II. Curtis said, 'I must have seen "To Hell and Back" ten times. I liked his demeanor and looks.' Curtis learned in Vietnam that when things got rough he had to rely on his own inner strength. He was proud of having survived combat although he did have a stress disorder. He is now critical of the kind of peer pressure he felt as a younger man to hang out with his buddies on the street and get high:

> I try to make a decent living and try to help our kids because they are so misdirected. So I guess I would tell them it's all right to be self-reliant cause nobody else is going to look out for you. That's the way it is. People don't care about each other too much any more.

David, a 30-year-old motel maintenance man in Florida (Caucasian), was another veteran who had learned the 'self-reliant' message from males in his family. For him this message meant working hard to achieve economic self-reliance. All his male relatives worked two jobs. He described his father as a workaholic who was never home but was 'out there', bringing home the bacon. David saw that he had an obligation to keep a roof over his head and to keep 'above water, not to drown'. David felt that the world was a dangerous place:

> You have to be careful in this day and age; you can't just go out and trust anybody. It would be nice if you could but it's just not like you can do that. You have to watch out who you get involved with. I'd like to be able to open up to people more but you can't because there are too many creeps out there; you've got to watch yourself; you got to be careful.

David felt that the 'self-reliant' message had a protective element, where he had to be on his guard to keep from getting hurt and to stay out of trouble. Both David and Curtis had gotten into fights when they were younger. David had learned how to defend himself from his father:

> I wasn't taught to come up swinging but when I'm pushed to my breaking point, then I go off. My Dad never taught me to go around smacking people. He taught me how to fight, to make damn sure I could protect myself if I would have to fight. He taught me how to box. He set up a ring in the basement and all the kids in the neighborhood used to come over to my basement to prove themselves.

The 'self-reliant' message has a fairly high correlation with the 'tough guy' message. Men who are self-reliant do not let others push them around.

David ran away from home when he was 18. Like many other men who want to strike out on their own at that age, he joined the Army, where he learned to stand up for himself. In those days David took crazy risks. He fought and drank a lot. 'At age twenty-one I was god damn mean. You couldn't tell me a god damn thing!' he said. David admitted that he had learned right from wrong by making mistakes, like the time he was arrested for stealing televisions and had to spend three weeks in jail.

David had recently gotten married. His wife was pregnant. Although he admits to feeling more responsible both for himself and for his family, he now feels strapped down because he has to take care of his wife and children. Judging from correlations with the 'self-reliant' message, other men felt this pressure to be breadwinners as they grow older. Neither 'breadwinner' nor 'faithful husband' has a significant correlation with the 'self-reliant' message at age 18 but older men demonstrated a correlation between these messages. On the family front, 'self-reliant' has a negative correlation with the 'nurturer' message at age 18 and with older men. Men who are self-reliant do not want to be tied down, and see sex as an adventure, as evidenced by strong correlations with the 'adventurer' and 'playboy' messages. They value the work ethic and jump over hurdles to achieve their goals, striving to be perfect and accomplishing much ('superman'). The 'self-reliant' message had a strong correlation with 'sportsman' at age 18 and was rated by respondents as being the third most important message.

Being self-reliant means trusting your own instincts and having the self-esteem to act upon those instincts. Simon, a 54-year-old self-employed therapist from Massachusetts (Caucasian), gets a sense of accomplishment from doing things on his own. He is a rebel, not in the sense of breaking laws, but rather in the sense of a unique individual who does not conform to social conventions. Simon said that being self-reliant was fun because there were always challenges to be overcome. He does many things by himself and does not easily ask for assistance. Simon felt that being self-reliant implied passing a test, where a man has to stand on his own two feet. As he grew older he felt himself reacting more meaningfully to others, and the 'self-reliant' message grew less important.

Simon learned the 'self-reliant' message at home where his parents told him, 'When you have something to do, you do it by yourself.' True to their teachings, he defied his parents and learned to do many things on his own. Simon, like Curtis and David, ran away from home. Because his hero was Jesus Christ, he joined a seminary at age 17. Jesus had a strong belief system that guided Simon's behavior. Simon stated that an important part of being self-reliant was developing a set of values and holding to those values. His own principles were so strong that he left the church. Simon was not a company man:

> I didn't like hypocrisy or sham. I had my own principles I wanted to adhere to and try to live a life consistent with those principles. If this is how you think, then this is how you act. There was just too much of that craziness around. I never wanted to join it.

As Simon matured, he gained competence, which he said was a part of the 'self-reliant' message:

> If it's not correct now, I want to fix it. It's not as critical to be that competent all the time doing things on my own. I don't worry about being competent anymore because I know I am and do things well. I am willing to ask other people for ideas and advice, which I would have never done before. It all started when I began to feel comfortable with who I was; then I could make myself open and vulnerable to others.

John, who also came from New England, had a similar approach to the 'self-reliant' message. At age 26, he was a cook (Caucasian) in a restaurant in Vermont. As the oldest of four children, John had to take care of himself. He saved to buy his own things and did not ask his parents for money. He did not want to be a burden:

> I would rather do it on my own and not ask anyone's help. So I was not feeling guilty, that I was robbing somebody of something else. I also got

satisfaction that I did everything myself without help. But it was mostly that I wasn't taking away from others.

John felt that asking for help was unmanly. He said, 'You don't want to be weak. You want to be strong and be able to handle everything.' John admitted that he has troubles living up to the demands of the 'self-reliant' message. He said that it would have been much easier to cop out. When he was a teenager he even contemplated suicide because he had so many things he felt he had to accomplish. He used the expression, 'I had to handle everything', implying that he had to be a superman and could admit neither his fallibility nor his vulnerability. John felt that when he was having trouble, he did not have to share his difficulties because he had the inner strength to handle situations himself.

John has tried to avoid becoming dependent upon people, which has had a negative effect upon his personal life:

I'm not real strong in stating my own needs. I'll just sort of say, 'Well that's OK, I'll take care of it myself.' Maybe in the back of my mind I hope others will realize I need them without me saying it. I know that there are ways in which I try to be self-reliant which aren't beneficial to me. I shouldn't be as tough, but I don't always do it.

John wants to be stable financially before he gets married and starts a family. He fears he will not be worthy of love if he is not self-reliant, 'I have this fear that if I met someone who was good enough, someone that I wanted to marry that she wouldn't think enough of me because I'm not self-reliant and taking care of everything.'

One of John's childhood heroes was Clint Eastwood. He liked that 'stoic, unemotional righteousness'. John said that as a little kid he thought it would be real neat to be like that but he also realized that such portrayals of supermen were a little comical because it was impossible to be as self-reliant as the characters Clint Eastwood portrayed in his movies:

What I liked about this image was that stars like Clint Eastwood did it easily. It wasn't hard for them to be self-reliant. They did it without feeling the pressure and worry, the anxiety that they might not be able to do it all.

These comments suggest that the 'self-reliant' message carries a certain style, where men walk through life handling difficult situations without showing their fears and doubts. In order to be self-reliant, men learn to maintain a stiff upper lip: to exhibit feelings is unmanly.

Stoic

Ignore pain in your body. Achieve even though it hurts. Don't admit weakness.

'Stoic' comes from Greek and refers to a specific philosophy of existence that states that a man's duty is to accept cheerfully whatever happens – poverty, disease, persecution, slavery, or even death – secure in the knowledge that all is for the best. It is a manly virtue to be stoical – strong, calm and unmoved by good or bad fortune. Whether slave or emperor, the true stoic stands beyond hope or fear, believing that he has the strength to endure, and hence approaches the immortality of the Gods. The 'stoic' message encourages men to control emotions and deny wounds. A stoic bears hardships with a stiff upper lip.

> The strongest message I received dealt with holding things in, denying feelings and gutting things out to the end. The message was implicit: You are not a man unless you can do this. (No matter how painful the situation was.)
>
> 32-year-old Caucasian teacher

Male stoics strive to be invulnerable and do not show that their feelings get hurt.

Dan, a 31-year-old psychiatric aide (African–American) at a boys' home, learned the 'stoic' message from his father:

> When he was dying, my father said he didn't want any crying at his funeral. That was a real big thing for him. Men were supposed to be hard. There were no feelings shown, regardless of how much pain we were enduring.

Dan said his grandmother and his mom also gave him this message. Crying is feminine, and boys are not supposed to be like girls; therefore they should neither cry nor show emotions. Dan explained that men are also supposed to be inflexible:

> If I could sum up stoic with one thing, it just meant being strong, being able to stand there and endure whatever life dishes out and you take it. And not show any, if this can be called weakness, crying, not crying or bending at all, just being sturdy and solid.

Dan had learned as a young man growing up in an inner city neighborhood to stand up to others and not let them know you are afraid. If he showed fear, other men would take advantage of him. At age 18, Dan signed up for the Marine corps, where his stoical tendencies were strongly reinforced. In his current job he has learned that you cannot be soft with teenagers or they will take advantage of you. Dan had an incident at work where, when one of the adults was not as forceful as he should have been with a youth, the youth hit him in the eye.

Stoicism is in some cases necessary for male survival.

Johnny, a 41-year-old lawyer (Caucasian), also learned to be a stoic from his parents. His father, a graduate of West Point, who was a career Army officer, did not preach the virtues of stoicism but rather set a silent example. His mother told Johnny that he should emulate his father and hold in his feelings. Johnny had a brother three years older who used to beat up on him. When he would complain to his mother, she would insist he defend himself. His high school experiences at a military academy only served to reinforce his stoical upbringing. He learned there the manly virtues of strength, toughness, and bravery, which have served him well in his chosen career, law:

> Law is a highly competitive, assertive profession and I've chosen the most competitive, assertive branch in the fiercest arena of all, New York City. There are few more aggressive jobs in the world than being a litigator. I spend all of my time preparing to do battle or fighting in court.

Johnny said that being a stoic required having long term goals and being willing to accept the pain, loss, and deprivation that comes from trying to reach those goals. He gave as an example his participation in the New York Marathon where he had to stretch the limits of his physical endurance. He described how he would practice for this race:

> It would gradually become more painful and difficult and psychologically I would get this tremendous urge to stop, yet not only did I almost never give in but I used to punish myself by adding extra miles. I'd go out to run ten miles, and around the seventh or eighth I'd start to drag and my body would start saying 'Quit!,' and I'd say, 'God damn it! I'm going to run eleven miles!'

Johnny, the father of three children, has learned through his first and second wives a different style of parenting than the unemotional stoic household in which he was raised. His first wife had an uncle whom Johnny said, 'was so gentle and loving. He called his sons "sweetheart". He was also real physically affectionate.' His second wife has taught him how to enjoy his children:

> I didn't enjoy my kids when I first had them, and part of the reason was I was very uptight. I was carrying on the models of my parents in terms of strictness and standards. I didn't like noise. I didn't like mess. I didn't like chaos. I didn't like all the things which come with children if you are going to let children grow up free and enjoy their companionship. My second wife made it so much fun that I learned to enjoy the things I hadn't enjoyed, all of which revolved around order and authority that are involved in this whole stoicism thing.

Negative correlations between the 'stoic' and 'nurturer' message back up the notion that men who are stoics are not nurturing fathers. The 'stoic' message has significant positive correlations with ten of the fifteen classical male messages used in this study.

Floyd, a 45-year-old shoe repair man from Vermont (Caucasian), learned the 'stoic' message from his father and his football coach. His father emphasized that it was important to keep your obligations. Floyd explained how his father taught this message: 'Plug it out; stick to it; don't admit any weakness; don't complain; don't be a burden on others; don't owe anybody; do it yourself.' On his high school football team Floyd was an Iron man, playing both offensive and defensive tackle. Floyd explained how he learned this message from his coach:

> He made mincemeat of my body. Any time I got hurt he was pissed off. Rather than seeing me as the victim of an unfortunate incident, he would get angry because it could hurt his team. He wanted me right back in action every time I'd get hurt. He used to yell at us and make us feel bad because we had been injured, like we were letting him and our teammates down.

A stoic holds himself aloof, has a few good friends, and does not make himself vulnerable. Floyd felt that as a younger man he avoided the companionship of woman. He suggested that stoics like to hang out with other men, tough guys, and tell their war stories. Women do not appreciate the gutsy things men do to maintain their stoical verneers. Floyd said, 'There's a sense of the young stoic choosing other males for friends and forming a close camaraderie which doesn't include the gentler sex.'

Floyd also learned that a part of the stoic message is not to spoil himself. A true stoic denies himself pleasures and sacrifices for others. He goes to a secondhand store rather than buying new clothes. Floyd has always bought and maintained old cars. He was taught not to eat expensive food and just get by on the basics. Floyd earns his living recycling old shoes. 'Be frugal', Floyd explained. 'Don't treat yourself well. Don't baby yourself or buy things that will make your life easier for you. Save for tomorrow rather than spend today.'

Randy also came from New England. A 42-year-old electrician in the Coast Guard (Caucasian) who grew up in New Hampshire, Randy learned that men who do physical work take risks and can get hurt. One aspect of the stoic philosophy which Randy expressed was a resignation to life that came from the attitude that nothing changes:

> I get real mad about the way Vietnam vets are wronged, but what's there to do? Everybody in my family has been in the military and we know the way the government treats vets. Nothing's going to change. It's the reality of life.

A stoic accepts what life gives without complaining. A fatalistic attitude about life teaches that things cannot be changed, no matter what you do.

As a youth in New Hampshire, Randy learned that there is no such thing as pain. 'You just live with it, no matter how bad you feel,' he said. 'You've got a job to do. You can't let a little pain stop you.' This attitude had proven especially useful in the Coast Guard, where when Randy was on watch he could not let other men down. He would keep the ship running even though he was seasick or not feeling well. Randy described one incident in the Bering Sea, where being a stoic saved his life:

> We had been called to rescue a small boat in rough seas, 25 to 30 foot waves. The only way to get people off the ship was to jump on a rope ladder hanging from our ship. I was on the small boat because I was the one who did the inspection to see if it could be saved. We just couldn't save it, so everybody had to abandon the small boat and get up the ladder that was swaying wildly in the storm. Waves were splashing around. It was freezing cold and there was no way you could keep dry, and it got to a point where it's real easy to sit down and say, 'To hell with this!' At times like that you have to reach inside yourself and say you can do it. If you don't you would freeze to death, so the 'stoic' message can be a real lifesaver.

Randy had the attitude that each man has a choice about how to deal with difficulties, either making this pain traumatic or trivial. 'How you deal with that pain is the way you are going to live', he said. 'You can be miserable or you can be happy.' The stoic philosophy implies that you do not get overwhelmed by hardship. Randy feared that a person who gave into one tough moment might cave into everything else and become totally impotent. He used the analogy of being in the driving seat and controlling your emotions. 'You know,' he said, 'you can't let something else drive you. You gotta be your own driving force.'

Stoical behavior has disastrous consequences for male health (Julty, 1980). A man who is a stoic will ignore pain in his body and guts it out rather than go to a doctor, thinking that going to a doctor and admitting being sick are signs of weakness. Stoics think it is self-indulgent to spend money on health care or to take a day off from work and rest in bed. As a result men in the United States die at a greater rate than women in all age groups (Goldberg, 1976). The 'stoic' message taken to extreme can be very destructive to males.

Rebel

Defy authority and be a non-conformist. Question and rebel against the system.

In contrast to stoics who may be resigned to their fates, rebels often struggle with the circumstances of their lives. Men rebel for a variety of reasons. Some who question authority because they feel the world is out to destroy them, rebel in order to survive. Others rebel because certain experiences have made them angry and hostile. Some rebel because they are concerned about justice. These revolutionaries join political causes and dedicate themselves to overthrowing the system.

Popular culture contains many images of the 'rebel' message. Rock music has many anti-establishment themes. A rebel has a heroic image, standing up for the underdog against powerful forces. Cultural heroes that reinforce this behavior are Robin Hood, who stole from the rich and gave money to the poor, and David, the Jewish soldier who slew the giant, Goliath. Rebels gain the respect of other men when they fight against injustice.

Men who participated in this study indicated that the 'rebel' message was not very influential in their lives. At age 18 it received the second lowest average score, and 23 per cent of the respondents said it had no influence. The 'rebel' message had high variance ratings, which means that for some men it was extremely influential, while for others it had little or no influence. As men grew older the variance score remained high, which indicates that for some men the influence of this message increased sharply, while for others there was a strong decrease.

Skip, a 41-year-old unemployed African–American, had grown up in inner city streets in an environment where rebels had status:

> The pimps, the gamblers, the funeral home operators were the ones who stood out in my neighborhood. They wore nice clothes and were seen as a success. They had finesse and were cool. We respected them because they got over on the man.

Skip's father had been a hustler. Men in that culture used craft, cunning, and strength to survive:

> I remember the 'I don't give a shit' attitude. The hell with this world. I'm going to stand on my own two feet and not care about what happens to anybody else.

Many minority men are rugged individuals because they live in cruel worlds where they do not feel they can trust anybody else. Since it is hard for minority men to acquire jobs which give them self-respect, many adopt a survival mode of hustling with its attendant 'cool' rebel pose (Majors and Billson, 1992).

As Skip grew older, the direction of the 'rebel' message changed. He said he was deeply influenced by the black power movement and antiwar activities:

> What's changed basically is that my reasons for non-conforming, or not being respectful have changed. The rebellion against the system legally is now based on a wider scope. It's expanded to include the world situation, not just a block or a small neighborhood in the city.

As a mature man, Skip is no longer interested in being top dog, the coolest man around. As Mac, another man interviewed for this study, said, 'Who wants to run the streets when you are 40? I want a little comfort.' When he was younger, Skip used to follow the actions of his buddies on the corner 'religiously'. 'Now,' he said, 'I can examine and make determinations based on my own inner feelings rather than just someone else's criteria of how I should act. I can make decisions.' Skip said that when he was younger he was rebelling to prove himself to his peers:

> When I was much younger, the need to rebel was more urgent. Perhaps time has mellowed me and I've learned to set an agenda, and I'm learning to cope with time.

Tony, a 31-year-old therapist, grew up in an American Indian household. His father is an Indian from Minnesota. His mother is Caucasian. Both his parents had drinking problems. Tony thought that the value he attached to the 'rebel' message came out of that pathological environment:

> Part of alcoholism is this stubborn kind of individualism, to the point of self destruction. I'm going to do it my way and I don't care if I hang because of it. My father pretty much goes his own way and does what he wants.

Tony said that nonconformists were looked up to in his house. 'The worst thing you could do,' he said, 'was to become a sort of stuffed shirt, follow the rules kind of person.' Tony's parents taught him it was better to be a rebel than fail. Thumbing your nose at the world was a heroic gesture:

> To me it's a real tragic position, because the heroism of the rebellion was just in their own minds. They rebelled against the system by bitching and moaning and not doing anything constructive. My family in general tends to feel pretty helpless against what they see as a very cold, cruel world, a dog eat dog world. Their values were you do whatever you need in order to get by as opposed to trying to make a difference in the world and living with integrity.

As a child Tony said he did not receive clear directions from his parents about how he ought to behave; therefore he learned to do what he wanted and not get caught. Tony started out his life doing the things juvenile delinquents did – shoplifting, petty burglary, vandalism, drugs, and promiscuous sexual behaviors, which he described as antisocial. He earned the respect of his peers because he could think of crazy things to do. Like Skip, Tony was influenced by the 1960s, where he said he found a meaning to the 'rebel' message beyond getting high. Attracted to the beat culture, he moved to the West Coast where he hit the skids and ended up in a mental hospital, saying at age 21 he needed help to get off drugs. He found some direction to his life through Christian mysticism and community organizing.

True to his 'rebel' message Tony does not follow the teachings of a traditional church but rather has developed a spiritual practice that combines eastern religions with Christian values. Tony said that in his earlier life he did not have a clear vision of what he could be if he was not going to be 'a man in a grey flannel suit'. The only alternative he knew was to be a criminal, dealing drugs, with part time jobs like his dad. At first he thought the only way to be a rebel was to get into trouble. As a therapist he has grown to value creativity over destruction and hopes to help people find happiness using their talents to make the world better. In his current life he sees himself rebelling against 'the forces of death that I see in the world.'

Fred, a 28-year-old machinist (Caucasian), who grew up in a working class community, traced the influence of the 'rebel' message in his life to a stormy relationship with his father, whom Fred described as a real 'bookman', who played by the rules. Fred, who had attended Catholic grade schools and high schools, started to notice his father's own hypocrisy and decided at the age of 13 that he was going to rebel:

> I noticed there was a real dichotomy between who he was presenting himself as and who he really was. I knew that hypocrisy was there and didn't want to sell myself in the same way he did.

Fred started to rebel at an early age. As he grew older, he skipped school and hung out with tough kids. Although he did not join any of the gangs in his neighborhood, Fred took great pride in being able to go amongst them. He achieved a kind of status in high school by being able to break the rules and not get caught:

> I think part of the rebellious thing had to be not only to know the system and play it like everybody else, but in order to be a rebel, you had to be better than the system; you had to go a couple of extra yards. There was a kind of endurance thing there.

Rebels are tougher than other guys. They prove their masculinity by outwitting, outsmarting, and outlasting other men.

A rebel gains status. He becomes a hero by standing up to the powers that be. Fred belonged to a group in high school that took pride in its ability to rebel. Other boys were achieving respect from their peers by getting good grades, starring in sports, or dating attractive girls. Fred and his crowd earned their esteem by breaking rules:

> It seemed that those of us who were breaking the rules also happened to be the same people who were socially aware about the war in Vietnam. We were into drugs, ran the black market, were real streetwise, and didn't deal with the typical things that guys do. We didn't care about our grades. The competition about athletics wasn't there for me. Stuff about sex and conquering girls wasn't there either.

Fred said that rebels respond to a higher morality. In school he was influenced by radical Catholic priests to question the system. 'When I got into high school, being a rebel meant not necessarily agreeing with what I was taught, to question, to argue', he said. 'The teachers were encouraging us to develop our own ideas on issues and to present them.' Fred felt that grade school rules were silly. His own sense of right and wrong led Fred to jail for his convictions. He had the following to say about this experience:

> The thing that's coming to my mind right now was that the last time for not going along with the system I became aware that they had me where they wanted me. I was kinda in their power structure but it was like they didn't get me. I did not conform to their ideas. They did the most powerful thing they could to me and I survived that.

Rebels take great pride in being able to survive outside the system.

George, an 18-year-old high school student (Caucasian), was a middle class kid who had grown up to question authority. George feels that he is a rebel on the inside. He wears whatever clothes he likes. He does not care what other people say. George feels it is important to question authority. 'Rules cause prejudice,' he said, 'and you ought to question them. You shouldn't do what society says.' George is motivated by a strong sense of fairness:

> My mom, sometimes when I was younger, would expect me to do things simply because she told me to; that used to lead to arguments, and bothered me because I think that's not fair. The idea of fairness is really on my mind.

From George's perspective a rebel looks carefully at all sides of an issue and follows his own conscience, not going along with the crowd. A rebel identifies with the underdog.

The 'rebel' message does not have positive correlations with the other male cultural messages used in this study but rather has significant negative correlations. Young men who value the 'rebel' message do not want to be like their fathers. They rebel against traditional family responsibilities ('breadwinner'). They do not respect the law. They do not do well in school. They do not value the work ethic. (All of the older men interviewed for this message were either unemployed or had nontraditional jobs.) As rebels grow older, they do not strive to be the best they can. Their strong individualism prompts them not to care so much about others ('good samaritan') and they do not accept their traditional gender roles as sportsmen.

Each of the older men interviewed for this message indicated that the nature of their rebellion changed as they grew older. Mac was a rebel until he was worn down by the prison system, and he married at age 35. At that point he said he was more interested in a revolution to improve the plight of African–Americans than he was in personal revenge. As men mature they seem to come to grips with whatever it is that causes their rage and turn their rebellious interests towards broader social concerns. As Fred stated, 'They acquire a heightened sense of social awareness.'

Tough Guy

Men don't touch, show emotions, or cry. They don't let others push them around.

Tough guys are street smart. They have stamina. As many coaches say to boys and men, 'When the going gets tough, the tough get going.' They stand on their own two feet and do not take any 'shit' from anybody. They prove themselves by defying authorities. They do not back down from challenges. Tough guys also shut themselves off emotionally, which makes it hard for them to get close to others. The 'tough guy' message had a negative correlation with 'nature lover' and 'nurturer'.

The correlations of 8 of the 11 messages which had a significant relationship with 'tough guy' both at age 18 and over time increased. This indicates that taking on classical male attributes requires men to be tough guys. In spite of these correlations between the 'tough guy' message and classical male messages, the 'tough guy' message had the greatest decrease over time, which indicates that as men grow older this message has less influence in their lives. The tribulations of being tough take their toll upon men, they value this message less as they age.

Brian, a 44-year-old high school teacher (Caucasian), grew up in a tough working class area of Detroit, where he learned to be a tough guy:

> I can remember having rivalries, physical rivalries with boys on my block from the age of six on. My father also told me don't let other people push you around. If you let someone push you around there is something wrong with how you look at yourself and the way you are leading your life.

Brian's father was an immigrant who came over from Poland and had learned to defend himself in his factory job in Detroit. Part of the 'tough guy' message for Brian was almost chivalric in its treatment of women. Knights in the Arthurian legends put women on a pedestal to protect them. Brian said that tough guys do not hit women. This protector aspect of 'tough guy' is reflected by the strong relationship between 'tough guy' and 'breadwinner', which increases over time. Brian remembers his father getting very angry and hurling things around the house but never striking his mother. However, such paternalistic relationships with women may also apply to nonrelatives. The 'tough guy' message had a significant correlation with the 'playboy' message both at age 18 and over time.

Brian explained the correlation between 'tough guy' and 'sportsman':

> One of the ways to avoid fighting was to be a fairly good athlete, because you didn't have to prove yourself with fights, but you could prove yourself on the football field, the hockey rink, or the basketball court. You can gain a kind of toughness and aggressiveness in those sports where people will let you alone and look up to you.

Brian himself played four years of football in high school. Sports provide an important outlet for masculine aggressiveness where boys can prove themselves in ways that are not as destructive as the ways they challenge each other in the streets.

Brian commented that his peer group did not very much value doing well in school:

> If you were a brain you were put down by most of the guys, although you could get a few points if you played sports. It was OK to be smart in certain areas of math, to have a mechanical aptitude. The best you could be was somebody who was going to be an engineer, who was quarterback on the football team, and was street wise.

Brian said that he did better in school than others because 'his parents wouldn't accept less'. In keeping with the high correlation between 'tough guy' and 'warrior', Brian wanted to be a paratrooper after high school but did not get accepted because of poor eyesight. When he graduated from college, he became a teacher in an inner city high school, because he knew he was tough. He explained, 'My self-consciousness was like, hey, you're the kind of guy that can hang tough and you don't have to teach in the suburbs or some place like that.'

Brian felt a strong correlation between 'tough guy' and 'self-reliant'. As he put it, 'As long as I have a strong back, nothing will go wrong.' He had learned through a variety of jobs that he could always support himself. In his case, since he was a teacher, he had learned to use his brain rather than brawn. Knowing he can rely on his own inner resources made him confident, like having a good friend whom you could call on in tough times. Being able to stand up to adversity gave him self-confidence. He would survive no matter how hard life became.

Brian felt there were certain advantages to being a tough guy. He does not back down. Nor does he feel guilty or bitter. If he has something hard to do, he does it, not losing sleep at night worrying about whether he can do it. Tough guys know how to get a job done and do not hesitate about carrying out their objectives. He said he never backed away from a challenge or a test. When he had something particularly difficult to do, he would tell his friends what he was trying to accomplish, so he felt he had to keep his word to them and not back down. Brian said that a disadvantage was that he often felt like a loner.

Pancho, a 37-year-old Puerto Rican drug counselor, grew up in a tough neighborhood on the south side of Chicago. He learned the 'tough guy' message on TV when he used to enjoy James Cagney and the *Untouchables*. Gangs were a big thing in Chicago when he was a boy. Every neighborhood had its own turf boundaries, taverns, and hallmarks that provided safety for those who knew the codes, but danger for any stranger entering gang turf. Pancho, who was overweight, started to hang out with some tough guys across the street. He looked up to them and wanted their approval:

> I was a very good boxer and because of my weight I could wrestle and throw people around. In that type of neighborhood you always look for

respect. You get it either by intimidating or being the tough guy or hanging around with the older guys.

At a young age Pancho learned to carry a pistol. In his group you were not a part of the crowd if you did not go to jail. The best thing you could be was to be labelled as crazy, a man who had no moral convictions, who would do anything to maintain his honor. No one ever messed with a guy who had that reputation.

In retrospect Pancho says that he and his boyhood buddies were insecure. Their 'tough guy' veneer hid inner fears. As Pancho put it:

> You are taught by all the guys not to show any emotions. So you always had to maintain and keep up that image all the time. You needed to carry yourself that way because if they saw you show any kind of feelings you weren't looked up to as having much respect, especially from the older guys. If you are going to be in a gang war, or if somebody comes after you with a bat, or if someone shoots at you, you have to take the attitude he is out to kill you. You can't be sensitive in cases like that.

People have said to Pancho, 'How can you be like that? How can you be so cold? You could just say that to somebody and not think anything of it.'

Don, a 21-year-old part-time mechanic (Caucasian), grew up in a very different environment in an affluent suburb of Minneapolis. Unlike Brian and Pancho who grew up in the inner city, Don did not have to fight to prove himself. Don learned to be a 'tough guy' from his father, who never showed any emotions. He said that his father worked all the time and never really talked to him. Don's peer group taught him to keep a stiff upper lip. He used to hang out with them, shooting baskets and riding a skateboard. Don also learned about the 'tough guy' message from television and the media, from heroes like Lee Marvin and Charles Bronson. He learned that tough guys get by in the world. Paul Newman, whom Don characterized as a fast talker, was one of his heroes. Such tough guys in the media get the good jobs, the attractive women, and the other accoutrements that make them into attractive playboys.

Don received reinforcement for being a tough guy from women. Don learned from his mother, who was a competent housewife, not to inject himself into domestic affairs. Don said her attitude was: 'I'll run the household while the men go to work.' Don reported that his girlfriends did not want him to express his emotions. 'They just aren't ready for a man's emotions. One girlfriend of mine didn't want to hear me complain.' Don has also learned to be guarded in his feelings about women. 'One woman used my feelings against me', he explained. 'I told her something personal and she threw it in my face when we were having an argument.' Don feels that a tough guy does not show his vulnerabilities by asking for help, remains cool and aloof, and stays calm.

Sam, a 29-year-old Vietnam veteran from Montana, said he was told by his mom to be a good guy and act appropriately, while around his father and the fathers of all of his friends, he learned to repress his feelings. His father expressed anger but no other emotions. Sam said that the 'tough guy' message was everywhere in his rural community. Sam had a friend from Montana whom he described in the following way:

> I had some friends who wouldn't let their sons come home from a fight until they won. That particular kid died in Vietnam and knew he was going to die in Vietnam. A mutual friend of ours saw him in the Marine Corps where he was still trying to prove to his father that he was OK. He didn't come back. He went to that length to prove to his father that he was a tough guy!

Sam understood that taking the 'tough guy' message to the extreme meant challenging death. Not all men win that challenge.

In the Navy, Sam was trained to be a killer:

> It put an enormous layer on top of 'tough guys don't feel'. Vietnam made it real difficult to unlearn that stuff, keeping it in because there was so much invested in the tough guy thing. There's a phenomenon in Vietnam called numbing out. When you operate there it's with a certain mindset – you can't feel in combat and survive.

To Sam, joining the Navy was a logical extension of his experiences in sports where he had learned to prove himself. The Navy provided a legitimate avenue through which he could prove to the world how tough he was.

By being tough guys, men think they will get rewarded. Sam found out just the opposite when he returned from Vietnam. He had thought there was societal approval for the tough guy:

> John Wayne was pretty well thought of. What happened with Vietnam to a lot of us is that we thought it was going to be our ticket to adult manhood. And when the very thing you think is going to insure your inclusion insures your exclusion, it's very hard. We came back not being able to get jobs, not being able to be socially accepted if people knew. If you put Vietnam veteran on your resume, people thought you were a baby killer ... I grew up thinking there is some kind of honor in this, and what did I get? Yahoos spitting on me!

Sam said there were incredible feelings of alienation and anger among veterans, but that they refused to acknowledge those feelings. A friend of his described how the Marine Raiders would carry on in their Veterans of Foreign War (VFW) posts:

> They'd get together and they'd drink and have a good time, remembering the good old days, but if somebody starts getting emotional they are immediately ostracized. They don't want to hear it.

Sam said that many tough guys drink and do drugs to avoid going into what he calls 'a grieving pool', a reservoir that contains hurts. They are afraid to go down into the pool for fear they will drown. Sometimes the pressure would build up in the pool and it would run over the dam. He also saw the pain as a wind in a balloon, building up pressure, until finally it explodes in a heart attack or a violent act. Sam said he knew of many tough guys living in the mountains. 'Western Montana attracts a lot of, they call them bush vets. They are so afraid of their own violence that they live like hermits, fearing social contact.' Sam knew a veteran whom he believed was dying from exposure to Agent Orange who could not get any benefits and was living in a cave. Tough guys guts it out on their own. They neither put out emotional feelers asking for assistance nor build supportive networks to help them through rough times.

Superman

Men are supposed to be perfect. They don't admit mistakes.

Superman is a male stereotype, a character who has had a strong influence upon cultural images of masculinity. The male message 'superman' is itself a characterization of masculinity. Superman, a popular television and movie figure, exemplifies the ability of an ordinary Joe to transform himself into a hero with superhuman capacities. Disguised as mild-mannered Clark Kent, a newspaper reporter, Superman saves the world, fights for truth and justice. By championing law and order, he rescues people in distress. Always in control, he does not show his emotions and never loses. An adventurous warrior who never ages, Superman has great strength and does things for the right reasons. He can fly and is invincible. Superman is a patriotic guy loyal to his country who takes care of those he loves.

The German philosopher, Friedrich Nietzsche, developed the idea of supermen who, because of their superiority have the right, if not the obligation, to dominate weaker people. Neitzsche (1967) taught that all men are dominated by what he called the 'will to power', and that they should obey this will. His teachings became the backbone of Fascism, which in Europe during the 1930s and 1940s preached that men who belonged to a super race had to take over the world.

In spite of the strong presence of superman images in US culture, this message was not rated very highly by men who participated in this study. Respondents ranked the 'superman' message as the twentieth most important male message. Twenty per cent said this message had no influence in their lives at age 18 and the influence of this message decreased significantly during the course of men's lives. Tendencies of being in control, being unemotional, and being tough were expressed in significant correlations with the 'superman' message. The correlations that were significant at age 18 decreased over time.

Kirk, a 48-year-old Lutheran pastor (Caucasian), identified with Superman when he was a young boy. He learned about the 'superman' message from his father and his older brother. Kirk described his father as a stern and demanding lawyer with high moral standards. His brother was an excellent student and athlete. Kirk said he always admired his older brother, who did things easily. He learned from a coach to go all out. In his high school in a suburb of Philadelphia he was student council president. At his church, where he plays a superman role as pastor, people look up to Kirk because of his leadership skills.

Being a superman takes a toll on men who realize, as they grow older, that they cannot maintain the same rigorous pace they had when they were young. Kirk put it this way: 'As I get older, I am starting to realize some of my physical limitations.' Kirk was a star athlete in high school and has always kept himself in good shape. He is starting to realize that his body cannot keep up with the superman standards he had as a youth:

> I never realized there that that there were physical limitations to what I could do. I have to remind myself of that. If I tire out or find myself exhausted, I have to realize I can't do everything, even though I would like to.

Kirk has also grown to realize that, unlike the fictional Superman, he cannot save the world. Having spent most of his adult life involved in political causes, Kirk is now more intentional about how he spends his time. 'I'm not sure about saving the world', he said. 'I don't think I can save the world, but I think I can contribute to change.'

Ken, a 27-year-old ex-con (Caucasian), identified with the perfectionist aspect of the 'superman' message. He had grown up in a working class community and described his drive for perfection in the following way:

> It's like I'm always striving for more than maybe I should be doing, trying to be Superman. It's great as long as it don't wear you out and give you ulcers because you're worrying about getting everything done. Anytime you've got time there's always something to do.

Ken had learned to be a perfectionist both from his father and from four years in the Air Force. He said both his father and grandfather were veterans who exhibited the same high adherence to impossible standards. He put it the following way:

> As I was growing up, my Dad was a perfectionist, so I learned a great deal of it from him. There were times he was overly a perfectionist. If I'd vacuum the floor and there would be one piece of dust, he'd make me do the whole floor over again. I thought he was just that way. Then when I was 17, I went into the Air Force, and I found out that they weren't much better. They taught the same thing. In Basic Training they taught you how to fold towels and stuff, like if one was a 32nd of an inch off they'd make you fold it all over again. You had to look down at all of them like that. Sometimes, even if they were perfect, they'd throw them on the bed and make you do them again, just to strive for

perfection. And with that in mind, you know, and then after I got out of that and into the job field, I found out that there was a lot of competition in the job field, and I almost had to strive for perfection and work my hardest in order to compete in the job field. There's such competition out there.

Ken described a situation where his father ordered him to do 500 push-ups. When he finished, his father demanded he do more, Ken said he collapsed and his father took off his belt and started 'whipping his butt'. Ken joined the Air Force at age 19 to get away from his Dad but ran into the same behavior patterns of domineering men making irrational demands upon him to behave like a superman.

Ken had two children by a previous marriage and felt worn down by the drain of working full time, keeping up the house, and raising children. As did Kirk, Ken felt that the 'superman' message makes it hard for men to be good, loving husbands. The 'superman' message had a negative correlation with the 'nurturer' message, both at 18 and over time. Ken felt that men are pulled in many different directions by the expectations society places on them. After the quiet time he had spent in jail, society seemed like an anthill with everybody scurrying around 'in a rush, a mad panic, like they can't slow down; they got to keep up with the world'.

Jose, a 41-year-old adult educator (Hispanic), identified with that aspect of Superman that transforms himself into a superhero. Jose had grown up in Mercedes, Texas and had spent many years in the migrant stream surrounded by macho men:

> Growing up in the mid-50s in a Chicano community, my childhood development was very much influenced by all the traditional things that Chicanos should be: Shouldn't cry, should be tough, you shouldn't let people push you around.

Jose's father ran away when Jose was eight years old. Since Jose was the oldest son, he had to set a model for the rest of the family. He was strongly influenced by uncles who lived in the same community and soon learned that in his culture he was expected to make the decisions because he was the man.

Jose was fascinated by the fact the Superman had an alter ego, Clark Kent, who was powerless and weak:

> I'm living in this world, this environment, where everything is real tough, and nobody's really dealing honestly with their feelings, with their economic situation, and really putting on a show in public.

Jose felt that the macho adult men in his community were putting up a big bluff that was not very sincere. He would have preferred them to be tough and powerful as well as honest and tender. Jose had often faced difficult confrontations because of the 'superman' message. As he put it, he would get into fights believing he was all powerful and had gotten into trouble. 'Without thinking you jump into it', he said. 'I've got to keep myself in check.' Jose would be the first to admit that his pride gets hurt and that he has a hard time admitting mistakes. He still tries to keep up a front, although at the technical college where he works, he counsels his students to be cautious about the 'superman' role.

Edward, a 33-year-old community organizer (Caucasian), came from an entirely different background than Jose. Edward's father, an insurance executive in Wisconsin, was very involved with his children and used to take them fishing. Edward learned the 'superman' message from television and movies, suggesting that 'superman' represented a rite of passage:

> Watching my two young boys brought back some memories of my own. Through the media, comic books, it seems pretty typical to have a super hero. They spend a lot of time playing that, and spend a lot of time looking for that on the cartoons, the right channels that have that. I mean you weren't watching other cartoons if there was some sort of super hero on – you know, Superman or Bat Man or Submariner, Iron Man. I clearly remember watching all those, loving super heroes. The thought that they were invincible. They could do things that you couldn't do: they could fly. They could embody the ideal in a lot of ways, physically and mentally.

Edward thinks that young boys look for men who become their super heroes. They emulate them and learn from them the ways of being men. Edward had looked up to his own Jesuit teachers in high school who set standards for compassion and social justice. Edward saw the 'superman' message gave many men a hyper sense of their own abilities, that they will be muscular, strong and good looking. Many men take great strides to live up to these standards, lifting weights, jogging, and even taking steroids to achieve superhuman strength.

The 'superman' message gives men unreal expectations for themselves. In the real world they will not have great adventures, be warriors, or conquer evil. In his neighborhood Edward watches many young boys practicing karate, learning that as supermen they can hurt other people and that might makes right. Edward saw that the 'superman' message was a kind of escapism for men who dreamed of gaining power and controlling others. Supermen have to prove their dominance over and over again, which was demonstrated in the correlations between the 'superman' message and 'hurdles'. They may be fired up on their missions, but they also get worn down by the futility of trying to realize their childhood fantasies of grandeur, which helps explain the decrease in the correlations with 'superman' over time. 'The ultimate male superman,' Edward said, 'is God.' 'God is omnipotent, invincible and all-knowing, a divine state out of reach for us mortals.'

Conclusion

The low ratings given the male messages in this factor, 'Rugged Individuals', point to a curious aspect of the US culture. Men are often portrayed in popular culture as being rugged individuals. However, the 560 men who participated in this study indicated that the influence of male messages like 'rebel', 'tough guy', 'stoic' and 'superman' was not as strong as other cultural gender norms. Furthermore, the influence of all the messages in this factor decreased over time. If men do not value being rugged individuals, why do popular male images so often depict this aspect of masculinity? Are the male authors who construct plays and novels and television dramas about men trying to glamorize a painful part of the masculine experience, making the lonely behavior of men seem heroic? Are they projecting their own insecurities about masculinity onto fictional characters? The messages that make up the factor 'Rugged Individuals' are widespread but do not seem to be that popular with men, especially older males.

John Donne's famous sonnet states that no man is an island, but in modern societies cultural norms like those highlighted in this chapter encourage them to be islands. The individualistic culture requires males to construct moats around themselves and not let down their drawbridges to let others come close or to allow emotions to gush outwards. The Greek word 'idiot' refers to one who attempts to lead a private life, ignorant of and unconcerned about the public domain. Modern capitalist societies, by requiring its men to be rugged individuals, may be raising male idiots – men who try to stand independent of others and consider it a mark of their masculinity to withdraw from social concerns. Rather than taking others' needs into account, they do whatever they want. Rather than acknowledging mistakes, they insist they are right and force their views upon others. Rather than admitting their vulnerabilities, they maintain a tough exterior and die in all age groups at rates higher than women. Rather than building a life based upon the needs of others, they scorn other people's needs as weaknesses. Rugged individuals are kamikaze pilots. When they finish their missions they self destruct, never knowing the joy of shared enterprises or deep love.

This factor, 'Rugged Individuals', expresses a tragic flaw in the male character. Millions of unknown soldiers are slaughtered in wars created by men. The brutality implied by messages like 'tough guy', 'superman' and 'stoic' not only murders men but also kills them spiritually. In their rush to prove their masculinity, that they are not feminine, rugged individuals die inside, drowned in their own pain, emotionally throttled by a culture that expects them to be superhuman. They trust in their country and the goodness of other men but often end up in an emotional cesspool, blaming themselves for their failures. After all, if they were rugged enough, they would be on the top of the pile!

What makes these heroic feats especially difficult is the emphasis from the 'stoic' message which deprives men of the comfort of expressing their emotions as they strive to live up to the difficult standards of masculinity. The emphasis of the messages within 'Rugged Individuals' denies men the soothing effects of emotional release and will not let them reach out for help. No wonder there is so much addiction and abuse among males! Gender expectations wind young boys up and program men to go on difficult missions, while at the same time telling them not to trust anybody and discouraging them from expressing feelings.

Many stories related in this chapter tell tragic tales about the depths men go to to get approval for their masculinity from other males.

Part III

Differences Between Men

Chapter 9

Different Lenses

I am definitely influenced by Hispanic culture and think that this is a man's world yet – and always will be.

60-year-old Hispanic professional

The male messages presented in this book provide central themes for masculinity, an ideology that exists at two distinct but interrelated levels. At the social level there are commonly held assumptions about how men ought to behave. These norms, or stereotypes, constitute cultural notions of masculinity. At the individual level each man has specific experiences from which he constructs a gender identity that has some common elements with the dominant male paradigm but also contains unique features.

Within any country a wide variety of subcultures nourish many different understandings of masculinity and reflect different emphases separate cultural groups place upon dominant male messages. These specific cultural groups provide lenses which define how an individual views dominant cultural norms. Each subculture has its own expectations for men so that individuals raised within subcultures view the dominant norms for male behavior with different lenses, which filter certain aspects of the dominant masculine paradigm, thereby emphasizing differing standards for male behavior. Men construct their identities from the images and values reflected within those subcultures as well as dominant modes of masculinity reflected within national boundaries.

This chapter will discuss how men – from different generations, different communities of origin (city, suburban, rural), different classes, different racial groups, and gay men view these messages. This chapter will neither include a discussion of how men from different geographic regions of the United States[1] construct separate notions of masculinity nor a discussion of how different ethnic groups, e.g. Italians, Norwegians interpret these messages. It is assumed that both of these variables, geographic place of origin and ethnicity, would affect responses to dominant male messages, but this study did not discriminate along these lines.

Generational Differences

By far the strongest lens that provides differing visions of how men ought to behave is generational difference. Men raised in different time periods have different values. In *People Puzzle*, Massey (1979) states that by the time children reach 15 they have formed a core set of values. They have spent considerable energy interpreting their cultural norms and their identities reflect those values. The way a young person sees the world at that age reflects contemporary cultural norms that prescribe how that person thinks the world ought to be. Understandings gathered during the key period of value formation provide impetus for what a person thinks is good, right, or normal.

Men raised in different decades have differing values based on current views that applied to the world they grew up in. Thus, men who formed their values in the 1920s usually are very patriotic. The experience of World War I led to a climate where people cared deeply for their country. Men who grew up during the depression (1930s) tend to have economic insecurities; saving money is an important value for them. Men raised during the 1940s were influenced by World War II. Because they were involved in the total commitment to win the war, they may worry about the status of their country within a world of nations. Men who entered their teenage years during the 1950s lived in an affluent consumer oriented society where men were breadwinners. During the 1960s television brought the civil rights and antiwar movements into everybody's living rooms, and men learned to challenge authority and question the system. The 1970s was the 'me' generation, which led males to introspection and cynicism. In the 1980s males turned to the business community to generate affluence and away from government to solve problems. Massey argues that these generational values

Table 9.1   Influence of different male messages upon cohort groups[2]

Messages	Average response on 5-point scale (0–4)							Mean
Age	< 19	20–29	30–39	40–49	50–59	60–69	> 70	
N =	91	99	146	97	58	21	13	
Adventurer	2.15	2.25	2.59	2.56	2.20	2.58	2.00	2.38
Be Like Your Father	1.64	1.75	2.08	2.11	2.16	2.54	1.85	1.96
Breadwinner	2.15	2.01	2.43	2.68	2.80	3.13	2.69	2.42
Control	2.02	2.34	2.51	2.65	2.82	2.75	2.23	2.45
Good Samaritan	2.40	2.47	2.67	2.52	2.78	2.75	2.46	2.55
Hurdles	2.06	2.13	2.41	2.46	2.09	2.50	1.69	2.26
Law	1.80	1.69	2.23	2.53	2.17	3.13	3.58	2.17
Playboy	1.87	2.16	2.40	2.57	1.93	2.35	2.15	2.25
Rebel	1.75	1.89	1.84	1.57	1.49	0.96	0.85	1.69
Scholar	2.76	2.47	2.51	2.99	2.81	2.86	3.00	2.67
Self-reliant	2.08	2.20	2.46	2.65	2.40	2.66	2.07	2.37
Technician	1.82	2.31	2.24	2.35	2.17	2.67	2.69	2.22
Tough Guy	1.59	1.94	2.34	2.43	1.95	2.54	1.69	2.11
Warrior	1.58	1.28	1.71	1.68	1.26	2.00	1.92	1.58

influence an individual throughout life. They can be changed but usually only through crises like a divorce.

Table 9.1 indicates how men from different age cohort groups respond to the male messages. The average numbers indicate how influential those messages were upon respondents at age 18.

Table 9.1 reflects some of the generational differences mentioned by Massey. For example, the 'breadwinner' message was most influential for men in their forties, fifties and sixties raised when the virtues of a traditional nuclear family were extolled. *Playboy* magazine, which came out in the 1950s, spurred an interest in the playboy role. According to Table 9.1, this interest is highest in men who were forming their values during the 1950s and 1960s. During the 1970s and 1980s with the proliferation of the women's movement, herpes, AIDS, and other sexually transmitted diseases, the influence of this message decreases. The influence of the women's movement can be seen in the younger men who have a lower average for the 'control' message and do not feel they have to be as controlling as older men who were raised with the idea that men had the right to dominate others.

Older men in their sixties and seventies most valued the 'law'. They were taught to be patriotic and thought it was a man's duty to uphold the law. Conversely, men who formed their values during the 1960s and 1970s, a period of rebellion marked by opposition to the Vietnam War, indicated that the 'rebel' message was more influential. Older men in their sixties and seventies who were influenced by the experiences of World War I and II had the highest responses to the 'warrior' message. They believed it was a man's duty to fight for his country. Conversely, younger men have lower than average scores for both 'tough guy' and 'warrior', reflecting a rejection of war that came about from the Vietnam experience and was further magnified during the 1970s and 1980s by aversion to the use and production of nuclear weapons.

The breakdown in the traditional family can be seen in responses to the 'be like your father' message, where older men who lived in traditional male dominated families felt the influence of this message more strongly than younger men raised in families during the 1960s and 1970s when divorce and single female-headed households became a more common occurrence. Many boys growing up during these decades lost contact with their fathers.

The values men adopt are molded by the specific circumstances in which they are raised. Table 9.1 indicates that events in the culture have a profound impact upon men's gender identities, so that men from different age cohorts will have different notions about how men ought to behave. This helps explain intergenerational conflict where fathers and sons argue about what is important because they have significantly different values by virtue of being raised in specific time periods: A forty-year-old father who formed his values during the 1960s might express dismay about his son's conformity; or a boy raised during the 1960s might have heard his father complain about him not developing a career because his father was raised during the depression when the most important concern was income security.

According to Table 9.1, men younger than 19 score below the mean for all these messages with the exception of 'rebel' and 'scholar'. This indicates that men who formed their values during the 1980s might be adopting different values than men of previous generations. Rebelling against traditional male values, these men are forming new forms of masculinity, using scholarship and not their muscles to get ahead in the world.

Community of Origin

> My idea of what is male oriented has changed through the years. I grew up in a small town with a small town attitude of what a man should be like. However, I now live in a larger city and have found some of my ideas have changed (how to love or be loved) but others have grown (how a man should act to be accepted by society).
>
> 26-year-old manager of fast food restaurant

Attitudes about masculinity vary according to the region in which boys grow up. Boys raised in rural areas have more classical views of masculinity, where men have to be tough and work with their hands. Boys raised in the suburbs are exposed to more educated men, while boys in urban areas are exposed to a wide variety of masculine models. Table 9.2 indicates these differences.

These six messages describe classical male behavior. With the exception of 'self-reliant', the rural men value these messages more than men raised in the city or in the suburbs. The higher score for 'self-reliant' with suburban men suggests that suburban men break off their roots when they move to their own 'castles' in the suburbs, where they live independently. Men in rural areas and small towns complete fewer years of schooling than other men (Hogan, 1981, p. 121). Since education plays a big role in introducing men to different notions about how men ought to behave, it should not be a surprise that rural men score higher on classical male messages.

Table 9.2   Impact of area grown up in upon male messages

Messages	Area grown up in						
	Suburbs	Rural	City composite	Small city (< 100,000)	Medium city (100–500,000)	Large city (> 500,000)	Mean
Number	199	101	249	81	50	118	
Breadwinner*	1.45	1.84	1.78	1.88	1.71	1.74	1.67
Law	2.23	2.39	2.01	2.37	1.78	1.87	2.16
Law*	1.42	1.75	1.62	1.82	1.67	1.37	1.57
Self-reliant	2.50	2.42	2.31	2.44	2.48	2.01	2.37
Tough Guy	1.95	2.47	2.17	2.15	2.40	1.97	2.12
Work Ethic*	2.07	2.32	2.16	2.17	2.33	1.97	2.18

* refers to responses over time. Those messages without * indicate responses at age 18.

Men in rural areas have more respect for the law and more traditional views about their roles in a family (breadwinner). Men in the suburbs who express less influence for the 'breadwinner' message than men in rural areas or cities are more likely to adopt nontraditional family roles. Suburban men also demonstrate less influence for the 'tough guy' message. Men raised in urban areas who face as teenagers constant challenges to prove their masculinity through fighting or other acts of physical daring value this message more. In cities boys tend to solve conflicts with their fists, while in the suburbs they use their wits. (Compare in Chapter 8 the responses to 'tough guy' message by Pancho, who was raised in inner city Chicago, to Don, who was raised in suburban Minneapolis.)

At age 18, men from the city have less respect for the law. Of the three categories men in the city are the least self-reliant, indicating that a city offers rich opportunities for building friendships and participating in social groupings. Respect for the work ethic is highest in rural areas and lowest in large cities of over 500,000. There are more examples of unemployed men in the city, while men in rural areas work hard to survive off the land. Men in large cities have fewer opportunities to earn a living through manual jobs like farm labor.

Where a man grows up affects his view of the world. As a boy who wants approval, he views various role models who reflect the values of that neighborhood and adopts a native identity, doing the things expected of men in those particular neighborhoods. Thus, a boy raised in a farm neighborhood who sees men working hard and hunting will probably grow up to value the work ethic and want to prove himself as a hunter as soon as he becomes an adolescent. A young boy growing up in a working class urban area may want to be a machinist or factory foreman when he grows up. Boys raised in the suburbs may aspire to professional jobs because that is how men in their neighborhood earn a living. Although men from the suburbs, the city, and from rural areas do reflect significant differences on six of the male messages studied here (three at age 18 and three as older men), over 85 per cent of the cultural conditioning they receive as men seems to be similar regardless of the various areas in which they are raised.

Class Differences

Sociologists have stated that social class plays an important role in how people see themselves (Crompton and Mann, 1986; LeMasters, 1975). People in different classes have different attitudes, values, and lifestyles. Social class depends upon income, occupation, and education. Class status influences the amount of resources available to an individual, which determines the level and quality of schooling and provides an important predictor of how successful a man will ultimately be. Men from the lower social classes leave school and enter the work force earlier than men from the upper classes (Hogan, 1981). Class position affects not only to what a man aspires but also what he attains (Hogan, 1981, p. 137):

This analysis suggests that the social milieu in which men are raised has an important impact upon their ability to achieve the transition to adulthood in an expeditious manner and in a normative fashion. Men who grow up in a home in which the father is employed in a blue-collar or farm occupation have a reduced probability of completing college, and lower status origins complicate the transition to adulthood of those men who complete college.

Men from the upper classes have better houses, health care, educations, occupations, and have more social and economic resources available to help them pursue their dreams. Men from the lower classes who earn less money, do not receive as much schooling, and hold lower status jobs with lesser occupational attainments, have a hard time surviving, let alone realizing their dreams (Sennet and Cobb, 1973).

The following quotation from Paul, a graduate of Yale Law School, sheds light on how different class backgrounds influence a man's gender identity:

> I feel that as a man I am constantly at bat. In my job and in my career I face these incredible obstacles; it's almost as if a fierce pitcher is bearing down on me all the time from the mound with vicious curve balls and blazing fast balls I'm supposed to hit. Every now and then I connect and hit a home run, but the satisfaction does not last long because I'm up at bat again. Many times I strike out or make an out.

All men who come to this plate face life's circumstances and want to hit a home run. Some get a few singles. Most strike out. Paul, with his private school and university education, has been well trained for this game. He has attended the best batting schools and stands at the plate with a Louisville Slugger. Men from the lower classes do not necessarily receive different male messages than upper class men but rather have very little training in how to successfully slug it out at the plate. Their schooling as men does not prepare them to be batting champions. Most men from lower classes stand at the plate with a tooth pick and fail to connect meaningfully with the few occupational and educational opportunities that come their way. As Eric indicates in Chapter 5, men from the lower classes get to the major leagues by rigidly adhering to the 'work ethic' message. They get similar male messages as upper and middle class men. But their training as men in how to survive in the various slums where they live does not prepare them for the big leagues in transnational corporations.

Table 9.3 indicates that class backgrounds do not provide great differences in terms of the influence of male messages that set expectations for how men ought to behave. The responses below indicate that at age 18 there were statistically significant responses by men from different classes to only three messages, or 13 per cent of the total, and with older men there were significant differences for only four messages, or 17 per cent of the total. This implies that over 80 per cent of the gender-role conditioning received by men from different classes is similar.

Table 9.3   Differences in responses of men from different classes to male messages

	Class		
	Lower	**Middle**	**Upper**
Number	91	339	32
Breadwinner	2.77	2.35	2.33
Faithful Husband	2.24	1.96	2.34
Law*	1.36	1.63	1.57
Playboy*	1.27	1.42	1.79
Sportsman*	1.76	1.62	2.08
Technician*	1.95	2.04	2.41
Tough Guy	2.51	2.05	1.84

* refers to responses over time. Those messages without * indicate responses at age 18.

Table 9.3 indicates that men raised in lower classes have more traditional family roles (breadwinner) than men raised in middle class homes. Upper class men have the highest ratings for 'faithful husband', which may come from patriarchal assumptions that men have a duty to obey their wives, an obligation to shelter women from the cruel world.

Men from the lower class find the influence of the 'tough guy' message more important than men from middle and upper classes. Men in the upper class have the lowest rating for this message. Privileged upper class men might have to prove their masculinity on sports fields, or in schools by earning good grades, or even with women, but they do not have to fight to protect themselves in the same physical way that characterizes life for lower class men living in rough neighborhoods.

Older men raised in lower class homes have less respect for the law. Many men from the lower class who are hostile to the social order break the law in order to survive. For these men society is not just and hence its laws are not respected. Men raised in middle class homes seem to have the greatest regard for the law. These 'pillars of society' are busy upholding the traditions and values of the social orders they inhabit.

Over time men raised in upper class homes are most influenced by the 'playboy' message, the 'sportsman' message, and the 'technician' message. This may be because they have more money and time to be sexually active, pursue sports activities, and master technological gadgetry. Imagine an upper class man buying a farm, a sail boat, a vacation home, or an airplane, mastering technical skills in order to maintain his investment. Men from the lower classes indicate over time the lowest influence for the 'technician' message. Even though these men have to work with their hands, many lower class men are laborers and hold jobs which do not require technical expertise. Over time men from the lower class have the lowest score for the 'playboy' message. Lacking financial resources, they may not feel as attractive and may not engage in romantic activity as much as more affluent middle and upper class men.

Most of the literature on gender conditioning has focused on white middle class men and women. This study indicates that dominant notions of masculinity overpower class differences in regard to how men ought to behave, e.g. 'being a man' is more important than being an 'upper class man'. Even though class distinctions are very oppressive to many men, male gender conditioning is mostly similar regardless of their class of origin. Male participants in this study shared similar notions of masculinity. Class differences may limit what men accomplish with their lives, but males seem to construct much the same gender identities. This similarity in views of masculinity may be unique to the United States, which maintains a myth of upward mobility where men from all classes believe they can achieve success. In other countries where class distinctions are more rigid, and individuals from the lower classes do not believe it is possible to escape their class background, wider differences might appear between how men from different classes view masculinity.

To date, most studies of male behavior have focused on the lives of middle class men. This analysis justifies this approach to understanding male behavior because middle class men are in the majority and there do not seem to be many significant differences between the different classes in terms of the influence of cultural expectations that set norms for male behavior.[4] However, studies show that men from the middle class are more likely to adopt more liberal attitudes about their gender role conditioning (Schaffer, 1981, p. 308).

Race and Ethnicity

The United States is a multicultural society consisting of people from a variety of races and ethnic groups. According to the 1990 census, the largest minority group in the United States consists of African–Americans who constitute about 12 per cent of the population. Hispanics are the next largest with 9 per cent, while Asians constitute 3 per cent. Men learn within these cultural groups different assumptions about what constitutes appropriate male behavior, values they have acquired, in many cases, from foreign countries. Research studies indicate that men from the first generation coming into this country have views of masculinity that most closely approximate gender norms in their host countries, while by the third generation men from different minority groups tend to have assimilated the dominant WASP values for appropriate male behavior (Yorburg, 1974). Likewise, within a specific racial or ethnic group there tend to be widely divergent different views of masculinity, so that Hispanics include Puerto Ricans, Mexicans, men from Central America, Brazilians, Chileans, etc. Because each of these countries of origin has its own norms for male behavior, it is incorrect to assume that Hispanic men hold common values about masculinity. Mexicans living within the United States are generally called Chicanos, but within that group, there exists a wide variation of beliefs. Chicanos differ from men with Hispanic surnames whose families have lived in the Southwest for 300 years and are well acculturated to illegal immigrants who cannot speak English. It is also hard to generalize about the experience of African–Americans who, although they have lived in the United States for many generations, have very varied experiences, that can range from being a poor farmer in Mississippi to a Supreme Court judge.

In the United States, Caucasian males have been the dominant race and have imposed their notions of appropriate male behavior. Cultural traditions within the United States have even argued that white males have a manifest destiny to colonize other men and convert them to their superior ways (Horsman, 1986). Superior attitudes about the white race have led to ethnocentric assumptions about Western culture and the inferiority of other races. Such racist notions have made it difficult for men of color to achieve equality.

> The 'white myth of superiority' along with institutional racism – and the inherent double standards – were direct contradictions to the Ten Commandments/Bill of Rights in developing positive male self con-cepts, and did result in creating conflict and complications in the role development of both white and black males, with far reaching adverse consequences for the growth and development of the American male.
>
> 56-year-old, African–American Social Worker

Within the United States all men are not treated equally. Racial tensions based on prejudice have created mistrust between men. One 34-year-old Hispanic professional even stated, 'Never accept what Caucasians tell you to be true!' Deep divisions along racial lines determine how men behave.

The next section of this chapter will discuss three different minority groups of men – African–American, Hispanic, and Asian.[5] Specific findings from African–American respondents will be included, while generalized research statements will be presented about Hispanic and Asian–Americans. Because of the small size and diversity of the sample of Hispanic and Asian–American men, no attempt will be made to summarize their responses to the survey instrument. These generalized statements suggest the kinds of lenses Hispanic and Asian men may be using to interpret dominant cultural norms in the United States. A danger in discussing how minority men respond to male messages is in inaccurately stereotyping their behavior. Within each group there are always wide varieties of opinion about appropriate male behavior. However, there exist within each group some common similarities that allow generalizations about expectations for men within specific cultures.[6]

African–American

Much has been written recently about the plight of African–American men in the United States (Duniere, 1992; Gary, 1981; Hale-Benson, 1986; Kunjufu, 1985; Wilson, 1978). These studies have elaborated a thesis that African–American men are becoming an endangered species because the dominant white society makes it difficult for black men to assume successfully traditional male roles. White society systematically keeps African–American men from achieving prestige and power, the hallmarks of manhood. Out of frustration and desperation some African–American men adopt antisocial behaviors in order to survive. The following provides statistical evidence of the difficulties experienced by African–American males:

> While the conditions of all other groups (including women and recent immigrants) have improved in the past 25 years, six million young black males age 15 to 24 are more likely than their counterparts to be unemployed, to be involved in the criminal justice system, and to commit suicide. In November 1987 the black teenage unemployment rate (34 per cent) was nearly twice the rate for all teenagers (17.4 per cent); the black unemployment rate was three times as high as in 1960, and both unemployment and labor force participation of young black males had deteriorated dramatically relative to whites since 1960. Almost half (46.2 per cent) of young black males under 18 are in households below the poverty line; 42 per cent live in female-headed households, two-thirds of which have below poverty incomes. (Marshall, 1988, p. vii)

As of 1986, one out of every two African–American children born in the United States is born into poverty (Gibbs, 1988, p. 25). More African–American men are in prisons than attend colleges or universities.[5] Many African–American males born into poverty are locked into the lowest stratum of society. The survival rate for African–Americans is therefore threatened by poverty, overcrowding, poor health care, and minimal protections against accidents and violence. Homicide is the leading cause of death among African–American males aged 15–24. Some African–Americans, born into middle class communities, are able to escape some of the violence and terror of street life, but many African–American men live in extremely dangerous conditions described below:

> With a touchy paranoia born of living battered lives, they are desperate to be real men. Killing is only machismo taken to the extreme. Incursions to be punished by death were many and minor, and they remain so: they include stepping on the wrong toe, literally; cheating in a drug deal; simply saying 'I dare you' to someone holding a gun; crossing territorial lines in a gang dispute. My brother grew up to wear his manhood on his sleeve. And when he died, he was in that group – black, male and in its teens and early twenties – that is far and away the most likely to murder or be murdered. (Staples, 1987, p. 60)

African–American men often respond to these conditions by adopting a 'cool pose' which projects a tough exterior to the world and does not admit vulnerability (Majors and Billson, 1992). African–American men learn to be bicultural. In their own culture they are raised by women, their mothers, and have to assume at a young age important responsibilities around the house as the male of the household. Because three and a half times as many black households as white households are headed by women (Clay, 1975), African–American males score higher on androgyny scales than whites do (Franklin, 1984, p. 56). African–American men tend to participate in more egalitarian marriages where they are more supportive of their wives' working than are Caucasian men (Schaffer, 1981, p. 293). The stresses upon African–American men contribute to a divorce rate for middle class blacks double the percentage for white couples. African–American men find it hard to assume the breadwinner role because the dominant society holds them back. Many attend inferior schools, are not able to get good jobs, and hence are not able to live up to many expectations the dominant society has for men. Learning to dominate with a fiercely competitive spirit is often seen as crucial for black male survival, while in the dominant white society, passivity and noncompetitive behaviors are expected of African–American males. Such contradictory expectations are frustrating for African–American males, who have to figure out whether they want to do things the white way or the black way. In order to succeed in a white world, African–American males feel they have to be twice as good because they stand out and people are watching them. Because American society is based upon white masculine gender-role paradigms, African–American males must learn those paradigms as well as the roles and rules expected of them within their own culture. Dan, one of the men interviewed for this study, described how he had to adjust to different cultures:

> I wear a number of faces. At the university I'm a student where I can't be the same tough guy I have to be on the streets. When I go to work I try to act like a professional. When I go home I try to be a provider, or whatever. I'm Dad. I'm there to respond to others. My defenses are down. When I'm walking through the streets of the inner city my guard is up. These different faces are functional, necessary for my survival in that particular area.

Such expectations upon African–American men create tensions and anxieties to the point that African–American men are admitted to mental hospitals at twice the rate of white males (Gibbs, 1988).

Table 9.4 reports the differences in responses of African–American men and Caucasian men to messages used in this survey.

Table 9.4 indicates that, at age 18, African–American men and Caucasian men have statistically significant scores on only four messages and therefore have fairly similar notions of masculinity. At age 18, African–American males have a higher score for the 'warrior' message than Caucasian men because, as young men, they must in many cases be ready to do battle in order to survive. As Curtis put it, 'Fighting when I was a kid helped me remove some of my frustrations.' Many young African–American men angered by their life circumstances rely upon the 'warrior' message to help them release hostilities toward a racist world. At the same age African–American males scored lower than Caucasian men for 'stoic' and 'self-reliant', which indicates that they depend upon others for their well-being and talk to others about their pain more than do Caucasian men who may not confide in others as much as African–American

Table 9.4   Statistically significant differences between African–American and Caucasian males

Messages	African–American mean	Caucasian mean
Number	58	451
Adventurer*	2.33	2.38
Breadwinner†	2.35	1.58
Control†	2.22	1.80
Money†	1.94	1.72
Nature Lover†	2.61	2.86
Nurturer†	2.62	3.10
Self-reliant*	2.04	2.43
Stoic*	2.23	2.31
Superman†	1.31	1.26
Tough Guy†	1.51	1.16
Warrior*	1.86	1.54

* Influence as reported at age 18.
† Average age for African–American males, 35; average age for Caucasian males, 38.

males. Ratings for the 'adventurer' message are so similar that one can conclude that both African–American and Caucasian men place similar value upon this male gender-role expectation, although they may learn different ways to be adventurous depending upon the contexts in which they are raised. Since the differences in response to the 'adventurer' message are not very profound (0.05), it can be assumed that at age 18 African–American and Caucasian males differ in their responses on only three, or 13 per cent, of the dominant male messages in the United States.[7]

Older African–American males score at statistically different levels on seven or 29 per cent of the messages used in this study. This increase in difference over responses at age 18 indicates that, as African–American males grow older, they develop different male identities than their Caucasian counterparts. Most specifically, they value control, money and being a breadwinner more than Caucasian men. For an African–American male, being in charge of the family is an extremely important role, which unfortunately, judging from the statistics on single female-headed households, few are able to achieve. African–American men do not have the luxury of being nature lovers and nurturers. Working hard to survive, they are more involved in the roles of superman and tough guy than older Caucasian men.

The injuries of racism are the result of 250 years of slavery and 100 years of legally enforced segregation. In 1954 segregation was ruled illegal by the US Supreme Court. In spite of this legal ruling, African–Americans continue to receive prejudiced treatment where on average they live in more poverty, receive less education, and die at younger ages than whites. The difficulties of surviving place severe strains upon African–American men requiring them to adopt different coping mechanisms than their Caucasian counterparts. Older African–American males have to be supermen, to be tough, and to work hard in order to survive. Rather than being able to live out the American dream of affluence and comfort, many African–American males live in a nightmare of violence and unfulfilled expectations.

Hispanics

Hispanics form a cultural or ethnic group that involves many different cultures and races and reflects varied cultural traditions. In spite of these differences, notions of masculinity in Hispanic cultures revolve around the concept of machismo which has been defined as follows:

> The expression of exaggerated masculine characteristics, ranging from male genital prowess to towering pride and fearlessness. It also is a specific counterphobic attitude toward women, and the anxieties of life and death. (Aramani, 1972, p. 69)

Adult Hispanic males who believe in the myth of machismo invest considerable energy to prove their manliness. A macho man believes he is stronger and tougher than others. His sense of manly honor demands repayments of insults to himself and his family; revenge is usually physical and inevitable. Male supremacy and sexual prowess must be demonstrated. Characterized by an exaggerated masculinity, machismo manifests itself as aggressiveness and intransigence. It often covers up for male insecurity, especially among lower class men who experience low levels of employment. Machismo historically implies the qualities of gallantry, generosity, charity, and courage. A macho man, in the traditional sense, takes care of those around him whom he loves, family members and neighbors. Positive traits associated with machismo include dignity in conduct, respect for others, love for the family, and affection for children (Ruiz, 1981).

Hispanic families tend to be male dominated:

> The husband and father is the autocratic head of the household. He tends to remain aloof from the rest of the family. Few decisions can be made without his approval or knowledge. He is free to come and go as he pleases without explanation to or questions by other family members. In essence the father represents authority within the family. All other family members are expected to be respectful of him. (Murillo, 1971, p. 103)

The father is responsible for the economic support of the family. If he cannot provide adequately for his family, he loses respect.

Machismo may well be a prejudice about Hispanic male behavior and may not manifest itself very deeply within the United States. This myth is most closely related to Mexican–American men. The closer a man is to the Mexican culture, the more closely he may behave according to macho principles. Other Hispanic men who come from the Caribbean islands, Central or South America may not exhibit macho characteristics. Research among Mexican–American families even indicates that patterns of conjugal decision making tend to dispel the macho myth of male dominance (Hawkes and Taylor, 1975).

The degree to which Hispanic men portray characteristics different from the dominant patterns for male behavior depends upon the degree to which the men have been acculturated. Mendoza and Martinez (1984) developed a grid to evaluate cultural assimilation. This grid measures degrees of assimilation of the dominant culture and degrees of extinction of native cultural customs. It includes four different categories:

1. *Cultural resistance* – Active or passive resistance to dominant cultural patterns as depicted by lack of assimilation.

2. *Cultural shift* – Substitution of one set of practices with alternate cultural characteristics as exhibited by simultaneous assimilation and extinction.

3. *Cultural incorporation* – Adaptation of patterns that are representative of both cultural groups as demonstrated by assimilation without extinction.

4. *Cultural transmutation* – Alteration of certain elements of both cultures to create a third and somewhat unique subcultural identity. (p.74)

A discussion of Hispanic notions of masculinity would have to include an examination of how well a particular individual or group had assimilated to the US culture. A man from category one or two above would tend to be monocultural. An example from category one might include a recent immigrant who fled violence in a country like Guatemala, who lives in a place like Tucson, Arizona among other Guatemalans and does not speak English. An example of cultural shift might include a third generation Puerto Rican who does not speak Spanish, living in a suburb in Indianapolis. An example of cultural incorporation might include a second generation Chicano teacher in Denver who speaks Spanish and feels equally at home among Hispanics and in Anglo culture. Such a bicultural individual would be comfortable moving between both cultures. A totally distinct culture would be the Zoot suit culture which became popular in Los Angeles in the 1960s and 70s, or the Puerto Rican culture in New York which is a blend of island traditions and urban street smarts.

Unfortunately, this study does not include enough Hispanic men to make any observations about distinct Hispanic understandings of masculinity. By the year 2000 Hispanics will constitute 11 per cent of the population of the United States (Schaefer, 1990). Further studies will have to be conducted to determine what unique contributions these individuals are making to norms for appropriate male behavior and how their understandings of masculinity differ from dominant norms in the United States.

Asians

Recently many immigrants have left Asia and come to the United States, where the Asian population consists of 25 distinct subgroups with the largest percentages being Filipino, Chinese, Vietnamese, Korean, Indian, and Japanese. Once again, variety, rather than homogeneity, characterizes this ethnic group. Individuals from Asia share diverse cultural patterns and religions. People from the Philippines tend to be Catholic. People from India worship mostly Hindu traditions but also include Moslem, Jain, and Sikh beliefs. Many Chinese are either Buddhist or Taoist, while Japanese Buddhism is quite different than that practiced on mainland China. Many people in Japan consider themselves Shintoists.

Elders and men in most Asian societies are given higher status. Father is given the dominant status within the family, although he is subservient to grandfather and great-grandfather. Within the Asian culture children tend to honor and obey their parents. The pressure to succeed academically is very strong. Many Indians and Chinese migrate to Western countries with professional backgrounds to pursue higher education and stay here because there are more opportunities for them than at home.

The way Asian–Americans view behavior is influenced by their cultural perspective:

> The personality characteristics Asian–American men display are thought to be the result of cultural values that emphasize the need for control of emotional expression, self-control, sensitivity to the reaction of others, and the need not to behave in a manner that would reflect badly upon the family. Several points have to be made, however. First, not all Asian–American men fit this pattern. Large within-group differences exist.... Second, Asian–Americans do display a wide range of emotional reactions such as anger, insecurity, and jealousy to a number of different situations. Third, personality descriptions such as 'passive' and 'introvert' are considered negative in Western cultures, whereas in Asian cultures they are often seen as virtues reflecting filial piety (respect and obligation to parents), modesty, and respect for authority. (Sue, 1990, p. 157)

Many Asian men experience cultural stresses in the Western culture and have a hard time adapting to a culture very different than their own. Because of different facial characteristics, they experience prejudice and often are not able to get jobs commensurate with their academic training. Many recent Asian refugees – Cambodians, Vietnamese, Khmer, and Hmong – have experienced tremendous personal losses, did not have time to prepare to leave their countries, and fled because of dangers to their lives. Because of these hardships, they had to leave family members behind and experience homesickness, loneliness, and depression. Because many of these males speak no English, they cannot get jobs, which leads to a decrease in their status as men and increased feelings of powerlessness.

Many feel that their values are being eroded because of exposure to American culture.

Gay Men

Kinsey *et al.* (1948) discovered that homosexual behavior among men is widely spread throughout the male population in the United States. His study reported that 37 per cent of all men had at least one homosexual experience resulting in orgasm. Until very recently homosexuality has been viewed as a psychological disorder. In 1969 homosexual men and women in New York City resisted the tyranny of the New York police in an event that subsequently became know as the 'Stonewall Rebellion'. Ever since that time, gay men have been asserting their identity by 'coming out of the closet'. In 1973, the American Psychiatric Association removed homosexuality from its list of mental illnesses.

Research on gay men demonstrates that in general they fit the same characteristics as other men (Morin, 1975; Weinberg and Williams, 1974). Homosexuals cannot be isolated according to any particular traits with the exception that their sexual identity is gay. Homosexual men acquire gender identities similar to heterosexual men (Parker and Thompson, 1990), a finding collaborated in this study which had a population that declared itself to be 9 per cent gay and 3 per cent bisexual. A T-test of comparison run between homosexual and heterosexual respondents indicated no significant differences at age 18 and only two significant differences over time, where older heterosexual men indicated that the 'be the best you can' message was more influential than did gay men (2.41 vs 2.28; $p < 0.05$), while older gay men indicated that the 'superman' message was more influential than did older straight men (1.37 vs 1.28; $p < 0.05$). As did the adult minority respondents, adult gay men might feel alienated from the dominant heterosexual norms for masculinity because of prejudice directed against them and as a result start to generate different masculine identities as they grow older.

Gay men are not seen in popular culture as 'real' men because, by having sex with men, they behave like women. Because heterosexual behavior is seen as normal, many gay men (as will be seen below) report feeling different and hence insecure about their masculine identities. Many straight men feel threatened by gay men. Their dislike of homosexuality has been described as homophobia, which is an aversion to homosexuals and a desire to inflict punishment upon them (Weinberg, 1972). Gay men are often despised. Survivors in a world of disdaining families; hostile peers, violent attacks, and fanatical persecution, gay men experience prejudices which contribute to feelings of alienation. A gay man learns about himself in contrast to rather than as part of the larger society and often feels that his sexual identity is neither affirmed nor supported by the larger society. This experience of duality was confirmed by respondents who volunteered the following comments about being gay:

Growing up gay is very confusing, because all the messages you receive don't quite fit. It took me thirty years to feel good about the female side of me. Surprisingly, that made me feel more 'male'.

This culture's messages about a male supposedly being tough, aggressive, and dominant have never impressed me. Sometimes, I'll admit I like to play act these qualities, especially if I am with heterosexual men. Personally, I prefer men who are warm, caring and friendly.

I would say that when I was growing up, I had to hide my 'real' self when it came to my true feelings. Being a homosexual during the 1950s and 60s wasn't easy; in fact it was damn hard.

I have often wished that I had been born in, say, 1961 – instead of 1941. I can't help but believe that the entire process of 'coming out' – including accepting my own self – would have been so much easier. As it was, and I can't think of reasons other than cultural pressure – I did not actively start coming out till July, 1976 – when I was 35½, and was goddamned sick and tired of concealing my true self/nature. By then I was experiencing physical symptoms in addition to emotional ones.

Almost two years have passed since the 'coming out' process began, and I feel like I'm in a good position now to look back at my earlier life. I suppose I could blame society for my not wanting to accept my homosexuality; part of my problem with dealing with my orientation was that I never believed I fit any of those wonderful stereotypes that abound in this culture. The message I received (or at least interpreted) was that gays were bizarre weirdos with high voices and limp wrists; to be normal was to be a sports fanatic (I wasn't), a family man (complete with bitchy wife and 2.5 children, God forbid), and in complete control of one's emotions. This culture doesn't provide any image of gay life; historically it was viewed as an illness, and presently it's still looked at as a curiosity – something for people to gawk at on the news. Simply put, I do not meet this society's expectations as a man. I'm beginning to realize how much I've allowed other people's expectations to rule my life. I'm through with that. It's really very simple – society doesn't provide me with any recognizable role models, so I say screw society in general and live my life (finally!) the way it should be lived: free of guilt, free of fear, free of need for acceptance from people who I have no idea why I should be trying to please anyway.

I always knew I was different so it was fairly easy for me to reject traditional male models during high school. I rebelled against them and paid a high price in the social sense in high school. Then in college I 'mainstreamed' and became more traditional to gain more acceptance. Now I've found I can selectively choose from both sets of experiences.

As a gay man and as a cross-cultural trainer, I have thought a good deal about male identity development in this culture. It seems to me that in the absence of positive role models, many gay men like myself come to an identity later than their peers – we were denied a gay adolescence in a conformity-ruled high school environment – and so only slowly and painfully come to identity in our 20s and 30s (hence at least some of the 'adolescent' nature of the gay community like sexual experimentation, drug use, etc.).

Even though at age 18 there were no significant differences between gay and straight responses to the male messages used in this study, some gay respondents indicated that they did not identify with these messages, that their experience of becoming a man was essentially different than what they perceived the heterosexual society expected of men. Because of their sexual orientation, they had a gut feeling about their gender identities that they were different from other men. Gay men have to fight against social pressures to renounce their gayness and become 'normal'.

A gay male suggested when interviewed for this study that being gay was not so much a dichotomy with being straight but rather could be seen on a continuum. Homosexual men are loving of other men. Some heterosexual men are emotionally expressive to men but do not have sex with them. This continuum is not so much about sexual orientation but rather about how a man expresses his feelings towards other men. On this continuum, all men are homosexual in the same way that all men are feminine. Some men refuse to acknowledge their feminine sides, while others are in touch with their feminine sides and celebrate nurturing aspects of their being. In a similar way, some men who are intensely homophobic and do not recognize tender feelings towards other men would be at one side of this continuum. Bisexual men who can live in both cultures and express their love and sexuality with both men and women would be at the middle of this continuum. Gay men would be on the opposite side to homophobic men on this continuum that recognizes a man's love for other men. In this way all men could be rated as to how gay they are, insofar as they express love for other men, just as all men could be ranked according to how much they are in touch with the feminine sides of their personalities. In this way 'being gay' is not a sickness or an abnormality, but rather is a name for an emotional orientation where men are openly expressive towards other men. All men are capable of acknowledging their gayness, although some homophobic men deny that being emotionally open towards other men is something they want.

The conclusion to Chapter 6 of this book discusses how alienated most men are from each other. All men can learn from gay men more about being supportive to men. By acknowledging that they have homosexual tendencies, men can learn to celebrate their capacity for loving men. Under current cultural norms, where homosexuality is seen as a deviance, homophobic men deny themselves male nurturance that could greatly enrich their lives.

Conclusion

Masculinity, a social construct, consists of many different points of view. Each individual has his own notions of appropriate male behavior which he learns from his environment, so that rather than there being one, commonly accepted view of masculinity in any country, there are many different masculinities. Different perceptions of masculinity, like so many squares on a quilt, come together to produce an overall pattern that contains the similar elements used in this study. Each man constructs his own gender identity from these common themes.

Masculinity is a dynamic concept. The experience of becoming a man is open to a wide number of differing perspectives. Each different cultural group contributes its own understanding of male behavior which may or may not accord with the dominant understandings of masculinity. Each man has experiences in life which help him determine how to behave. Depending upon when a man is born, where he is raised, his religious training, his class, his sexual orientation, and his ethnic group or race, an individual will construct his own unique gender identity that contains characteristics he has acquired from the dominant culture, from his subculture, and from his own unique experiences. Many different notions of masculinity experienced within an individual's social history contribute to that man's gender identity. Both within an individual and within the broader culture there are antagonistic and clashing views of appropriate male behavior. Each man's experiences provide a lens through which he views the complex experience of being a man. These lenses constitute a set of eyeglasses that he wears as he travels through life.

Male behavior in any country can be represented by using the model of a marketplace. Imagine the marketplace as a downtown of a large city. Different men come into that public intersection wearing their different lenses. Some are speaking different languages. Some are on foot. Others are driving. The rich are in cabs, while the poor are begging. The point of this analogy is that, like the financial marketplace of Adam Smith, there seems to be an invisible hand at work in this male market. In spite of the vast difference between the background of all the men in the market, the behavior of these men contains similarities. The vast majority seem to follow certain patterns of behavior. Although there might be outbreaks of violence or accidents, certain social standards are respected. There may be an occasional terrorist, but on the whole there are enough common assumptions that in most societies the intersection works. This study indicates that dominant norms for masculinity are so powerful they override differences brought about by class, race, sexual orientation, age, and place of origin. Men get to their offices and reach their destinations, even though each unique individual may see that marketplace differently because of his unique lenses. The invisible hand is the dominant male paradigm that contains male messages used in this study. This paradigm promotes similar behavior among male members of a society even though those males may be clashing sharply because of economic, ethnic, and cultural disagreements.

Notes

1   This author has tried to raise funds to carry out a study that would indicate the unique contributions of these different regions to masculinity in the United States. So far, he has been unsuccessful. Such a study would require random digit telephone dialing to over 200 men in each of five different geographic regions in the United States and would cost about $75,000.

2   An analysis of variance was used to eliminate variables that did not have a significance score of less than 0.05 in tables 9.1, 9.2, 9.3 and 9.4.

3   Twenty per cent of the men in this sample said they grew up in lower class homes. It is hard to determine how representative a sample of class divisions in the United States this is because the United States census bureau does not keep data according to class differences.

4   The sample used here may not be truly representative of the lower class. Some men from the lower classes had difficulty participating in this study. In order to include the view of lower class men, this researcher distributed this questionnaire at an inner city laundromat and has conducted a workshop on male gender conditioning at a prison. Many men in those environments had a hard time relating to the methodology used in this study. They were neither used to thinking in such abstract concepts about their masculinity nor were they comfortable sharing their thoughts about manhood with a stranger who was a university professor. Many lower class men who are illiterate could not fill out a questionnaire as complicated as this. The men who did respond to this questionnaire who said they came from the lower class were all fairly well educated; therefore they may reflect values more indicative of the middle class status they have achieved even though they were raised in lower class homes.

5   A racial group left out of this discussion is American Indian, a group that constitutes approximately one per cent of the population in the United States. Only seven individuals who identified themselves as American Indians participated in this study. Furthermore, there has been precious little written about masculinity in American Indian cultures. Such notions revolve around the concept of being a warrior. (See discussion by Harvey in Chapter 7.) Being a warrior in American Indian culture involves much more than hunting and fighting. A warrior is expected to take care of tribal members, to pass on tribal traditions, to honor the Earth, and to be responsible for his family.

6   Because of the small size of this sample, the conclusions presented below should be seen as tentative, suggesting some generalized trends, but requiring further experimental verification.

7   The findings of this study in regard to the behavior of African–American men may be influenced by racial bias. African–American respondents to this research instrument administered by a Caucasian professor might present a guarded image of their views of masculinity. They may have tried to impress the professor and may not have been willing to express themselves openly, afraid to let a Caucasian man know how they really feel. A similar study conducted by an African–American researcher could determine the degree of racial bias in this study.

Chapter 10

Message Therapy

Self-esteem has a lot to do with how I view myself as a man. Also the people I meet bring out different sides of my manhood.

18-year-old high school student

Stanley Kubrick's movie, *Full Metal Jacket*, describes how in basic training soldiers are trained to be killers. Symbolically, all men wear rigid jackets which restrict their movements. As boys, they go through a similar kind of basic training into the rigors of masculinity. Without going to a specific camp, each boy has to discover how to provide for himself, how to achieve security, and how to interpret his world with a masculine schema. In modern technological societies men on their own without any recognized rites receive uniforms woven by cultural messages and the special attention they receive because of their male features. Like suits of armor, these uniforms provide a coat to protect the little boy within from a mean male world. These jackets also project an exterior that broadcasts what type of mannikin lives inside. Puppets pulled by gender-role norms, men are conditioned to wage war, support families, fight battles, coach teams, ignore sickness, hunt animals, play sports, camp in the woods, create problems, solve problems, build temples, join the Boy Scouts, despoil the environment, climb mountains, deny feelings, minister to the sick, and write books. Some men, wolves in sheep's clothing, do not understand why they act in destructive ways.

Through gender-role conditioning men enter adulthood with gender identi-ties that provide a specific persona, but most do not begin to understand why they wear that uniform until they reach their thirties. Their identities contain many myths about masculinity. The process by which they construct their gender identities is unconscious. One commentator on male gender has even compared the condition of men to that of fish swimming in the ocean (Brannon, 1985, p. 2). A fish has no understanding of how the water sustains him, just as a man has little appreciation of how cultural attitudes shape his behavior. Being clear neither about cultural expectations nor gender identity formation creates confusion amongst men. When does a boy know he is a man? When he gets drunk? When he gets laid? When he graduates from high school? When he marries? When he has his first child? When he divorces? When he joins the military? When he earns his first pay check? When he leaves home? Without rites of passage there is little clarity about what it means to be a man. Sifting through male messages to comprehend the type of jackets they wear represents a prime developmental challenge for all men.

Understanding the role of male messages that set standards for masculinity can help an individual develop ego integrity. Since the gender-role conditioning process is so implicit, i.e. it is neither taught in schools nor examined critically in families, men resemble drivers at night who have received a destination but neither understand the terrain they are travelling through nor why they turn in certain directions. Pulled by strong inner drives, they are on automatic pilot, not driven by an ego that has an authentic self-understanding, but rather by a little boy trying to live up to the demands of others. Becoming conscious of how gender norms influence behavior helps men figure out their own values. Such an awareness can start a therapeutic process whereby a man ceases being a puppet. He can then cut the metaphorical strings that are moving him around and achieve ego integrity by developing his own identity for his life's journey. Analyzing male myths can help men avoid some of the stresses of masculinity.

Gender-Role Strain

As researchers have pointed out, masculinity is full of risky and failure-prone expectations (Doyle, 1983; Jourard, 1968). Many problems occur when men develop their gender identities. Men who acquire negative self-images feel they are less masculine than other men. Full of hidden anxieties about whether they are properly gendered beings, males practice unhealthy behavior trying to prove their masculinity. They experience conflict when they cannot accomplish all the demands placed upon them and shame when they feel they cannot live up to standards spelled out by modern male messages. Conforming to the expectations for masculinity established by cultural conditioning creates many different kinds of strain:

1. Men are confused by contradictory male messages in complex contemporary societies.

2. Men are frustrated because they cannot live up to masculine standards.

3. Men are expected to perform destructive acts.

4. Men experience shame about their manhood.

These are now considered in turn.

Contradictory Male Messages

Difficulties in figuring out how to be a man in contemporary society come from the variety of roles available. Examples of men from different cultures, as well as constantly changing media images create a multiplicity of male models. As one respondent put it, 'I am mostly confused about my role as a male – receiving a multitude of messages (family, job, church, friends, support group, reading, self).' Male cultural messages place contradictory expectations which cause anxiety as men try to figure out how to live. A tough guy who is a neighborhood bully might feel bad because he also receives the 'good samaritan' message. A husband will not remain faithful if he follows the urges of the 'playboy' message. A rebel who breaks the law will get in trouble. A breadwinner who spends all his energies working to support his family cannot also nurture them. And a farmer who uses high doses of chemicals in order to create a profit has a hard time reconciling his farming practices with the demands of the 'nature lover' message. These contradictory pulls that exist within cultural beliefs cause 'gender-role strain' (Pleck, 1981) within the lives of individual men.

Each message has both a good and a bad aspect: The 'technician' message stimulates men both to create new medicines that save lives and to manufacture toxic chemical weapons. Warriors protect their families and loved ones but slaughter enemy children. Tough guys stand up for their rights but also hurt people. An executive does the best he can for his corporation even though his company creates environmental havoc. An adventurer takes bold steps to change the world, but also drops bombs on innocent civilians. Bosses develop an admirable degree of self-control but control the hopes of others. Stoics get the job done, even if it kills them in the process. Nature lovers grow flowers within suburban sprawls. Scholars reconstruct ancient cultures but also research biological weapons. Men who value money steal for it. Rebels break laws attempting to build a new social order. Presidents who defy international laws to promote the interest of their own countries push for the creation of the United Nations. Because of pressures to conform, a man may be forced against his moral principles.

Trying to reconcile the contradictory pulls of these messages is confusing. Men are told on their jobs to behave in upsetting ways. Social institutions require them to go against ethical teachings. Behaviors they exhibit at work cause tensions at home. Unique ethnic cultures provide messages that conflict with dominant male paradigms. Masculine demands within their gender identities make it difficult for males to develop genuine relationships. Demands to provide both for themselves and the people they love block spiritual development. Men face many dilemmas in the process of determining the kind of men they want to be.

Masculine Frustration

Being a man is frustrating. Men feel inadequate because society places unrealistic demands upon them. Ricardo mentioned biting his nails up to age 18 because he was anxious about his manhood. Joe explained how he was scared when he was young because he did not think he could live up to the standards expected of men:

My example is this: Say you've grown up and you're told not to cry, and yet crying is a natural thing. You're told it's bad and you can't stop doing it. It's like saying, 'A good man's nails never grow.' And your nails keep growing so you can't be a good man. It's a bind, a kind of fear, 'I don't want to let people know my nails are growing.' I feel ashamed of myself because I can't live up to these expectations and I live in fear that others are going to find out that I'm not what I'm supposed to be.

Adolescent males face cultural demands to be handsome, brilliant, athletic, kind, rich, sexy, devoted, skilled, tough, sensitive, rebellious, obedient, muscular, adventurous, brave, bold, and successful. Some teenagers with strong egos set their courses to scale such heights, but others neither receive the appropriate training nor have sufficient self-esteem to hazard such bold missions. Of course, there are the super stars who seem to accomplish the rigors of masculinity with ease, but the vast majority of males achieve neither fame nor fortune. They spend their years disgruntled because they cannot realize social expectations for their gender. Many men who achieve modicum levels of success feel like impostors. Even though others see them as succeeding, inside they feel a sense of failure because of unrealistic standards for male behavior.

Male Destruction

Most countries expect their male citizens to serve in the military where men are trained to defend their homeland. Men have deep instincts that urge them not to become the killers they are trained to be. Male dominated societies expect men to maintain a patriarchal world order at all cost, even if it requires using such awesome weapons as nuclear bombs. Male messages create societies that damage both human beings and the environment that sustains them (Baker, 1987, p. 10):

> Being a man meant suppressing certain natural instincts, among them the instinct to behave sensibly. Much later I understood the primitive wisdom that had created such irrational standards for boys to measure up to. It sprang from the fact that in perilous times a man may be required by his country to face death in battle. To fulfill that duty it helps if in early life you have been taught that being a man often requires conduct that is neither sensible nor natural, but nevertheless is honorable.

Why do men become so destructive?

Males honor those who live up to the demands of masculinity. War heroes are celebrated in novels, histories, newscasts, and television shows. Boys have to memorize the names of heroes who, as Bob Dylan said, 'have guns in their hands and God on their side'. Men reward those who uphold militaristic values by publishing autobiographies, writing biographies, bestowing medals, creating sculptures, paying generous salaries, and building halls of fame to house memorabilia of warriors who have exemplified male standards with distinction.

Such advertising, celebrating the honor of devotion to classical masculine ideals, encourages naive boys to swallow a bitter pill (Theroux, 1987, p. 235):

> I have always disliked being a man. The whole idea of manhood in America is pitiful, a little like having to wear an ill-fitting coat all of one's entire life. (By contrast, I imagine femininity to be an impressive sense of nakedness.) Even the expression, 'Be a man!' strikes me as insulting and abusive. It means: Be stupid, be unfeeling, obedient, and soldierly, and stop thinking. Man means 'manly' – how can one think 'about men' without considering the terrible ambition of manliness? And yet it is part of every man's life. It is a hideous and crippling lie. It not only insists on difference and connives at superiority, it is also by its very nature, destructive – emotionally damaging and socially harmful.

Living up to the cultural demands of masculinity is not only stressful and confusing. It is insulting, requiring men to disavow their humanity and embrace death, force, and brutality to gain the approval of other men.

Some men are reluctant to do what cultural messages demand, as illustrated by the following statement:

> I felt a lot of isolation due to my basic gentle nature and masculine physical nature. I got double messages of 'be good, honest, etc.' but the macho issue was more important.
>
> 34-year-old plumber (Caucasian)

Men are supposed to prove they have hard balls, but testicles are sensitive organs. Men have gentle tendencies that need protection from the rigorous demands of masculine conditioning.

> I find that our culture today really 'pushes' the macho, heroic male message, especially in the media. Personally, I feel my own male conditioning was developed through my own 'gut' feelings about who and what I want to be, and not through society's sports heroes or fashion models.
>
> 18-year-old construction worker (Caucasian)

Males blame themselves when they cannot live up to the inhumane demands their cultures place upon them.

Masculine Shame

Men feel a variety of different types of shame about their masculinity. Shame is the belief that the essence of my being is inadequate, unworthy or defective. Shame is distinct from guilt which is incident specific. Shame is more general, referring to a state of being. A person who experiences what John Bradshaw calls toxic shame feels flawed: 'Repair seems foreclosed since no change is really possible. In its ultimate sense, toxic shame has the sense of hopelessness' (Bradshaw, 1988, p. 19). Human beings experience shame when they are told that they are not good enough. Males are shamed for their inadequacies in the family, their coarseness with women, and their lack of sensitivity to the nurturing needs of children.

Males feel mortified when they cannot live up to society's expectations. They are ashamed if they cannot make the team and embarrassed by what male tribes expect of their members. Male shame also comes from female reproach about macho behavior. Each man in today's society hears manhood criticized:

> The quality of 'maleness' has guided those who require the model that 'maleness' depicts. Unfortunately, the model has changed over time and across people that one encounters. If acceptance is an important need in a man, then confusion will surely ensue. Personally, the role of men in society has come under great criticism recently. Relating to the 'male dominant' society has acquired a negative connotation. Previously, the male was supposed to be the dominant force in the family and the society. Now we are criticized for leaving the woman out of it. This is a qualitatively good evolution, but let us not 'cut down' a slow learner. Men and women should emphatically support each other and boost each other's efforts – not detract and criticize.
>
> 25-year-old salesman (Caucasian)

Men feel guilty about their inadequacies, almost as if they are born in mortal sin, committing the crime of being male.

Men learn shame in many different ways. Mothers angry at males discredit their son's being. Minority men feel devalued and insulted in a white culture. Lower class men feel shame about their social status. Men learn through cultural conditioning to be ashamed about their sexuality, a rich part of their being rigidly controlled by social norms. Gay men may fear their sexual desires are not normal. Curious boys experimenting with sexuality often bear emotional scars for life because of sexual contact with other boys. Older men doubt themselves when their sexual performance declines. Boys feel deep shame if they cannot earn the respect of other boys through the tough behavior demanded of them. Males who are expected to be successful experience self-doubt when they lose their jobs and cannot pay bills. Even though most social institutions have only one place at the top, a man who gets passed over for promotion or does not graduate at the top of his class feels bad due to male competition. Men striving to get ahead in the world work so hard that they alienate themselves from those who love them and feel a profound sense of loss. Climbing an upward ladder to gain respect requires them to step on others and leave behind friends. Men feel inadequate when they cannot live up to cultural images on television and blame themselves. Minority men feel shame because they do not possess features equated with success. Males also feel shame about their gender, identifying with other men who are publicly upbraided for being criminals, child molesters, or murderers. Bowed down with shame, it is hard for men to take pride in their identities (Bradshaw, 1990, pp. 66–7):

> In the internalization process, shame, which should be a healthy signal of limits, becomes an overwhelming state of being, an identity, if you will. Once toxically shamed, a person loses contact with his authentic self . . .

> Once one's feelings are bound in shame, one numbs out. This numbing out is the precondition for all addictions, because the addiction is the only way the person is able to feel. For example, a chronically depressed man who becomes a super achieving executive through his work addiction can feel only when he is working. An alcoholic or drug addict feels high with mood-altering drugs. A food addict feels a sense of fullness and well-being when his stomach is full. Each addiction allows the person to feel good feelings or to avoid painful ones. The addiction mood alters the hurt and pain of the spiritually wounded inner child. The spiritual wound inflicted by toxic shame is a rupture of the self with the self. One becomes painfully diminished in one's own eyes; he becomes an object of contempt to himself.

The strain of trying to live up to the demands of masculinity creates deep wounds which must be healed if men are to achieve a healthy self-respect. Men try unsuccessfully to mask their feelings of shame through accomplishment (Bradshaw, 1988, p. 84):

> Unfortunately, accomplishments do not reduce internalized shame. In fact, the more one achieves, the more one has to achieve. Toxic shame is about being; no amount of doing will ever change it.

Angry individuals who act out of shame seek revenge for their wounds. They do not approach other men with trust but rather view them with suspicion, as competitors. The only way to heal such wounds is through love, but men must first learn to love themselves before directing their nurturing energy to healing others. The 'nurturer' message gives men permission to use their capacity for love, but most males do not celebrate their nurturing abilities because those aspects of masculinity are not honored in patriarchal cultures that venerate warriors and tough guys.

Many aspects of male gender-role conditioning are fatal to men who die at all ages at higher rates than women, who occupy more beds in mental hospitals, who commit more suicides, who live in the streets, and who languish in cells in prisons. Understanding the patterns of male gender-role conditioning can help identify the sources of male gender-role strain in modern societies.

Cracks in Patriarchy

Patriarchy, as much a way of thinking as a characterization of society, promotes norms that men are taught to value in order to promote a social order that benefits a few men, while it oppresses many others. Patriarchy, because it demands that men repress their emotions in order to carry out manly tasks, creates many of the strains described above. Men who successfully conform to standards contained within classical male messages that sustain patriarchy are rewarded when they become heads of state, generals, movie stars, corporate executives, and athletic heroes, while men who rebel against this social order are ridiculed, jailed, ostracized, or killed.

Previous studies about men have observed the grossest of male actions – the killings of soldiers, the driving competitiveness of business men, the obsession with winning that dominates sports, the greed of politicians, the lack of involvement of fathers in family life – and drawn from these observations the conclusion that male gender conditioning supports patriarchy. These accounts are accurate insofar as men are trained for patriarchal roles within contemporary societies, but this study indicates that classical male messages supporting patriarchy are not as influential as other, more positive notions of appropriate behavior men get from their homes, families, peers, and religious activities. A corporate culture promotes images of hard driving men, but these men have complex identities that differ from popular images.

An example of this discrepancy is the low rating given the 'money' message. Capitalist culture places a great deal of importance upon the value of money. Many social observers have commented upon how hard men work to earn money, a key to status and power. However, only one of the over five hundred men who responded to this survey instrument indicated that 'money' was the most important message in his life. Men are expected to earn money but the respondents to this survey rate it as the least important message in their lives, which indicates that classical notions of masculinity that support a patriarchal world order may not dominate men's identities. Rather than being shallow puppets driven by neoclassical advertising images, men develop their own unique identities that allow them to feel good about themselves. Men in the modern world have a hard time reconciling their own sense of self-worth with social institutions that expect them to compete for rewards.

Women help insulate men against the harsh demands of patriarchy. If boys were raised in locker rooms by stern coaches, they might grow up in a sequestered male environment that focused only on winning. However, findings in Chapter 2 indicate that boys are mostly raised by mothers who tend to be the nurturing parent. Not all men conform to the rigorous expectations of classical masculinity. Boys acquire messages about how to behave from significant women – their mothers, wives, girlfriends, sisters, aunts, friends, and co-workers. Because of these influences, men have within their identities personality traits typically considered feminine, which have been named by Carl Jung (1928) as the anima. This feminine side of the male personality contradicts the influence of patriarchal myths about masculinity.

This study shows that classical norms for male behavior – 'work ethic', 'self-reliant', 'be the best you can', 'tough guy', 'breadwinner', 'president', 'adventurer', 'control', 'stoic', 'hurdles', 'sportsman', 'playboy', 'superman', 'warrior' and 'money' – exist in contemporary culture, but their influence upon individuals is not as important as other messages which they receive from people who love them. As one respondent indicated on a questionnaire, 'I would say my family, friends and teachers have influenced me the most. Others that have influenced men are TV, sports, and movie heroes.' Men also have spiritual lives that motivate compassionate behavior.

The ordering of the patterns of male behavior in this study reveals the kind of behaviors valued by men. They find keeping the standards and working to be more influential in their lives than being lovers. But they also indicate that being bosses and rugged individuals is less important than being lovers. Men may be coached, forced, or cajoled by employers, fathers, friends, peers, and teachers to be subservient to patriarchy, but other values also motivate them. They are influenced by their culture to obey laws, to be the best they can, to love nature, to be good samaritans, scholars, technicians, faithful husbands, and nurturers. The social construction of masculinities provides both positive and negative models of male behavior. This is good news. If we are going to construct healthy male identities that nurture life on this planet, we cannot simply lecture men, hoping through punishment or ridicule that they will change. Putting men down or criticizing them creates shame and makes them defensive and hostile. This study points out positive aspects of male gender identities which can be reinforced in an attempt to rectify the wrongs of patriarchy.

> Men are not 'kings of the mountain' as commonly believed in our paternalistic society. We must co-exist in a loving and natural manner with the world around us. We can never close our minds to new ideas and concepts and always be willing to share our knowledge.
>
> (33-year-old unemployed Caucasian)

Men neither have to be puppets responding ignorantly to the harsh demands of classical masculinity nor resign themselves to live according to the dictates of a destructive patriarchal world. Masters of their own destiny, they can throw off straitjackets and choose how to relate to the world. The kind of clothes they wear will reflect their visions. A dominant vision for life in Western societies has been that of a race through a jungle where it is each man out for himself, playing the game of life according to patriarchal principles that reward men of action. As the bumper sticker says, 'The one who dies with the most toys wins!' A society with liberating expectations for men would restructure gender-role conditioning so that men do not have to obey patriarchal commands, but could dedicate their lives to equality.

No society is static. Earlier epochs of history revolved around an agrarian social order which allowed a kind of conformity that does not exist in technological societies. Modern challenges to classical masculinity by gay men, feminists, men from different racial and ethnic groups, peaceful warriors, and environmentalists cause discomfort for men who still want to be frontiersmen and elect leaders like Ronald Reagan to reinforce classical myths of masculinity. While these myths have existed for many hundreds of years, images of masculinity that establish norms for male behavior are slowly changing in an information-based economy. A classical paradigm for male behavior in the United States is the lone ranger living in a world of unlimited resources, who carves a home for his family in the wilderness, taking from the land and using force to get his way. Such rugged pioneer images cause great pain in the modern world, where men kill, rape, and pillage the environment. Males who follow these tough dictates are wound up to self-destruct. Individuals who understand how dysfunctional these classical notions of male behavior are in modern societies are starting to challenge gender-role expectations that promote the superiority of the male species.

The Role of Men's Groups and the Ways Men Change

Some males who question hazards associated with a patriarchal world order are joining men's support groups seeking new identities. In these groups they reveal themselves and find to their surprise that other males experience similar strain about gender conditioning, the full metal jackets they have been taught to wear. This is already happening in modern industrial societies, where small fledgling collections of men are finding ways to challenge patriarchy by creating new patterns of masculinity. These groups take many different forms that provide insights into patriarchal conditioning. Some support men going through divorce. Bisexual and gay men deal with issues of sexual orientation. Men of color discuss the impact of racism upon their gender identities. Some groups organize men against sexism. Others struggle for fathers' rights. Many promote personal growth. These groups provide support for men struggling with the unrealizable demands of the patriarchal societies they inhabit.

Men's groups allow men in modern societies to disclose to each other and to make deep contact with other men, overcoming psychological isolation from their brothers, speeding up a process of male intimacy that used to be part of a man's heritage. In agrarian societies men lived and worked together in cottage industries and family farms, which allowed trust through close male contact. They hung out in extended families with uncles, brothers, and cousins. In modern information-based societies where men work by themselves behind computer terminals, males fill the void that comes from not having intimate contact with other men with work, or drown their loneliness in alcohol or drugs. Men's support groups allow men to talk to each other about problems they are having living up to the demands of patriarchy without fearing that the men listening will pounce on their weaknesses. They teach men how to be expressive to other men. They allow a man to share with his brothers pain he has experienced because of the shackles of classical masculinity.

Most men resist change because they neither admit oppression nor feel they have to change. Secure in the comfort of their possessions, they do not realize their vulnerability until some crisis forces them to become aware of their shackles. Gender conditioning from 'stoic', 'tough guy', 'self-reliant' and 'superman' messages teaches men to deny they have problems. Men stick with the status quo until divorce, addiction, or stress related medical problems hit them. Because many men fear losing privileges, they will not change. Men's groups support individuals willing to try out new wardrobes.

Men also change their identities when they go through crises. It takes a crisis to crash through tough defenses. Most men respond to crises by being stoical. In its most extreme form male stoics respond to crises by committing suicide. In order to ask for help they have to be dissatisfied. Job loss, heartbreak, medical emergencies, and separations from their children have compelled many men to examine critically *their* classical male conditioning. Male stoics store deep pain within. As many as one fourth of the men in the United States are survivors of abuse (Johnson and Shrier, 1985). If they deny the pain that comes from the many different ways they are abused, they will spend the rest of their lives in misery, pushing people away, and making enemies. Each time that pain comes to the surface, trying to get out so that its owner may experience health, another crisis occurs. These crises force men to re-examine their behavior. Men have to realize that they are having problems before they take the first steps to developing healthy identities. They have to want to change. Nobody can force a man to undergo a hero's journey of personal self discovery.

There are sudden changes and developmental changes in men's identities. Chapter 3 outlines the developmental changes all men experience as they strive for ego integrity. At first, their gender identities are filled by the values of those who love them. They behave in certain ways because they want parental approval. Next, in their adolescence they act to gain support from peers, in order to be accepted into the brotherhood of men. In their twenties and thirties men strive for competence, but also in their thirties they start making choices about how they want to live. In their forties they start focusing on their own needs. Feeling they no longer have to please others, they adopt standards they respect. Some men change their gender identities because they realize life is a journey in a rich world with many different cultures. Thrilled by the adventure of new discovery, they eagerly try on many different jackets.

Why do men consciously change their gender identities? Men change because they receive new images of masculinity from the men they respect. They learn the language of feelings from women. In the supportive environment of a men's group, males can reward each other trying out multicolored coats. Men need role models of other men who have courageously challenged the assumptions of patriarchy, new warriors who follow the promptings of their hearts and not the commands of their pig parent pursuing male domination. Such a warrior challenges social conventions about masculinity by trying on different masculine costumes. A new warrior is self-nurturing. He makes conscious choices about how he wants to live his life. He is self-nurturing, rooted in his community and cares for others in that community. He knows how to parent himself and others. A friend who can make love to people without abusing them, he honors both his feminine and masculine sides. He admits mistakes. He plays with his inner child, has concern for others, listens well, and expresses his feelings. He selects his gender-role models or sexual orientation. He shares domestic chores. He attempts to be one with the Earth and seeks to be in harmony with larger rhythms. He is not afraid to ask for help. He embraces change because he appreciates his own growth. Men will open their hearts around other men who have opened their hearts.

Males who use men's support groups to experiment with new forms of masculinity have benefited from such changes. Because the love experienced within these groups helps heal wounds caused by gender-role strain, participants can relate to the world out of love instead of mistrust. Men who have opened their hearts do not have to live in fear that some 'devil will draw them into eternal damnation'. By spending less energy accumulating toys and trying to be the boss, they will have more friends. They will live longer and have more to look forward to as they age, knowing that life can be one great spiritual voyage. Male standard bearers who have struggled against the rigors of classical patriarchy can take pride in their courageous attempts to produce new patterns of masculinity.

Patterns of Masculinity

In spite of the wide diversity of cultures that influence the way individuals see the world, this study indicates that there are similarities in the ways that men construct their gender identities. Masculinity in modern technological societies contains common themes that connote different personality types. Each one of the factors used in this study – 'Standard Bearers', 'Workers', 'Lovers', 'Bosses' and 'Rugged Individuals' – describes patterns of masculinity that some men will incorporate into their identities more than others, while many men identify with aspects of each of these factors.

Men who value the messages found within the factor 'Standard Bearers' – 'scholar', 'nature lover', 'be the best you can' and 'good samaritan' – tend to be spiritual, have high moral convictions that motivate their behavior, and live according to principles that come from the *Bible*, the *Koran*, or other ethical teachings. They strive to improve the world. Their rewards come from realizing their standards and from helping others. Critical of those who hold different values, zealous standard bearers try to convert others to their points of view. Standard bearers tend to be crusaders who make sacrifices to convince others of the correctness of their values, believing that a good world would be one in which everybody adopted their standards.

The 'Workers' category contains the messages 'technician', 'work ethic', 'money' and 'law'. Men who identify with these messages tend to be hard workers who trust that their efforts will be acknowledged. Those who are not rewarded can become cynical and bitter. They strive to improve the world through action and appeal to community accepted ethical standards to create social cohesion. They believe that hard work will bring success, that perseverance will be rewarded, and that human beings are basically destructive. Laws, police, courts, and punishments are necessary in order to provide security.

These conforming men enforce traditions.

Men who are 'Lovers' ('breadwinner', 'nurturer', 'faithful husband' and 'playboy') value friendships. They value personal relationships and maintain interpersonal support systems. Sensitive lovers will make themselves vulnerable but, if they get hurt, will build a shell to protect them from future pain. They appeal to the good in others. Such a perspective leads to a cooperative vision of the world, communicating to build a beloved community. Male lovers feel responsible for the well-being of the larger group, understanding that the group will not be healthy if any member suffers.

Men who have been influenced by the messages within the 'Bosses' factor ('control', 'hurdles', 'president', 'adventurer', 'sportsman', 'be like your father' and 'warrior') see the world as a jungle that is best characterized by survival of the fittest. These social Darwinists have to climb to the top in order to survive. Like Plato and Nietzsche, they believe in a warrior class that has both the right and the obligation to lead others who have neither the wisdom nor the training to take care of themselves, let alone rule others. Men who value standards implied within the 'Bosses' factor strive to become members of the ruling class and to maintain its traditions. Their elitist perspective contains a certain *noblesse oblige* to care for others. Behaviors encouraged by the messages clustered within the 'Bosses' factor support the existing patriarchal order.

The factor 'Rugged Individuals' which contains the messages 'self-reliant', 'stoic', 'rebel', 'tough guy' and 'superman', prepares men for a free marketplace where every man is out for himself. This dangerous world of nuclear weaponry requires peace through strength to protect the wealth greedy men acquire. Each man has a chance to succeed. It is his fault if he fails. Rugged individuals distrust government interference. They hate paying taxes and bear arms for protection. These lone rangers have a libertarian philosophy of self-reliance, where they want freedom to pursue their own dreams without having to accommodate others. A social system built by rugged individuals thrives on competition. These men stand alone and do not admit vulnerabilities.

Studying male messages can be a kind of therapy, helping men become commanders of their own destinies as opposed to responding to the commands of various captains, bosses and fathers, who bark out orders to their subordinates. Each of these patterns of masculinity connotes a specific way of looking at the world. Understanding the impact of these factors upon the male psyche helps explain male behavior. These different factors illustrate the complexity of masculinity in postmodern societies. A holistic understanding of modern manhood demonstrates that men are not just rugged individuals (as many have emphasized), but also have high moral standards that motivate their behavior. Patterns of masculinity support patriarchy but also encourage men to rebel against the destructive aspects of patriarchy. Masculine ideology may have destructive tendencies but it also has prescriptions for a healthy planet. In order to construct a more nurturing world, men have to be liberated from the oppressive aspects of masculinity contained within the factors 'Bosses' and 'Rugged Individuals' and encouraged to pursue the behaviors implied by 'Standard Bearers', 'Workers' and 'Lovers'. Males have the potential to serve their fellow human beings in many positive ways. They should not allow the negative aspect of male gender conditioning to block that potential.

A strong conclusion of this research is that men's self images differ remarkably from the way their personalities are portrayed both in the popular media and in scholarly presses. This study has described how men see themselves. Their constructed gender identities – which contain notions like good samaritan, scholar, nature lover, be the best you can, and nurturer – provide positive motivations. That these findings differ so much from other accounts of masculinity indicates both a strength and weakness of this research. The strength of this study comes from the diversity of stories told. This is not one man's account of masculinity but rather reports on how a diverse sample of 560 men respond to male cultural stereotypes. The weakness of this study is that it is retrospective and relies upon the psychology of the remembered past. Such self-reports by participants in this study may be considerably more positive than the actual reality of their lives.

This study demonstrates that within the identities of men are complex messages that steer them towards healthy behavior. They can construct positive gender identities and discard negative messages that urge them to exploit others. In order to adopt healthy identities better suited for the challenges of the twenty-first century, men can search inside themselves to find what they truly value, replace those messages that cause strain, transform those that are not healthy, and accept those that bring joy.

Younger men still trying to figure out who they are can become more conscious of the impact of male messages upon their identities. Many of the 96 men interviewed for this study commented voluntarily that examining the role of male messages in their identity formation had been very helpful. Tony commented:

> I've had these thoughts sort of scoot by in my head, but to actually put them into words and say them to another person. It's real powerful. I feel like I'm coming out of the closet to you. I am talking about stuff that is my core. These are my core beliefs about life.

Bruce stated, 'I should do this very often, it's very therapeutic.' Malcolm said:

> Understanding these male messages is therapeutic insofar as I am now able to assess things in more concrete ways. I can think more now about my messages meaning something in my life. It gives you a perspective in knowing yourself, and that is a strong goal of mine, self-discovery, to know myself.

When a man achieves ego integrity, his self-concept reflects his reality. Each man has a pattern of the messages that he uses to construct his gender identity. A key developmental challenge is for each man to realize a vision that ennobles his existence. Achieving ego integrity requires men to live for that vision, not blaming others for problems, but taking full responsibility to achieve their goals.

A generative man conforms his dreams to a vision of a less androcentric and more just social order by challenging the negative aspects of classical masculinity to create a world where other humans can achieve their dreams. In its highest state, masculinity draws upon the positive features of male messages to create a world where all human beings achieve generativity and ego integrity. That struggle cannot take place blindly. It depends upon understanding the complex process by which men construct their gender identities.

Appendix: Methodology

This book summarizes a seven-year research study conducted during the 1980s. This research study had three stages. During the first stage a questionnaire was developed. This investigation began in 1982 in a class on male identity at the University of Wisconsin-Milwaukee where the author asked students to identify two gender-role messages they received from their culture that helped to define what it meant to be a man. Workshops with diverse groups of men – a support group for violent men, seminars for men interested in changing male identities, and meetings with school administrators – helped create a list of male messages further refined during 1983 with men from all major ethnic and racial groups, social classes, and ages. A list of 30 different messages generated by these activities was placed into a questionnaire. During 1984, 120 men in the Midwest responded to this questionnaire by indicating the degree of influence these messages had upon their lives. An item analysis helped remove items from this questionnaire that did not correlate with the whole instrument. Further refinement was done during a three-hour workshop at the Great Lakes Men's Conference held in Madison, Wisconsin during September 1984. As a result of these analyses a new questionnaire was developed with 24 messages.

During the second stage of this research project this questionnaire has been field tested, refined, and distributed for a final sampling. A second scale was added to the questionnaire asking men to indicate how the influence of these messages has changed since they were 18. This scale was added when respondents indicated during the first run of the questionnaire that, because the influence of these messages changed over time, they found it difficult to rate it. In this text, responses to this second scale will be reported as men's responses to these messages over time. The average age of the 470 respondents to this scale is 37. Eighteen was chosen because it is a time of transition, when men graduate from high school, leave home, join the armed forces, start working, etc. – events which help establish that year as an important moment between childhood and the responsibilities of adulthood. A field test of the new questionnaire was conducted during 1985 with a sample population of 200 men, 78 per cent of whom grew up in the Midwest. A reliability test done on this instrument produced a coefficient α of 0.80. Further refinements were made as a result of this test and the final distribution of the questionnaire was carried out from 1986 to 1989.

A factor analysis was conducted on the variables to determine how they might group together and has provided the basis for organizing the second part of this book, which presents case studies about these messages. Pearson's correlation was used to determine how different variables in this study correlated with each other. This analysis indicated positive and negative relationships between the 24 messages. Only those scores that were statistically significant ($p \leq 0.05$) will be reported. Furthermore, only those scores with a positive r value of greater than 0.250 will be considered to have a significant correlation. When the r score between two values falls below 0.250, no significant relationship will be reported because of the small percentage of respondents who considered that there was a correlation between the two variables. Negative scores are reported because of the interesting trends they suggest. An r score greater than 0.25 indicates that at least 6 per cent of the respondents thought there is a significant correlation between two variables.

During the final part of this research study four men were interviewed for each message to determine how that man got one gender-role message, how that message influenced that individual, and how he adapted to that message throughout his life. These men were asked to talk about the most important message in their lives. During this stage, in order to observe the influence of these messages upon working class men, the author joined an industrial bowling league in Milwaukee, Wisconsin and served as a counselor of men who had been ordered to receive counseling for their violent behavior as an alternative to incarceration.

A T-Test of comparison was conducted on the sample of men interviewed and the total sample of respondents. The only significant difference between these populations ($p \leq 0.05$) occurred for the 'nurturer 2' message, where the men interviewed indicated that over time the 'nurturing' message had a greater influence on their lives than the total population of men responding to the questionnaire. It can therefore be assumed that the 96 men interviewed are in most ways similar to the total sample of 560 men who filled out this questionnaire.

Objections might be raised about a methodology that asks men to recall the influence of these messages at age 18. After interviewing many men, some of whom have been over 60, the author is convinced that these messages are sufficiently powerful that individuals have strong recollections of their influence when they were younger. It is a significant demonstration of the importance of these messages that older men in their sixties and seventies have been able to recall clear details about them. Individuals have not complained about any difficulty in remembering that far back into their past, although the accuracy of their reactions can always be questioned. Although a sample that relies upon memory is influenced by the subjective interpretation by respondents, perception provides important interpretations of reality.

Comments from Respondents

The questionnaire used in this study contains an open stem asking respondents to state anything they would like to say about their own male conditioning or cultural messages that have influenced their identity as men. From time to time in the narrative these comments will be quoted anonymously. During the final stage of the research project 96 men have been interviewed, four men for each of the 24 messages, and their comments recorded and transcribed. Quotations from these interviews will appear in the text with a fictitious name, and a brief description of these people so named appears in the text. Summaries and interpretations of these narratives will appear in Part II of this book which describes the content and influence of these messages.

These interviews have been conducted to provide a broad overview of what these male messages mean. Interviewing these men and hearing how they have adjusted their lives to gender standards has been a truly remarkable experience. As the reader will appreciate, this diverse sample includes respondents from different race and class backgrounds, many of whom have been friends and acquaintances of the author. Some may object that personal knowledge of the people interviewed would bias the results of this study. Knowing many of the participants in this study has enhanced it, because of the trust level established between interviewer and interviewee. Most men will not disclose personal secrets to a stranger. Knowing many of the men interviewed provided this researcher with important insights into their personalities and behavior, while also enabling a degree of confidence with the interviewer that might not have been possible in a more 'objective' study conducted by a stranger. This author is greatly indebted to all those men who have shared their lives for this study.

How Representative a Sample is This?

A variety of validity checks, both indirect and direct, have been conducted to determine how validly these messages reflect the experiences of men in the United States. The factor analysis produced results that might have been expected: 'adventurer', 'money', 'hurdles', 'president', 'sportsman' and 'warrior' all grouped together with positive weights ($>.04$), and this factor contained negative weights for 'good samaritan', 'law' and 'scholar'. Another grouping produced the following sets of results: 'rebel', 'self-reliant', 'stoic', 'superman' and 'tough guy', with negative weights for 'technician' and 'nurturer'. A third grouping included the following messages, 'good samaritan', 'nature lover' and 'nurturer' which related negatively with 'be the best you can', 'breadwinner', 'money', 'hurdles', 'playboy', 'president', 'superman' and 'tough guy'. A person familiar with male behavior in the United States would expect these variables to be clustered in such a manner. That they do so group provides face validity for the messages used in this study, indicating that this research methodology has produced results which reflect common understandings of the experiences of men.

Table A   Rank ordering of those messages whose influence increased from time respondents were 18

Nurturer
Nature Lover
Scholar
Be the Best You Can
Good Samaritan
Work Ethic
Technician

Another validity check of this research methodology came from the second scale on the questionnaire which asked men to indicate how the influence of the messages has changed since age 18. Respondents indicated on a five point Likert scale that went from much less influence to much more influence (the midpoint was no change) how the influence of that message has changed in their lives. Gender research describes a process of development a man goes through in forming his gender identity. At first gender-role behavior is oriented to avoidance of punishment and the desire to satisfy needs. Later, gender-role behavior is oriented to following rules for appropriate gender behavior. Finally, as an individual matures, he or she shrugs off some of the rigid gender-role expectations and adopts a self-formed identity. In this research study, the influence of all the male messages decreased for the participants except the messages which are listed in Table A in a rank order, with the message that increased the most at the top of the list and the messages that increased the least at the bottom.

The average score for the influence of other more traditional messages decreased. Those messages listed above with the exception of 'work ethic' and 'technician' that increased are fairly nontraditional and reflect the values and behaviors that men adopt as they mature and cast off some of the rigid gender-role expectations from their younger years. This finding correlates with research on adult development.

A more direct test of the validity for the results of this study has been conducted by comparing demographic information about the sample of men who responded to this questionnaire with statistical information about men in the United States as provided by the United States Census Bureau. For this to be a valid sampling of men in the United States it should be a random sample of men from all parts of the country that includes men from all different age groups, races, and occupations.

One 'scientific' way to conduct such a study would be to create a random digit dialed telephone sample of men in the United States, getting over 200 men from six different geographical regions in the United States to respond to these messages, so that comparisons could be made between men who grew up in different areas such as the Southeast and the Midwest. Such a 'scientific' sampling would have enabled valid comparisons between men from different regions of the United States but would have cost in 1986 over $50,000. Proposals have been submitted to raise money for such a study but none has been funded.

Table B   Geographic characteristics of sample

Region of country	Number of respondents	Percentage
Northeast	70	13
Midwest	351	63
West	69	13
Southcentral	23	4
Southeast	14	2
Other	33	5
Total	560	100

Lacking financial support, the author has had to use a 'sample of convenience' where friends from different parts of the country have helped distribute the questionnaire, but the majority of respondents (64 per cent) grew up in the Midwest. This sample may not accurately describe how these messages influence men throughout the United States, but it does include men from all regions. The country was divided into sections which contain roughly equivalent numbers of individuals according to standard census divisions of the United States. Table B provides responses to a stem that asks men to indicate in what part of the United States they attended junior high and high school.

The category 'Other' includes either men from Alaska or Hawaii or men who attended junior high and high school in more than one place. The lack of men from the South is seen as a limitation in this study's ability to represent the experiences of all men in the United States. This sample is strongly biased towards men who live in and grew up in the Midwest.

Many of the individuals who responded to this survey came from Wisconsin and most specifically from the standard metropolitan statistical area of Milwaukee. An advantage of a Midwest sample, and most particularly a sample that includes individuals from the Milwaukee area, is that Milwaukee is commonly used as a test market by large corporations (Daniell, 1989). Individuals in this part of the United States fit a standard for average. If it can sell in Milwaukee, market researchers argue, it can sell anywhere in the United States. The age breakdown of Milwaukee's population, its household income, and education levels closely mirror national averages.

The majority of respondents to this questionnaire who have grown up in the Midwest can be seen as representatives of middle America. This sample is not overly influenced by respondents from areas like San Francisco, California; Newark, New Jersey; Dallas, Texas, or New York City, which might be seen to exhibit extreme tendencies of male behavior.

Seventy-three per cent of the respondents indicated they grew up in middle class families, 20 per cent in lower class families, and 7 per cent in upper class families. Although this sample may not exactly mirror class divisions in the United States, it does include a significant number of respondents from all classes.

In other demographic characteristics (age and race) with the exception of educational level, these respondents provide a representative sample of men in

Table C   Employment status

Status	Percentage
Employed	60
Unemployed	21
Part Time Employed	14
Retired	4

the United States. Eighty-two per cent of the men sampled were Caucasian. Eleven per cent were African–American. Four per cent were Hispanic; 2 per cent were Asian–American, and 1 per cent were American Indian. The average age of respondents was 30. Eighteen per cent of respondents were under nineteen. Eight per cent were over 60. Thirty-two per cent of the respondents were veterans. Fifty-one per cent had children. Nine per cent of the respondents considered themselves homosexual; 3 per cent bisexual. Table C indicates the employment status of respondents.

During the period that these data were collected (1985–1989), the unemployment level in the United States varied from 8 to 5 per cent. Even though experts have stated that the official unemployment rate is half the actual number of unemployed people, the unemployment rate for respondents to this questionnaire is considerably higher than might be expected from a representative sample of men in the United States. The high percentage of unemployment and part-time employment of this sample can be explained by the fact that many of the respondents were students.

Table D indicates the marital status of respondents. The 1987 edition of *Statistical Abstracts of the United States* indicates that during the year 1985, 53 per cent of the men in the United States were married and 18 per cent were single. The above table indicates that 54 per cent of the men in this sample had at one point in their lives been married. The high percentage of single men in this sample again indicates that many of these questionnaires were distributed through universities and high schools, and hence a high proportion of respondents were single.

Table E compares the occupational categories of men responding to this questionnaire with occupational categories of men according to *Statistical Abstracts of the United States* (1987).

The high percentage of professional men and the lower percentage of

Table D   Marital status

Status	Percentage
Married	40
Divorced	14
Single	43
Separated	3

Table E   Occupational categories for males in the United States

Category	Percentage respondents	Percentage males in U.S. labor force
Clerical and Sales	10	16
Craftsperson	11	20
Manager or Proprietor	11	12
Operative	5	15
Service	9	11
Professional	28	11
Unskilled Laborer	8	7
Other	18	8

unskilled labourers, operatives and craftspeople indicates a bias of this study, that it relies too much upon professional men and not enough upon people who work with their hands. The high percentage of respondents who replied 'other' comes from difficulties in interpreting the categories used in this study. These headings come from standard census tracts used by the US Census Bureau and provided opportunities for comparison. Some men, who checked 'other' said they were engineers, self-employed, musicians, or even retired. Many students did not fit these occupational categories. Many checked 'other' when they could not figure out into which category their employment fitted. A couple of men who worked for the Coast Guard also checked this category. It is significant that men from all occupational categories are represented in this sample.

Thirty per cent of the respondents had experience with a men's group. Men's consciousness raising and support groups are a phenomenon that began in the 1970s among men questioning traditional male gender-roles. The author of this book has been in four men's groups (one in 1974 in Philadelphia, another in 1976 in Milwaukee, a group for Batterers' Anonymous which he facilitated in 1987 in Milwaukee, Wisconsin, and an integration group he currently attends that grew out of a new warrior training experience held in Kenosha, Wisconsin). He also helped host the sixth annual conference for the National Organization for Changing Men in 1979, and attended a national men's conference in 1984. Men at these gatherings have expressed interest in this study and have helped distribute questionnaires throughout the United States. Many of the men in these groups and organizations have started to question traditional male values. It cannot be assumed that their values are representative of the values of all the men in the United States, although it can be assumed that they grew up with similar values.

The high percentage of men who have attended men's consciousness/ support groups skews this sample away from a representative sample of men in the United States towards a sample of men who have started to challenge traditional patterns about male behavior. These participants suggest new paradigms for masculine behavior that started to emerge in the 1970s. Because these men have thought seriously about their gender-role conditioning, their insights have made an important contribution to this study. These articulate men have willingly shared how they have formed their male identities. It has been the experience of this researcher that more traditional men, many of whom have not started to think about their gender-role conditioning, are often defensive and do not readily share information with a researcher about their self-concepts as men.

Men who responded to this questionnaire were better educated than the average man in the United States. The median educational level for men in the US is slightly below junior year in high school (10.7 years of schooling); whereas the median level of schooling for respondents to this questionnaire is 14.1 (sophomore in college). This is an inevitable drawback to doing this type of survey research, which requires a fairly sophisticated reading level in order to respond to a five page questionnaire. It must be concluded that the high proportion of educated respondents in this sample will skew the results towards reflecting the experiences of well educated men in the United States, as opposed to 'average' men in the United States.

In summary, this sample of 560 men who filled out the questionnaire designed for this study is better educated than average males in the United States, is overrepresented from the Midwest and underrepresented from the southern parts of the United States. The sample contains a disproportionately high percentage of professional men and a disproportionately low percentage of men who are classified as operatives (skilled industrial or mechanical). This sample, because it contains a majority of well-educated middle class, one third of whom have participated in men's groups is slightly more liberal than might be the norm for males in the United States. These participants also have more experience with nontraditional views of masculinity. In other key demographic variables (age, sexual preference, and race) this sample mirrors ratios for US males.

References

ARAMANI, A., 1972, Machismo, *Psychology Today*, January, 69–72.

ARCANA, J., 1983, *Every Mother's Son*, Seattle: Seal Press.

ARKIN, W. and DEBROFSKY, L. R., 1978, Military socialization and masculinity, *Journal of Social Issues*, **34**(1), 151–68.

BAKER, D., 1966, *The Quality of Human Existence*, Chicago: Rand McNally.

BAKER, R., 1987, Foreword, in E. Klein and D. Erickson (Eds), *About Men: Reflections on the Male Experience* pp. 1–15, New York: Poseidon Press.

BANDURA, A., 1969, *Principles of Behavior Modification*, New York: Holt, Rinehart and Winston.

BARTH, J., 1967, *The Floating Opera*, Garden City, NY: Doubleday.

BELL, D. H., 1982, *Being a Man*, New York: Harcourt Brace Jovanovich.

BELLAH, R. W., MADSON, R., SULLIVAN, W. M., SWIDLER, A. and TOPTON, S. M., 1985, *Habits of the Heart*, Berkeley: University of California Press.

BEM, S., 1974, The measurement of psychological androgyny, *Journal of Consulting and clinical psychology*, **42**, 155–62.

BEM, S., 1993, *The Lenses of Gender*, New Haven: Yale University Press.

BERGER, P. L. and LUCKMAN, T., 1966, *The Social Construction of Reality*, New York: Doubleday.

BERNE, E., 1976, *Beyond Games and Scripts*, New York: Grove Press.

BLUMENTHAL, M., 1987, No big deal, in E. Klein and D. Erickson (Eds), *About Men: Reflections on the Male Experience* (pp. 134–40), New York: Poseidon Press.

BOLEN, J. S., 1989, *Gods in Everyman: A New Psychology of Men's Lives and Loves*, San Francisco: Harper & Row.

BRADBURY, P., 1972, Sexuality and male violence, *Radical American*, **16**(6), 63–71.

BRADSHAW, J., 1988, *Healing the Shame That Bonds You*, Deerfield Beach, FL: Health Communications.

BRADSHAW, J., 1990, *Homecoming: Reclaiming and Championing Your Inner Child*, New York: Bantam Books.

BRANNON, R., 1985, Dimensions of the male sex role, in A. Sargent (Ed.), *Beyond Sex Roles* pp. 296–316, St. Paul: West Publishing.

BRENNER, H., 1976, *Estimating the Social Cost of National Economic Policy: Implications For Mental and Physical Health and Clinical Aggression*, a report prepared for the Joint Economic Committee, U.S. Congress, Washington, DC: US Government Printing Office.

BRENTON, M., 1966, *The American Male*, New York: Conrad McCann.

BRITTAN, A., 1989, *Masculinity and Power*, Oxford, England: Basil Blackwell.

BROWN, K. H., 1987, The bright side of fifty, in E. Klein and D. Erickson (Eds), *About Men: Reflections on the Male Experience* (pp. 295–8). New York: Poseidon Press.

BROYLES, W., 1986, *Brothers in Arms*, New York: Knopf.

BUTSCH, R. and GLENNON, L. M., 1983, Social class: frequency trends in domestic situation comedy, 1946–1978, *Journal of Broadcasting*, **27**(1), 77–81.

CAHILL, S. E., 1983, Reexamining the acquisition of sex roles: a social interactionist approach, *Sex Roles*, **9**(1), 1–15.

CHODEROW, N., 1978, *The Reproduction of Mothering: Psychoanalysis and the Sociology of Gender*, Los Angeles: University of California Press.

CLARK, W. V. T., 1940, *The Ox-Bow Incident*, New York: Time, Inc.

CLARY, M., 1982, *Daddy's Home*, New York: Seaview Books.

CLATTERBAUGH, K., 1990, *Contemporary Perspectives on Masculinity: Men, Women, and Politics in Modern Society*, Boulder, CO: Westview Press.

CLAY, W., 1975, The socioeconomic status of blacks, *Ebony*, September, 29.

CROMPTON, R. and MANN, M., 1986, *Gender and Stratification*, Cambridge: Greenwich University Press.

DANIELL, T., 1989, How marketers see Milwaukee, *The Milwaukee Journal*, May 14, b1.

DAVID, D. and BRANNON, R., 1976, The male sex role: Our cultures blueprint of manhood and what it's done for us lately, in D. David and R. Brannon (Eds), *The Forty-nine Percent Majority* pp. 1–48, Reading, MA: Addison-Wesley.

DEMOS, J., 1982, The changing faces of fatherhood: a new exploration in American family history, in S. Cath, A. Gurwitt and J. Ross (Eds), *Father and Child: Developmental and Clinical Perspectives* (pp. 425–50).

DOYLE J., 1983, *The Male Experience*, Dubuque, IA: William Brown Books.

DUBBERT, J., 1979, *A Man's Place: Masculinity in Transition*, New York: Prentice-Hall.

DUNIERE, M., 1992, *Slim's Table*, Chicago: University of Chicago Press.

EHRENREICH, B., 1983, *The Hearts of Men*, New York: Doubleday/Anchor Press.

EISLER, R., 1988, *The Chalice and the Blade*, San Francisco: Harper & Row.

ERIKSON, E. H., 1963, *Childhood and Society* (2nd ed), New York: Norton.

ERIKSON, E. H., 1968, *Identity: Youth and Crisis*, New York: Norton Press.

ERIKSON, E. H., 1980, *Identity and the Life Cycle*, New York: N. W. Norton and Company.

ERIKSON, E. H. and ERIKSON, J. M., 1981, On generativity and identity, *Harvard Educational Review*, **51**, 249–69.

FARRELL, M. and ROSENBERG, S., 1981, *Men at Midlife*, Boston: Auburn House.

FARRELL, W., 1974, *The Liberated Man*, New York: Random House.

FARRELL, W., 1986, *Why Men Are The Way They Are*, New York: McGraw-Hill.

FASTEAU, M. F., 1974, *The Male Machine*, New York: McGraw-Hill.

FEDERAL BUREAU OF INVESTIGATION, 1978, *Crime in the United States: Uniform Crime Reports, 1977*, Washington, DC.: US Government Printing Office.

FILENE, P., 1975, *Him/herself: Sex Roles in Modern America*, New York: Harcourt, Brace Jovanovich.

FLUGEL, J. C., 1970, *Man, Morals and Society: A Psychological Study*, New York: International Universities Press.

FORCEY, L., 1987, *Mothers of Sons: Toward an Understanding of Responsibility*, New York: Praeger.

FRANKLIN, C. W., II 1984, *The Changing Definition of Masculinity*, New York: Plenum Books.

FREIMUTH, M. and HORNSTEIN, G., 1982, A critical examination of the concept of gender, *Sex Roles*, **8**(5), 511–32.

FREUD, S., 1962, *The Ego and the Id*, New York: Norton.

FRIEDAN, B., 1970, *The Feminine Mystique*, New York: Dell.

FURSTENBERG, F., JR. and SPANIER, G., 1984, *Recycling the Family: Remarriage After Divorce*, Beverly Hills: Sage.

GARFINKEL, P., 1985, *A Man's World*, New York: Mentor Books.

GARY, L. (Ed.)., 1981, *Black Men*, Beverly Hills: Sage Publications.

GERZON, M., 1982, *A Choice of Heroes*, New York: Houghton Mifflin.

GIBBS, J. T., 1988, *Young, Black, and Male in America: An endangered species*, Dover, MA: Auburn House Publishing.

GILMORE, D. D., 1990, *Manhood in the Making*, New Haven, CT: Yale University Press.

GOLDBERG, H., 1976, *The Hazards of Being Male*, New York: New American Library.

GREEN, M., 1976, *Fathering: A New Look at the Creative Art of Being a Father*, New York: McGraw-Hill.

HALE-BENSON, J. E., 1986, *Black Children: Their Roots, Culture and Learning Styles*, Baltimore: Johns Hopkins University Press.

HARRIS, I., 1986, Media myths and the reality of men's work, *Changing Men*, Summer, 8–12.

HARRIS, I., 1988, *Peace Education*, Jefferson, NC: McFarland & Co.

HARRIS, I., 1991, The role of social conditioning in male violence, in E. Boulding, C. Brogagio and K. Clements (Eds), *Peace and Cultures and Society: Transnational Research and Dialogue*, pp. 166–76. Boulder, CO: Westview Press.

HARRIS, I. and DENISE, P., 1989, *Experiential Education for Community Development*, New York: Greenwood.

HAWKES, G. R. and TAYLOR, M., 1975, Power structure in Mexican and Mexican–American farm labor families, *Journal of Marriage and the Family*, **37**, 807–11.

HOFSTADTER, R., 1963, *Anti-intellectualism in American Life*, New York: Knopf.

HOGAN, D. P., 1981, *Transitions and Social Change: The Early Lives of American Men*, New York: Academic Press.

HORSMAN, R., 1986, *Race and Manifest Destiny: The Origins of American Racial Anglo-Saxonism*, Cambridge, MA: Harvard University Press.

JOHNSON, R. L. and SHRIER, D. E., 1985, Sexual victimization of boys, *Journal of Adolescent Health Care*, **6**, 372–6.

JOURARD, S. M., 1968, *Disclosing Man to Himself*, Princeton, NJ: Van Nostrand.

JULTY, S., 1980, Men's health issues for the '80s, *American Man*, **1**(40), 36–50.

JUNG, C., 1928, *The Relations Between the Ego and the Unconscious*, Princeton, NJ: Princeton University Press.

KAGEN, J., 1964, Acquisition and significance of sex typing and sex role identity, in M. Hoffman and L. Hoffman (Eds), *Review of Child Development Research* (Vol. 1) (pp. 137–67), New York: Russell Sage.

KEEN, S., 1991, *Fire in the Belly*, New York: Bantam.

KESSLER, S. J. and McKENNA, W., 1978, *Gender: An Ethnomethodological Approach*, Chicago: University of Chicago Press.

KINSEY, A., POMEROY, W., MARTIN, C. and GEBHARD, P., 1948, *Sexual Behavior in the Human Male*, Philadelphia: Saunders.

KOHLBERG, L., 1966, A cognitive-development analysis of children's concepts and attitudes, in E. F. Maccoby (Ed.), *The Development of Sex Differences*, pp. 82–172, Stanford, CA: Stanford University Press.

KOMAROVSKY, M., 1976, *Illiterate America*, Garden City, NY: Anchor Press/Doubleday.

KRIEGEL, L., 1979, *On Men and Manhood*, New York: Hawthorn Books.

KUNJUFU, J., 1985, *Countering the Conspiracy to Destroy Black Boys*, Chicago: African American Images.

LASCH, C., 1979, *Haven in a Heartless World: The Family Besieged*, New York: Basic Books.

LEMASTERS, E., 1975, *Blue Collar Aristocrats*, Madison, WI: University of Wisconsin Press.

LEVINSON, D., DARROW, C. N., KLEIN, E. B., LLEVINSON, M. H. and MAKEE, B., 1978, *The Seasons of a Man's Life*, New York: Ballantine Books.

LIDDY, G. G., 1990, *Will*, New York: Doubleday.

LINDSEY, L. L., 1990, *Gender Roles: A Sociological Perspective*, Englewood Cliffs, NJ: Prentice Hall, Inc.

LLOYD, R. and HETRICK, W. M., 1987, Community-based high school diploma programs, *Community Education Journal*, **14**(4), 46–8.

MAJORS, R. and BILSON, J. M., 1992, *Cool Pose: The Dilemmas of Black Manhood in America*, New York: Lexington Books.

MARSHALL, R., 1988, Forward, in J. T. Gibbs (Ed.), *Young, Black, and Male in America: An Endangered Species* (pp. i–ix). Dover, MA: Auburn House.

MARTIN, C. L. and HALVERSON, C. F. JR, 1981, A schematic processing model of sex typing and stereotyping in children, *Child Development*, **52**, 151–62.

MARTINEZ, J. L., JR, and MENDOZA, R. H. (Eds) 1984, *Chicano Psychology*, Orlando, FL: Academic Press.

MASLOW, A., 1968, *Toward a Psychology of Being* (2nd edn), New York: Van Norstrand Reinhold.

MASSEY, A., 1979, *People Puzzle*, Englewood Cliffs, NJ: Reston Publishing.

MEAD, G. H., 1934, *Mind, Self, and Society*, Chicago: University of Chicago Press.

MENDOZA, R. H. and MARTINEZ, J. L., 1981, The measurement of acculturation, in A. Baron, Jr, (Ed.), *Explorations in Chicano Psychology*, (pp. 71–84), New York: Praeger.

MILLER, S., 1983, *Men and Friendship*, Boston: Houghton Mifflin.

MORIN, S., 1975, Heterosexual bias in psychological research on lesbianism and male homosexuality, *American Psychologist*, **32**, 629–37.

MURILLO, N., 1971, The Mexican American family, in N. N. Wagner and M. J. Haug (Eds), *Chicanos: Social and Psychological Perspectives*, pp. 15–25. St. Louis, MO: C. V. Mosby Co.

NELSON, J. B., 1988, *The Intimate Connection*, Philadelphia: The Westminster Press.

NEITZSCHE, F., 1967, *Beyond Good and Evil: Prelude to a Philosophy for the Future*, London: Allen and Unwin.

OSHERON, S., 1986, *Finding our Fathers: How a Man's Life is Shaped By His Relationship With His Father*, New York: Faucett Columbine.

PARKE, R. D., 1981, *Father*, Cambridge, MA: Harvard University Press.

PARKER, S. and THOMPSON, T., 1990, Gay and bisexual men: Developing a healthy identity, in D. Moore and F. Leafgren (Eds), *Problem Solving Strategies and Interventions for Men in Conflict*, pp. 113–24, Alexandria, VA: American Association for Counseling and Development.

PERRY, D. G. and BUSSEY, K., 1984, *Social Development*, Englewood Cliffs, NJ: Prentice-Hall, Inc.

PETERS, T. and WATERMAN, R., JR, 1982, *In Search of Excellence*, New York: Harper & Row.

PETROVICH, M. and TEMPLER, D. I., 1984, Heterosexual molestation of children who later become rapists, *Psychological Reports*, **54**, 810.

PLECK, J. and SAWYER, J., (Eds), 1974, *Men and Masculinity*, Englewood Cliffs, NJ: Prentice-Hall.

PLECK, J. H., 1975, Masculinity–femininity paradigm, *Sex Roles*, **1**(2), 161–78.

PLECK, J. H., 1976, The male sex role: Definition, problems, and sources of change, *Journal of Social Issues*, **32**, 155–64.

PLECK, J. H., 1981, *The Myth of Masculinity*, Cambridge, MA: MIT Press.

PLECK, J. H., 1987, American fathering in historical perspective, in M. S. Kimmel (Ed.), *Changing Men: New Directions in Research on Men and Masculinity*, pp. 83–97, Beverly Hills: Sage Publications.

RICH, A., 1976, *Of Women Born: Motherhood as Experience and Institution*, New York: Norton.

RUDDICK, S., 1989, *Maternal Thinking Toward a Philosophy of Peace*, Boston: Beacon Press.

RUIZ, R., 1981, Cultural and historic perspectives in counseling Hispanics, in D. W. Sue (Ed.), *Counseling the Culturally Different: Theory and Practice*, (pp. 186–214), New York: Wiley.

SAHLINS, M. D., 1976, *The Use and Abuse of Biology*, London: Tavistook.

SARGENT, A., 1985, *Beyond Sex Roles*, St. Paul: West Publishing.

SATIR, V., 1972, *People-making*, Palo Alto, CA: Science and Behavior Books.

SCHAEFER, R., 1990, *Racial and Ethnic Groups* (4th ed.), Glenview, IL: Scott, Foresman & Co.

SCHAFFER, K. F., 1981, *Sex Roles and Human Behavior*, Cambridge, MA: Winthrop Publishers.

References

SEIDLER, V. J., 1989, *Rediscovering Masculinity: Reason Language and Sexuality*, London: Routledge.

SENNET, R. and COBB, J., 1973, *The Hidden Injuries of Class*, New York: Vintage Books.

STAPLES, B., 1987, A brother's murder, in E. Klein and D. Erikson (Eds), *About Men: Reflections on the Male Experience*, (pp. 59–62), New York: Poseidon Press.

STEIN, P. and HOFFMAN, S., 1978, Sports and male role strain, *Journal of Social Issues*, **34**(1), 136–50.

STOLLER, R. J., 1985, *Presentations of Gender*, New Haven, CT: Yale University Press.

STOLTENBERG, J., 1980, *Refusing to be a Man: Essays on Sex and Justice*, Portland, OR: Breitenbush Books.

STREICKER, L. D., 1989, *Fathering: Old Game, New Rules*, Nashville: Abingdon Press.

SUE, D., 1990, Culture in transition: Counseling Asian-American men, in D. Moore and F. Leafgren (Eds), *Problem Solving Strategies and Interventions for Men in Conflict*, (pp. 153–69), Alexandria, VA: American Association for Counseling and Development.

TENNIS, D., 1985, *Is God the Only Reliable Father?* Philadelphia: The Westminster Press.

TERKEL, S., 1974, *Working*, New York: Pantheon.

THEROUX, P., 1987, The male myth, in E. Klein and D. Erikson (Eds), *About Men: Reflections on the Male Experience*, pp. 235–8, New York: Poseidon Press.

THOREAU, H. D., 1970, *The Annotated Walden*, New York: Clarkson and Potter.

VAILLANT, G., 1977, *Adoption to Life*, Boston: Little Brown & Co.

VAILLANT, G. and MILOFSKY, E., 1980, Natural history of male psychological health: IX empirical evidence for Erikson's Model of the Life Cycle, *American Journal of Psychiatry*, **137**(11), 1348–59.

VAN GENNEP, A., 1960, *The Rites of Passage*, Chicago: The University of Chicago Press.

WEBER, M., 1958, *The Protestant Ethic and the Spirit of Capitalism*, New York: Scribner.

WEINBERG, G., 1972, *Society and the Healthy Homosexual*, New York: St. Martin Press.

WEINBERG, M. S. and WILLIAMS, C. J., 1974, *Male Homosexuals: Their Problems and Adoptions*, New York: Penguin.

WEITZMAN, L. J., 1979, *Sex Role Socialization*, Palo Alto, CA: Mayfield Publishing.

WHITBOURNE, S. K., 1986, *The Me I Know: A Study of Adult Identity*, New York: Springer.

WILSON, A. N., 1978, *The Developmental Psychology of the Black Child*, New York: African Research Publications.

WYKOFF, H., 1974, Sex-role scripting in men and women, in C. Steiner (Ed.), *Scripts People Live*, pp. 165–75. New York: Grove Press.

YORBURG, B., 1974, *Sexual Identity*, New York: Wiley.

Index

Index